PUBLIC POLICY
AND THE
PRACTICE AND PROBLEMS
OF ACCOUNTING

PUBLIC POLICY AND THE PRACTICE AND PROBLEMS OF ACCOUNTING

Ahmed Belkaoui

Q

Quorum Books
Westport, Connecticut • London, England

Library of Congress Cataloging in Publication Data

Belkaoui, Ahmed, 1943-
   Public policy and the practice and problems
of accounting.

   Bibliography: p.
   Includes index.
   1. Accounting—Standards—United States.
2. Auditing—Standards—United States.   I. Title.
HF5616.U5B39   1985   657'.0218   85-3568
ISBN 0-89930-105-3 (lib. bdg.)

Library of Congress Catalog Card Number: 85-3568
ISBN: 0-89930-105-3

First published in 1985 by Quorum Books

Greenwood Press
A division of Congressional Information Service, Inc.
88 Post Road West
Westport, Connecticut 06881

Printed in the United States of America

10 9 8 7 6 5 4 3 2 1

À la vertu des femmes des marins

CONTENTS

Exhibits   xi

Preface   xiii

**I. The Generally Accepted Accounting Principles and
   Financial Statements**   3

1.   The Meaning of the GAAP   3
2.   CPAs Owe Their Careers to a Fifteenth-Century Monk   6
3.   Development of the GAAP: From Chaos to Politics   9
4.   What Should It Be—GAAP, Special GAAPs, or OCBOA?   14
5.   Little GAAP versus Big GAAP   15
6.   The Saga of Sam's Delicatessen   20
7.   The Structure of Accounting Theory   21
8.   The Accounting Postulates   23
9.   The Theoretical Concepts of Accounting   25
10. The Accounting Principles   27
11. Financial Statements of Business Enterprises   33
12. Future Scope of Accounting   39
13. Letting the Accounting Tail Wag the Economic Dog   47

II. The American Institute of Certified Public Accountants   51

1.   The AICPA: Toward Less Standard Setting and More
     Self-Regulation   51
2.   Knowledge, Skills, and Abilities List   56

3. Work Activities List   63
4. Sunset Review   67
5. Peer Review: Does It Work?   69
6. Professionalism versus Commercialism in Accounting   75
7. Specialization in the Profession   77
8. Issues Identified by the Future Issues Committee   82

III. CPA Firms and Individuals   89

1. Should the Auditor Review and Evaluate Internal
    Accounting Control?   89
2. Should the Auditor Join the Privileged Few?   90
3. What about the Audit Committees?   92
4. What Is Independence and Is It Possible?   100
5. Are the Big Eight Invading the Middle-Market Turf?   103
6. Consulting for Law Firms   105
7. "Low Balling": A Popular Strategy   106
8. Accountants Are Working on a New Image   107
9. Bias and Bias Law Apply to Partnerships   109
10. Auditor Switch: Get the Right Accounting Firm and
    You Get the Opinion You Want   111
11. Checklist: Selecting CPA Services   112
12. Ex-Jewel Chief Profiles Ideal Accounting Firm   116
13. Direct Uninvited Solicitation: Client Chasing by CPAs   118
14. When Accountants Miss the Mark   120
15. Accountants' Liability   122
16. What's Behind the CPA-Client Relationship?   126

IV. The Financial Accounting Standards Board   131

1. The FASB: Structure and Functioning   131
2. Is the Board Doing a Good Job?   137
3. Accounting Standards Overload: A Hangman's Noose   139
4. The FASB's Conceptual Framework   145

V. The Securities and Exchange Commission   149

1. The Securities and Exchange Commission:
    A Tough Act Ahead   149

2.   The SEC, Insider Trading, and the Accountant   155
3.   Misleading Financial Statements and the SEC   157
4.   What Exactly Is the Position of the SEC on Nonaudit
     Services and Auditor Independence?   158

VI. Auditing   **161**

1.   The Auditor's Standard Report: Past, Present, and Future   161
2.   The Auditor's Standard Report: Content and Nature
     of the Opinion   167
3.   The Auditor's Standard Report: Meaning of "Present
     Fairly . . . in Conformity with GAAP"   172

VII. Conclusions   **179**

1.   The Generally Accepted Accounting Principles and
     Financial Statements   179
2.   The American Institute of Certified Public Accountants   180
3.   CPA Firms and Individuals   181
4.   The Financial Accounting Standards Board   181
5.   The Securities and Exchange Commission   182
6.   Auditing   182
     Selected Bibliography   183
     Index   195

EXHIBITS

1. The House of GAAP   5

2 . Control of the Big Eight Accounting Firms and the
    AICPA over Accounting Standards Approved by the SEC   13

3. Valuation Bases under Generally Accepted
    Accounting Principles   37

4. Deriving the Value-Added Statement   46

5. Structure of the Financial Accounting Standards
    Board (FASB)   133

6. Conceptual Framework for Financial Accounting
    and Reporting   147

7. Generally Accepted Auditing Standards   168

PREFACE

For the past twenty years, the accounting discipline and profession have been faced with accelerating public attention, most of it unwelcome. The attention has been triggered by inadequacies, issues, and unresolved problems facing the accounting world. It seems that most of the actors in the accounting world have lost some of their virtues. Responses to this new situation have arisen slowly but not always effectively. What has resulted is a trial of the accountants in a theatre of the absurd. The public not only does not clearly grasp these inadequacies, issues, and unresolved problems but does not understand what accounting and auditing are all about and does not understand the specific roles of the actors involved, namely the American Institute of Certified Public Accountants, the CPA firms and individuals, the Financial Accounting Standards Board, and the Securities and Exchange Commission.

This book is aimed at closing this communication gap by providing a critical examination of the role and issues facing the accounting and auditing disciplines, the accounting profession, the standard-setting process, and the oversight process—a critical examination of the role and issues facing the generally accepted accounting principles and the auditing process, the American Institute of Certified Public Accountants, the CPA firms and individuals, the Financial Accounting Standards Board, and the Securities and Exchange Commission (SEC).

The specific purpose of this book is to pinpoint what is right as much as what is wrong in the world of accounting as far as the public interest is concerned. Therefore, questions of public policy in need of correction, standardization, and legislation are put forward. Solutions advanced by the courts, the Internal Revenue Service, the SEC, the professional bodies and the literature are discussed. The book consists of seven chapters:

I. The Generally Accepted Accounting Principles and Financial Statements

II. The American Institute of Certified Public Accountants

III. CPA Firms and Individuals

IV. The Financial Accounting Standards Board

V. The Securities and Exchange Commission

VI. Auditing

VII. Conclusions

Each chapter examines a set of vital public-policy issues and solutions facing the accounting world.

The book serves two basic purposes:

To provide an exhaustive presentation of the solutions to issues facing accounting to practicing accountants, users of financial information, legislators, businesspeople, and the general public. Each of these groups has a need to understand better the working, the institutional, and the procedural structure of the *actors* in the accounting world; the public-policy issues facing them; and the potential solutions.

To provide academicians with a textbook to be used as a supplementary book in all financial accounting courses to expose the students to the issues facing the accounting world. Conventional textbooks in general elaborate on the body of knowledge in accounting without exposing the students to the institutional and public-policy questions facing the accounting world.

No book can be written without the help of numerous individuals and organizations. A special note of appreciation is extended to the American Institute of Certified Public Accountants, the *New York Times*, and *Crain's Magazine* for giving me permission to reprint portions of their work in this book.

Finally, to Hedi J. and Janice M. Belkaoui, thanks for everything.

PUBLIC POLICY
AND THE
PRACTICE AND PROBLEMS
OF ACCOUNTING

I

THE GENERALLY ACCEPTED ACCOUNTING PRINCIPLES AND FINANCIAL STATEMENTS

1. THE MEANING OF THE GAAP

Accounting has been defined either as the art of recording, classifying, and summarizing in monetary terms transactions and events that are of a financial character or as a service activity whose function is to communicate quantitative information, primarily financial, about economic entities to assist in decision making. Whether accounting is referred to as an art or a service activity, the implication in both cases is that it encompasses a body of techniques deemed useful for certain fields. Examples of fields for which accounting is useful include: (a) financial reporting, (b) tax determination and planning, (c) independent audits, (d) data-processing and information systems, (e) cost and management accounting, (f) internal auditing, (g) external auditing, (h) fiduciary accounting, (i) national income accounting, and (j) management consulting.

Although accounting is a set of techniques useful for specified fields, it is practiced within an implicit theoretical framework. This framework consists of principles and practices that have won acceptance by the profession because of their alleged usefulness and logic. Known as the "generally accepted accounting principles" (GAAP), they are a guide to the accounting profession in the choice of accounting techniques and the preparation of financial statements in a way considered to be good accounting practice. The GAAP, in fact, encompass the conventions, rules, and procedures necessary to define accepted accounting practice at a particular time. They represent the consensus at a given time about which economic resources and obligations should be recorded as assets and liabilities, which changes in them should be recorded, how the recorded assets and liabilities and changes in them should be measured, what information should be disclosed and how it should be disclosed, and which financial statements should be prepared. The GAAP are formulated by people on the basis of experience, reason, custom, usage, and, to a significant extent, practical necessity. The conventions, rules, and procedures have acquired the special status of being included in the GAAP, because they have *substantial authoritative support.* The inclusion of a principle in the GAAP may sometimes require a judgment of appropriateness.

The literature pertaining to the content of the GAAP has expanded over time to include volumes of statements, opinions, and other pronouncements from a variety of *authoritative* sources. It includes the pronouncements currently in force of the various standard-setting bodies, namely, the Financial Accounting Standards Board (FASB) statements of financial accounting standards (SFAS) and the interpretations, along with the Accounting Principles Board (APB) opinions and the American Institute of Certified Public Accounts (AICPA) accounting research bulletins. Other common sources of the GAAP are:

1. AICPA industry audit and accounting guides and statements of positions and AICPA accounting interpretations
2. Other identified publications of the FASB such as technical bulletins and of its predecessors such as APB statements
3. Publications of the Securities and Exchange Commission (SEC) such as accounting series release
4. Recognized and prevalent practices as reflected in the annual AICPA publication *Accounting Trends and Techniques*
5. AICPA issues papers, FASB concepts statements, textbooks, and articles

This profusion of sources may be viewed as an hierarchy. Exhibit 1 looks at the hierarchy as a four-story house—the house of GAAP. The authoritativeness of accounting guidance rests on the various official positions of the profession and the SEC.

First, the relationship of the accounting profession with the standard-setting body, in this case the FASB, was clarified by Rules 203 and 204 of the AICPA's Code of Professional Ethics. Rule 203 of the AICPA's Code of Professional Ethics holds that a member of the AICPA may not express an opinion that financial statements are presented fairly in conformity with the generally accepted accounting principles if the statements depart from an FASB statement or interpretation or an APB opinion or accounting research bulletin, unless the member can demonstrate that, because of unusual circumstances, the financial statements would be otherwise misleading. Rule 204 of the AICPA's Code of Professional Ethics requires AICPA members to justify departures from the Financial Accounting Standards Board that relate to the disclosure of information outside of the published financial statements, such as supplementary financial statements adjusted for the effects of inflation. Rules 203 and 204 force the AICPA member either to comply with authoritative accounting pronouncements or to be prepared to defend his or her choice at the member's own risk. In

EXHIBIT 1 THE HOUSE OF GAAP

Fourth floor	APB statements	AICPA issues papers	Other professional pronouncements	FASB concepts statements	Textbooks and articles
Third floor	FASB technical bulletins		AICPA accounting interpretations		Prevalent industry practices
Second floor	AICPA industry audit guides		AICPA industry accounting guides		AICPA statements of position
First floor	FASB statements	FASB interpretations		APB opinions	AICPA accounting research bulletins
Foundation	Includes the going concern assumption, substance over form, neutrality, the accrual basis, conservatism, materiality.				

Source: Stevin Rubin, "The House of GAAP," *Journal of Accountancy*, June 1984, 123. Reprinted with permission. Copyright © 1984 by the American Institute of Certified Public Accountants, Inc.

other words, Rules 203 and 204 constitute an endorsement of the FASB with some reservations by recognizing that, in unusual circumstances, literal compliance with presumptively binding, generally accepted accounting principles issued by a recognized standard-setting body may not always ensure that financial statements will be presented fairly.

Second, the SEC's relationship with a standard-setting body, in this case the FASB, was clarified in 1973 by SEC Accounting Release No. 150, which stated that "principles, standards and practices promulgated by the FASB will be considered by the Commission as having substantial authoritative support, and those contrary to such FASB promulgations will be considered to have no such support." It also stated that "the commission will continue to identify areas where investor information needs exist and will determine the appropriate methods of disclosure to meet these needs." This constitutes an endorsement of the FASB with some reservations in that the SEC has not delegated any of its authority or given up any right to reject, modify, or supersede FASB pronouncements through its own rule-making procedures. In fact, before the creation of the FASB, the commission had issued more than 200 accounting series releases (ASRs) on accounting, auditing, and financial matters, some of which are in conflict with or are amended or superseded with standards set by the standards-setting bodies.

Rules 203 and 204 and ASR No. 150 require that published financial statements conform to the accounting principles that are set by the FASB and other previous standard-setting bodies and that are currently in force, except in highly unusual circumstances. Given this situation, the accounting firms are constantly demanding more guidance that is subject to the AICPA's ethic rules and, therefore, is mandatory. The search for guidance is basically motivated by the concern about (a) fierce competition among accounting firms, (b) "shopping" by corporations for favorable accounting solutions, (c) merchandising of accounting solutions by some investment bankers and consultants, and (d) litigation against accounting firms from unhappy investors. Fortunately, the AICPA stepped in to provide guidance on accounting practice problems to its members. The best guidance is offered in a loose-leaf service, *AICPA Technical Practice Aids*, that contains unofficial responses to thousands of accounting questions; a telephone technical-inquiry service; a library-research service; a published annual survey of accounting practices, *Accounting Trends and Techniques*; and various other publications. The existence of this extensive guidance process indicates the confusion surrounding the true nature and composition of the GAAP.

2. CPAS OWE THEIR CAREERS TO A FIFTEENTH-CENTURY MONK*

Historians generally attribute the birth of accounting to the fifteenth-century Italian monk Fra Luca Pacioli. A friend of Leonardo da Vinci, Fra Pacioli was a mathematician who wrote a number of treatises on various branches of mathematics. In one of his textbooks published in 1494, Fra Pacioli included a section, "De Computis et Scripturus," that prescribed a system of record-keeping for merchants in the Italian city-states of the period.

The interesting thing about Fra Pacioli's treatment is that it describes a mathematically consistent scheme of double-entry bookkeeping based on

---

*Reprinted with permission from the September 24, 1984, issue of *Crain's Chicago Business.* Copyright 1984 by Crain Communications Inc.

the fundamental accounting model: Assets = Liabilities + Owners' Equity. As anyone who has taken a course in basic accounting principles will recall, this equation and the techniques of recording economic transactions in a chronological record (journal) according to principles of "debit" and "credit," posting these entries to ledger accounts, and computing the balances of these accounts are fundamental tools of the art of accounting.

A Simple Economy

On the North American continent, accounting had unprepossessing beginnings. The colonial American economy was predominantly agricultural, and business entities were mostly small, single proprietorships or family enterprises. It was not a money-oriented economy, and there was little need for sophisticated European accounting on the style of Fra Pacioli's model. Business records consisted mostly of accounts with persons, that is, receivables and payables. Therefore, financial statements as we know them were rarely prepared.

Debtors and creditors would get together occasionally to compare their accounts with each other's records and settle any differences. This in itself could be a formidable task, because with the chronic scarcity of cash that prevailed at the time, there was a great deal of bartering with inevitable disagreement about the relative values of various commodities.

To complicate matters further, various European currencies—English, Spanish, Dutch, and French—were circulated throughout the colonies, and records had to be kept to reflect these multiple currencies. These conditions continued into the early days of the republic. Despite the absence of the European style of accounting, businessmen of that time took their record-keeping seriously. Among this nation's founding fathers, for example, George Washington and Thomas Jefferson were noted for their conscientious maintenance of accounts. Jefferson personally kept highly detailed records of his business transactions and even devised a kind of cost accounting system for the nail factory ("nailery") that he operated for many years on his Virginia plantation.

The development of the United States as an industrial power gave great impetus to improvements in accounting practices. As a capital-importing nation, the young republic depended greatly on European investors for the funds needed to finance large-scale industrialization. British investors were particularly attracted to nineteenth-century growth industries such as railroading, mining, and brewing. Accustomed to the financial-reporting practices of European companies, these investors demanded the same kinds of disclosures from American enterprises in which they were interested. During the latter half of the nineteenth century, British investors also began sending independent auditors to the United States to examine the accounts of the businesses they were interested in. By the 1890s, however, an indigenous U.S. public accounting profession began to take root. In 1896 the state of New York passed the first accounting law and established certified public accountants as members of a legally constituted profession.

Enter Industrialization

As the United States evolved from an agricultural nation to one with a strong industrial and commercial orientation, business organizations of substantial size soon abandoned the primitive record-keeping methods that had been common in earlier days. The balance sheet was of overriding importance to lenders and investors of that era, but there were wide divergences of practice concerning the disclosure and valuation of items in this basic statement. At one extreme were those enterprises whose managements were uninhibited in their financial manipulations and their reporting. Shares of stock in these companies were issued for assets that were greatly overvalued, and in the unregulated securities markets of that time, the market prices of such "watered" stock were subject to wild swings upward and downward. During the recurring financial panics of the time, the holders of such shares often lost sizable sums of money.

At the other end of the spectrum were those companies for which extreme conservatism was the rule. For such companies, it was a mark of respectability to have a balance sheet in which assets were understated and liabilities were fully recognized or even anticipated. The cautious managements of these firms usually charged off every possible expenditure as an expense of the current period, thus creating so-called secret reserves, and they set up all kinds of explicit reserves in anticipation of remote future losses. This was before the introduction of the income tax and before there was much acceptance of rational cost-allocation theories like depreciation.

Income Tax Speeds Change

The advent of the federal income tax in 1913 had an immediate effect on accounting practices. Not only did it stimulate growth of the public accounting profession by providing a whole new area of services, but it began to divert attention from the balance sheet to the income statement, a trend that has persisted to the present. The United States Treasury did not show much enthusiasm for "conservative" financial reporting in which expenses were maximized and revenues minimized. So limits were soon set concerning items that could be deducted as expenses for any tax-reporting period and, similarly, taxable revenues were more sharply defined. Even though the coming of the income tax had a strong bearing on the shift in emphasis from the balance sheet to the income statement, the tax laws and regulations should not be credited with significant breakthroughs in defining the generally accepted accounting principles.

The United States experienced a period of economic boom in the 1920s, following a letdown and readjustment after the wrenching experience of World War I. During the latter half of the 1920s, public enthusiasm for securities trading reached previously undreamed of heights. Rising stock-market prices encouraged corporations to issue shares to a public that was eager to buy them.

In the relatively unregulated markets of that time, there were few rules governing the financial reports of companies whose securities were actively traded. Probably, few people cared about accounting as long as stock prices continued to rise. The cataclysmic stock-market crash of 1929 ended the speculative boom; it also signaled the end of the laissez-faire era of financial accounting in this country.

3. DEVELOPMENT OF THE GAAP: FROM CHAOS TO POLITICS

The GAAP phase has been subject to a constant reexamination and critical analysis. Three stages in this process may be identified: First, management had complete control over the selection of financial information disclosed in the annual reports (1900-1933); second, the professional bodies played a significant role in developing principles (1933-73); and third, in the stage that continues to the present, the FASB and various interest groups are moving toward a politicalization of accounting.

1. *Management-Contribution Phase (1900-33)*. This era was marked by the growth of the corporate form of business organization, the introduction of income taxation in 1913, the stock-market crash of 1925, and the passage of the securities act in 1933-34. All of these events had a tremendous effect on the growth of accounting. But above all, the influence of management in the formulation of accounting principles arose from the dominant economic role played by industrial corporations after 1900 and the increasing number of shareholders. The diffusion of stock ownership gave management complete control over the format and content of accounting disclosures. This intervention by management may be best characterized by the adoption of ad hoc solutions to urgent problems and controversies. The consequences of this dependence on management initiative include the following:

1. Given the pragmatic character of the solutions adopted, most accounting techniques lacked theoretical support.
2. The focus was on the determination of taxable income and the minimization of income taxes.
3. The techniques adopted were motivated by the desire to smooth earnings.
4. Complex problems were avoided and expedient solutions adopted.
5. Different firms adopted different techniques for the same problem.

The situation generated dissatisfaction during the 1920s. A lot of people were particularly outspoken in urging improvement in financial reporting. At the same time, Adolph A. Berle, Jr., and Gardiner C. Means in their book

The Modern Corporation and Private Property (New York: Macmillan, 1933) pointed to the corporate wealth and power of industrial corporations and called for the protection of investors.

2. *Professional-Contribution Phase (1933-73).* The second phase of accounting formulation from 1933 to 1973 was marked by the organization of various societies and agencies to regulate accounting practices.

First, government intervention came in the form of the Securities Acts of 1933 and 1934. In fact, by mandating independent reviews of public companies, the Securities Act of 1933 gave birth to the modern accounting profession. Some even alluded to the idea that accountants guaranteed their livelihood and paychecks through Uncle Sam's laws. In short, accountants benefit from a kid of white-collar welfare.

Second, the AICPA acted through the establishment in 1938 of the Committee on Accounting Procedure (CAP). Comprised of 21 volunteer CPA members, it contributed to the GAAP through the issuance of accounting research bulletins (ARBs). Each of the bulletins required the assenting votes of two-thirds of the CPA members before being issued. Fifty-one ARBs were issued between 1939 and 1959. In 1953 the first 42 ARBs were revised and reissued as Accounting Research Bulletin No. 43. Besides the ARBs, the CAP issued 11 accounting terminology bulletins (ATBs). One of the major characteristics of the ARBs and ATBs was that they were essentially *advisory*.

Third, following criticisms of the ad hoc nature of the ARBs and ATBs, the AICPA replaced the CAP with a new standard-setting committee called the Accounting Principles Board (APB). Comprised of 18 to 21 volunteer accountants, drawn from academia, the profession, industry, and the government, the APB contributed to the GAAP through the issuance of pronouncements called *opinions.* Each opinion required the assenting votes of two-thirds of the APB members before being issued. Thirty-one opinions were issued between 1959 and 1973. Besides the opinions, the APB issued four *statements* that contained recommendations rather than requirements. Of these statements, Statement No. 4, "Basic Concepts and Accounting Principles Underlying Financial Statements of Business Enterprise," constitutes the first major theoretical framework by the profession. In addition to the opinions and statements, the APB published fifteen *accounting research studies* (ARSs) intended but never used to serve as a logical support for the opinions. Although it contributed significantly to the development of the generally accepted accounting principles, the APB was criticized for the same reasons advanced against the CAP. The following criticisms were cited:

1. The CAP and the APB did not rely on any established theoretical framework.

2. The authority of the pronouncements was not really clear-cut.

3. The existence of alternative treatments allowed flexibility in the choice of accounting techniques.

4. The pronouncements reflected most of the time the views of the large CPA firms and the AICPA. It was even advanced that CPA board members were hard pressed to criticize poor accounting principles used by their own clients.

The dissatisfactions with the results of the APB and the CAP interventions were effective in bringing to the attention of the general public the accounting abuses dominating certain annual reports. In response to the stormy situation and the constant threat of governmental regulation, the AICPA appointed a seven-person committee, chaired by Francis M. Wheat, to study the process of establishing accounting principles and to make recommendations for improving that process.

   3. *Political Phase (1973-Present).* The 1972 report of the Wheat Committee led to the establishment of the *Financial Accounting Standards Board* as the official standard-setting body, with the responsibility of establishing and improving the generally accepted accounting principles in the United States. At the same time, the activeness of interest groups led to more political-ization of the standard-setting process. This situation is created by the generally accepted view that the accounting members affect economic behavior, and consequently, accounting rules should be made in the political arena. In fact, since its inception, the FASB has adopted a deductive and quasi-political approach to the formulation of accounting principles. The FASB conduct is better marked by, first, an effort to develop a theoretical framework or accounting constitution and, second, by the emergence of various interest groups, the contribution of which is required for the "general" acceptance of new standards. The standard-setting process, there-fore, has a political aspect. The following statement by the FASB indicates its awareness of this new situation:

The process of setting accounting standards can be described as democratic because like all rule-making bodies the board's right to make rules depends ultimately on the consent of the ruled. But because standard setting requires some perspective it would not be appropriate to establish a standard based solely on a canvass of the constit-uents. Similarly, the process can be described as legislative because it must be delib-erative and because all views must be heard. But the standard setters are expected to represent the entire constituency as a whole and not be representatives of a specific constituent group. The process can be described as political because there is an edu-cational effort involved in getting a new standard accepted. But it is not political in the sense that an accommodation is required to get a statement issued.[1]

   That the process of formulating accounting standards is becoming polit-ical is better expressed by a report released by the Senate Subcommittee on Reports, Accounting and Management, *The Accounting Establishment.* Known as the Metcalf Report, it charged that the Big Eight accounting firms monopolize auditing of large corporations and control the standard-setting process. Exhibit 2 shows the relationship of the major organizations, which suggests that the Big Eight accounting firms and the AICPA have control over accounting standards approved by the SEC. After emphasizing the need for the federal government to ensure that publicly owned corporations are properly accountable to the public, the report made the following recommendations aimed at enhancing corporate accountability:

1. Congress should exercise stronger oversight of accounting practices promulgated or approved by the Federal Government, and more leadership in establishing proper goals and policies. . . .

2. Congress should establish comprehensive accounting objectives for the Federal Government to guide agencies and departments in performing their responsibilities. . . . A comprehensive set of Federal accounting objectives should encompass such goals as uniformity, consistency, clarity, accuracy, simplicity, meaningful presentation, and fairness in application. In addition, Congress should establish specific policies abolishing such "creative accounting" techniques as percentage of completion income recognition, inflation accounting, "normalized" accounting, and other potentially misleading accounting methods. . . .

3. Congress should amend the Federal Securities laws to restore the rights of damaged individuals to sue independent auditors for negligence under the fraud provisions of the securities laws. . . .

4. Congress should consider methods of increasing competition among accounting firms for selection as independent auditors for major corporations. . . .

5. The Federal Government should establish financial accounting standards for publicly owned corporations. . . .

6. The Federal Government should establish auditing standards used by independent auditors to certify the accuracy of corporate financial statements and supporting records. . . .

7. The Federal Government should itself periodically inspect the works of independent auditors for publicly owned corporations. . . .

8. The Federal Government should restore public confidence in the actual independence of auditors who certify the accuracy of corporate financial statements under the Federal Securities laws by promulgating and enforcing strict standards of conduct for such auditors. . . .

9. The Federal Government should require the nation's 15 largest accounting firms to report basic operational and financial reports annually. . . .

10. The Federal Government should define the responsibilities of the independent auditors so that they clearly meet the expectations of Congress, the public, and courts of law. . . .

11. The Federal Government should establish financial accounting standards, cost accounting standards, auditing standards, and other accounting practices in meetings open to the public. . . .

12. The Federal Government should act to relieve excessive concentration in the supply of auditing and accounting services to major publicly owned corporations. . . .

13. The Federal Government should retain accounting firms which act as independent auditors only to perform auditing and accounting services. . . .

14. The Securities and Exchange Commission should treat all independent auditors equally in disciplinary and enforcement proceedings under the Federal securities laws. . . .

15. The Membership of the Cost Accounting Standards Board should not be dominated by representatives of the industry and accounting firms which may have vested interests in the standards established by the board. . . .

16. Federal employees should not serve on committees of the American Institute of Certified Public Accountants or similar organizations that are assigned to directly or indirectly influence accounting policies and procedures of the Federal Government. . . .

EXHIBIT 2 CONTROL OF THE BIG EIGHT ACCOUNTING FIRMS AND THE AICPA OVER ACCOUNTING STANDARDS APPROVED BY THE SEC

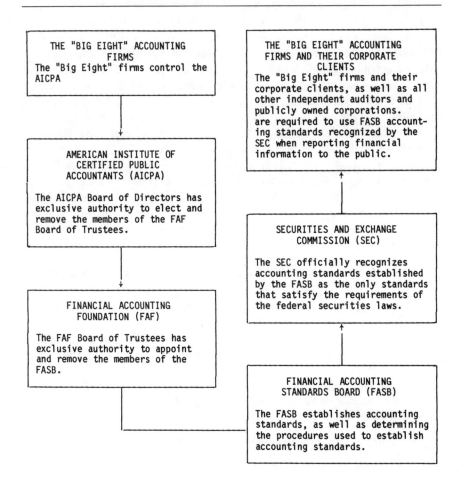

4. WHAT SHOULD IT BE—GAAP, SPECIAL GAAPS, OR OCBOA?

There is a change of perception of the GAAP. They are not perceived as being a rigid set of measurement rules. Their numerous applications differ, in fact, depending on the circumstances. On the one hand, we have the widely known GAAP for business enterprises; on the other hand, we have various and different special GAAPs such as GAAP for governmental organizations, GAAP for regulated business enterprises, GAAP for not-for-profit organizations, GAAP for investment companies, and GAAP for banks. There is even serious debate in favor of a special set of GAAP for small enterprises. This fact has been officially adopted by the FASB, which has either given small and closely held business some relief from certain financial-statement disclosure requirements—like the suspension in 1978 of the requirements to disclose earnings per share and segment information for companies whose securities are not publicly traded—or has distinguished between disclosure that should be required for all enterprises and that which should be required for only certain designated types of enterprises.

There is also more interest in alternatives to the GAAP, basically in financial statements prepared in accordance with other comprehensive bases of accounting (OCBOA). The motivations to switch to the OCBOA came from changes in the tax laws made by the Economic Recovery Act of 1981 and the increasing separation of tax accounting from the GAAP accounting, the increase in the number of partnerships, the subchapter S corporations and other entities that prefer to present tax or cash-basis financial statements, and the tentative conclusions of the AICPA accounting standards overload-study special committee in favor of the increased tax basis of accounting. Guidance to practitioners faced with the OCBOA statements is provided in the 1976 AICPA Statement on Auditing Standards No. 14 "Special Reports." Of the four types of reports identified, one is based on the OCBOA. To be classified as OCBOA, a basis must meet one of the four criteria:

1. A basis of accounting necessary to meet regulatory requirements. It is basically *GAAP for regulated companies.*
2. A basis of accounting that may be used for income tax returns. It is basically the *tax basis of accounting.*
3. A basis of accounting based on cash receipts and disbursements with or without out some accrual support. It is basically the *cash basis* or the modified *cash basis of accounting.*
4. A Basis of accounting resulting from the application of a definite set of criteria. *Current-value financial statements* or price-level *adjusted financial statements* are good examples.

The use of the OCBOA statements presents more problems to both users and CPAs:

1. To the users, they may not appear as an acceptable or known alternative to the GAAP. This may be aggravated by the requirement that the auditor's report include a middle paragraph that:
   - a. States, or preferably refers to the note to the financial statements which states, the basis of presentation of the financial statements on which the auditor is reporting
   - b. Refers to the note to the financial statements that describes how the basis of presentation differs from the GAAP and that may state the monetary effect of such differences
   - c. States that the financial statements are not intended to be presented in conformity with the GAAP

   This middle paragraph may be perceived by the less-than-sophisticated user as a qualification by the auditor rather than an informational statement.
2. To the practitioners, the OCBOA statements may present problems due to the lack of comprehensive guidance similar to the one available for the GAAP statements. To alleviate the situation the AICPA Technical Information Service (TIS), a consultation services department, may be used by an AICPA member to obtain assistance on any accounting or auditing problem by letter or toll-free telephone call.

But what should it be: GAAP, special GAAPs, or OCBOA? Those in favor of more uniformity and comparability would argue for the GAAP; those in favor of more flexibility and better avenues to deal with varying circumstances would argue for the special GAAPs. Those arguing for unique circumstances or against standards overload would argue for the OCBOA.

5. LITTLE GAAP VERSUS BIG GAAP

In the long run, after all the ramifications of this perplexing problem have been explored, it may well be that the only practical solution is to exempt certain companies from having to adhere to the standards issued by the FASB. The basis for such an exemption would have to be arbitrary. There is no rational justification for insisting that the protection afforded by the disclosures required under Board pronouncements should be provided to investors in one type of business entity but not to others.

Marshall Armstrong, former chairman of the FASB,
Journal of Accountancy (August 1977), 88.

The quotation by Armstrong refers to the problem of small business being overburdened by administrative and accounting costs in order to comply with irrelevant rules and to the need for relief in the form of exemptions. When one considers that more than one-half of this country's manufacturing, trade, and retail sales are produced by medium-sized and small businesses that are not listed on the New York or American stock exchanges, the gravity of the problem is further magnified. The question is whether any real difference exists between large and small businesses and among the needs of their respective information users to justify differences in the accounting rules in the form of two GAAPs: a little GAAP for smaller and/or closely held businesses and a big GAAP for large companies.

Differences between Large and Small Businesses

With respect to the differences between large and small businesses, the question is to identify those companies for which more relief from existing financial-reporting requirements should be made. A definition is needed to distinguish between small and large companies on the basis of the real differences that exist between them. The FASB tentatively defined a *small company* as follows:

A company whose operations are relatively small, usually with total revenues of less than $5 million. It typically (a) is owner-managed, (b) has few other owners, if any, (c) has all owners actively involved in the conduct of enterprise affairs except possibly for certain family members, (d) has infrequent transfer of ownership interests, and (e) has a simple capital structure.[2]

It also defined a *public company* as follows:

A company (a) whose securities trade in a public market on a stock exchange or in the over-the-counter market or (b) that is required to file financial statements with the Securities and Exchange Commission. A company is also considered a public company if its financial statements are issued in preparation for the sale of any class of securities in a public market.[3]

It follows that a *large company* is any company that is other than the above-defined small company, and a *private company* is any company that is other than the above-defined public company. Although these definitions show the real differences between small and large companies and public and private companies, they do not indicate whether the disclosure and reporting relief should be provided to private companies, to small companies, or to private and small public companies.

Differences among Users of Financial Statements

With respect to the differences among users, the issues are to identify (a) whether there are real differences between the needs of users of financial statements of public companies and users of financial statements of private companies and (b) whether there are real differences among users regarding the degree of their reliance on financial statements of private companies as sources of information. Empirical research on both questions presents conflicting evidence. One study asserted that financial analysts and public stockholders are the primary users of the financial statements of public companies, whereas owner-managers and creditors are the primary users of financial statements of private companies. It follows that different groups may be perceived to have different information needs. Another study, however, reported that bank loan officers and security analysts have a high degree of similarity of preferences for various types of information that are typically included in the financial statements. It also attributed the few instances in which those two groups might have a difference in preference for information to a difference in focus (for example, cash-flow analysis for bankers versus earnings per share for security analysts). This last finding has been the prevalent position of standard setters when it comes to defining the needs of users. Statement No. 4 of the Accounting Principles Board identified the following different user groups: owners, creditors and suppliers (both present and potential), management, taxing authorities, employees, customers, financial analysts and advisors, stock exchanges, lawyers, regulatory or registration authorities, financial press and reporting agencies, trade associations, and labor unions. Although it acknowledged that these groups have different needs, the statement observed that "the problem of ascertaining specialized needs of a large number of users, the cost of attempting to serve those needs on an individual basis, and the confusion that might result from disseminating more than one set of information about the financial results of an enterprise's operation militate against attempting to serve all needs of users with special-purpose reports." It also identified one of the basic features of financial accounting as the presentation of "general-purpose financial information that is designed to serve the common needs of owners, creditors, managers, and other users, with primary emphasis on the needs of present and potential owners and creditors." This basic feature of financial accounting is based on the presumption that "a significant number of users need similar information." As we might expect, the FASB adopted similar positions. Its stated objective for financial reporting is to serve the needs of users of financial statements in general and not the particular needs of specific users.

Another indication of the FASB's view was expressed in an FASB exposure draft issued before the issuance of FASB Statement No. 14, "Financial Reporting for Segments of a Business Enterprise":

The Board believes, however, that there is no fundamental difference in the types of decisions and the decision-making processes of those who use the financial statements of smaller or privately held enterprises. . . . Information of the type required to be disclosed by this statement is as important to users of the financial statements of those enterprises as it is to users of the financial statements of a large or publicly held enterprise. Accordingly, this statement applies to all financial statements that present financial position or results of operations in conformity with generally accepted accounting principles.

There seems to be no awareness by the standard setters that small and closely held companies are in an economic environment completely different from that of large and publicly held companies.

Many, however, will disagree with the APB Statement No. 4 and the FASB positions on the nature of the user and his or her further needs and with most of the empirical findings that there may be no basic differences in the needs of users of financial statements. The intuitive and at the same time accurate view is that principal users of public company financial statements are financial analysts and public stockholders, and financial statements of smaller and/or closely held businesses are usually directed toward owner-managers and bankers and other credit grantors.

Official Positions on "Little GAAP"

The need for differential measurement, reporting, and disclosure on the basis of either size (small versus large) or ownership (public versus private) has been a concern of the profession since 1952. More recently, the AICPA's accounting standards division began a study of the application of the GAAP to smaller and/or closely held businesses by forming in 1974 the Committee on Generally Accepted Accounting Principles for Smaller and/or Closely Held Business (the "little GAAP" Committee). Four basic questions were asked in a discussion paper distributed to more than 20,000 members:

1. Are any differences in the application of the generally accepted accounting principles appropriate?
2. If there were differences in the application of the generally accepted accounting principles, on what basis should the different applications be determined?
3. If there were differences in the application of the generally accepted accounting principles, what differences would be appropriate?
4. If there were differences in the application of the generally accepted accounting principles, what impact would this have on the independent CPA?

The "little GAAP" Committee studied the responses and concluded generally in its 1976 report that there is strong support within the profession as a whole for reconsideration of present practices with respect to the application of the generally accepted accounting principles to the financial statements of smaller and/or closely held businesses and with respect to standards for reports of CPAs on such statements. More specifically, the report (pages 8 and 9) contained the following conclusions and recommendations directly related to the issues being considered:

[Conclusions]

- . . . The same measurement principles should be applied in the general-purpose financial statements of all entities, because the measurement process should be independent of the nature of users and their interest in the resulting measurements.

- • . . . The nature of the information disclosed and the extent of detail necessary for any particular disclosure may well vary depending on the needs of users.
- • . . . [There should be a distinction between] disclosures . . . required by GAAP [and] additional or analytical [disclosures] in the financial statements of all entities.

[Recommendations]

- • The Financial Accounting Standards Board should develop criteria to distinguish disclosures that should be required by GAAP . . . from disclosures that merely provide additional or analytical data. . . . The criteria should then be used in a formal review of disclosures presently considered to be required by GAAP and should also be considered by the Board in any new pronouncements.
- • The AICPA auditing standards division should reconsider pronouncements concerning a CPA's report on (a) unaudited financial statements, including those accompanied by an "internal use only" disclaimer, (b) financial information presented on prescribed forms, and (c) interim financial statements of smaller and/or closely held businesses.
- • . . . The Financial Accounting Standards Board should amend APB Opinion No. 15 ["Earnings Per Share"], to require only publicly traded companies . . . to disclose earnings-per-share data.

The official reactions to these recommendations were positive. The AICPA created the Accounting and Review Services Committee (ARSC) and gave it the status of a senior committee. Its objective was to reconsider all aspects of AICPA pronouncements applicable to the association of CPAs with unaudited financial statements, a project that is basically small-business oriented. Since then the ARSC has issued statements on standards for accounting and review services (SSARs), which establish and delineate the CPA's involvement with unaudited financial statements of companies. The ultimate result is to give to small businesses the possibility of appearing "unaudited but OK."

The FASB reacted favorably to the report. In 1978 it issued Statement No. 21 "Suspension of the Reporting of Earnings per Share and Segment Information by Nonpublic Enterprises," which suspends the earnings-per-share and segment disclosures as requirements for reporting by private companies. It also started including in its pronouncements size tests that exempt small and private companies from certain requirements. The AICPA was not, however, impressed with the FASB efforts. Thus in 1980 the Technical Issues Committee of the AICPA Private Companies Practice Section began a project to identify significant measurement and disclosure requirements of the generally accepted accounting principles that either (a) are not relevant to the financial statements of most small and medium-sized privately owned businesses (private companies) or (b) do not provide benefits to the users of those statements sufficient to justify the costs of applying the principles.

In 1982 the committee issued its report *Sunset Review of Accounting Principles.* It recommended changing or eliminating eleven accounting and disclosure requirements that the committee believed either should not apply to private companies or do not sufficiently benefit the users of private companies' financial statements to justify their costs. The eleven issues examined were: (1) deferred income taxes, (2) leases, (3) capitalization of interest, (4) inputed interest, (5) compensated balances, (6) business combinations, (7) troubled debt restructurings, (8) research and development costs, (9) discontinued operations, (10) tax benefit of operating loss carryforward, and (11) investment tax credits.

The ball was once more in the FASB's court. Would it go toward the creation of a "little GAAP," or would it treat the problems faced by small business within the standards-overload problem. The more logical approach for the FASB would be to treat the standards-overload problem first, which would alleviate the problems faced by small business. Creating a "little GAAP" would be practically and logically unsound. Most of the objections to having two sets of GAAPs are convincing.

Examples of objections are as follows: (a) improvements in reporting to one group of users should also result in improving the reporting to other groups; (b) all companies operate in the same environment, face similar economic conditions, and could have the same types of transactions; (c) most companies belong to either trade associations or industry groups that typically summarize financial statements of companies in the association or the group, and different accounting requirements for different companies within the same group could distort financial comparisons; and (d) most private companies would eventually become public.

6. THE SAGA OF SAM'S DELICATESSEN*

I met with my old friend Sam Applemeister last week and was delighted to learn that his business, Sam's Delicatessen, Inc. was doing well. So well, in fact, that Sam had been stricken with a bad case of "compliance syndrome."

"I've been doing my own accounting," he told me, "but now I can afford to hire you and I want my financial statements to be really professional."

"That's a good idea," I told him. "I'm sure you'll find the information in your financial statements will be valuable. For instance, you'll have a ' "Statement of Changes in Financial Position.' "

"What's that?" Sam inquired.

"Well, in its simplest terms," I replied, "it tells you where your cash came from and where it went. It's all spelled out in Accounting Principles Board Opinion no. 19."

---

*Charles Chazen and Benjamin Benson, "Fitting GAAP to Smaller Businesses," *Journal of Accountancy*, February 1978, 46-47. Reprinted with permission. Copyright © 1978 by Charles Chazen and Benjamin Benson.

"I already know where it came from and where it went," exclaimed Sam. "All I care about is what's left at the end of the year."

"Sorry Sam," I said, "it's required if you want full financial statements."

"O.K.," he responded, "but if it weren't for my catering business there wouldn't be that much to account for."

"The catering business, Sam?" I asked.

"Sure," he said. "In addition to the retail trade, my take-out business has really grown and a big part of my income is from catering parties."

"Oops," I replied, "you may be subject to Statement of Financial Accounting Standards no. 14, *Financial Reporting for Segments of a Business Enterprise*, in which case you'll have to segregate the revenues, profitability and identifiable assets of the retail and catering lines. You must also provide information about your major customers."

"But I don't have those figures," complained Sam. "We do all of our business out of the store, and I don't keep records about how much business we do with each customer."

"That's all right," I told him. "We can help you set up a management information system."

"I don't know how that information can be of value to anyone except my competitors, but if I can afford to own the building that the store is in, I guess I can afford such a system."

"Do you own the building personally?"

"Yes," he replied. "I made a small down payment and there is a long-term lease from the corporation that provides for the mortgage payments and all other expenses."

"Well, it looks like this comes under Statement of Financial Accounting Standards no. 13, *Accounting for Leases*. Ordinarily we would have to consider the fair value of the property, any bargain purchase options, the estimated economic life of the property, estimated residual value, the lessee's incremental borrowing rate and some other factors. In your case, because of the relationship of the lessee and lessor, we'll have to make the accounting match the economic substance rather than the legal form."

"It sure sounds complicated," said Sam, scratching his head. "But as long as my earnings are there I still want to go ahead."

"Don't worry about your earnings. Under Accounting Principles Board Opinion no. 15, your earnings per share will be clearly stated."

"What do you mean, 'earnings per share'?" cried Sam. "There are only 100 shares issued and I own them all."

"Don't panic, Sam," I told him. "You said you wanted proper financial statements."

"I do, I do," he said, wiping away his tears, "but how much will all of this cost?"

Taking out my pencil, I figured it out. "Here's good news, Sam," I said. "It looks as though you won't have to worry about earnings per share after all."

7. THE STRUCTURE OF ACCOUNTING THEORY

A full appreciation of the current and future scope of accounting depends on an understanding not only of accounting techniques but also of the structure of accounting theory from which the techniques are derived. The development of a structure of accounting theory to justify better the existing techniques and rules is important. The primary objective is to modify the postulates, concepts, and principles of accounting and to formulate a coherent accounting theory to enable accountants to improve the quality of financial reporting.

In general, the *structure of an accounting theory* contains the following elements:

1. A statement of the objectives of financial statements.
2. A statement of the postulates and theoretical concepts of accounting dealing with the environmental assumptions of the accounting unit. These postulates and theoretical concepts are derived from the stated objectives.
3. A statement of the basic accounting principles based on both the postulates and theoretical concepts.
4. A body of accounting techniques derived from the accounting principles.

The development of these elements—postulates, concepts, and principles of accounting—has always been one of the most challenging and difficult tasks in accounting.

1. The *accounting postulates* are self-evident statements or axioms, which are generally accepted by virtue of their conformity to the objectives of financial statements, that portray the economic, political, sociological, and legal environment in which accounting must operate. They include the entity postulate, the going-concern postulate, the unit-of-measure postulate, and the accounting-period postulate.
2. The *theoretical concepts of accounting* are also self-evident statements or axioms, which are generally accepted by virtue of their conformity to the objectives of financial statements, that portray the nature of accounting entities operating in a free economy characterized by private ownership of property. They include the proprietary theory, the entity theory, and the fund theory.
3. The *accounting principles* are general decision rules, derived from both the objectives and the theoretical concepts of accounting, that govern the development of accounting techniques. They include the cost principle, the revenue principle, the matching principle, the objectivity principle, the consistency principle, the full-disclosure principle, the conservatism principle, the materiality principle, and the uniformity and comparability principles.

An understanding of these elements and the relationships of accounting theory guarantees understanding of the rationale behind actual and future practices. The financial statements presented in the formal accounting reports are merely a reflection of the application of the theoretical structure of accounting. Improving the content and format of financial statements is definitively linked to improving the theoretical structure of accounting.

Foremost on the agenda of the standard-setting bodies should be the clarification of the elements of accounting theory, namely, the postulates, concepts, and principles.

8. THE ACCOUNTING POSTULATES

The *accounting postulates* are self-evident statements or axioms, generally accepted by virtue of their conformity to the objectives of financial statements, that portray the economic, political, sociological, and legal environment in which accounting operates. They include the entity postulate, the going-concern postulate, the unit-of-measure postulate, and the accounting-period postulate.

The Entity Postulate

The *entity postulate* holds that each enterprise is an accounting unit separate and distinct from its owners and other firms. It defines the accountant's area of interest and limits the number of objects, events, and their attributes that are to be included in the financial statements. The transactions of the enterprise rather than the transactions of the owners are to be reported.

One way of defining an accounting entity is to define the economic unit responsible for the economic activities and administrative control of the unit. This approach is better exemplified by the consolidated reporting of different entities as a single economic unit, regardless of their legal differences.

Another way to define an accounting entity is in terms of the economic interests of various users rather than the economic activities and administrative control of the unit. In other words, the interests of the users rather than the economic activities of the firm define the boundaries of the accounting entity and the information to be included in the financial statements. This view justifies the possible data expansion that may result from the new scope of accounting as it attempts to meet all of the potential information needs of users.

The Going-Concern Postulate

The *going-concern postulate*, or *continuity postulate*, holds that the business entity will continue its operations long enough to realize its projects, commitments, and ongoing activities. The postulate assumes either that the entity is not expected to liquidate in the foreseeable future or that it will continue for an indefinite period. Such a hypothesis of stability reflects the expectations of all parties interested in the entity. Thus the financial statements provide a tentative view of the financial situation of the firm and are only part of a series of continuous reports. Except for the case of liquidation, the user will interpret the information as computed on the basis of the assumption of the continuity of the firm. The major role of the going-concern postulate is that it justifies the valuation of the assets on a non-liquidation basis and forms the basis of all types of accounting allocation. It is regrettable, however, to report that all accounting allocations are arbitrary and incorrigible.

The Unit-of-Measure Postulate

The *unit-of-measure postulate* holds that accounting is a measurement and communication process of the activities of the firm, which are measurable in monetary terms. It implies two main limitations of accounting. First, accounting is limited to the production of information expressed in a monetary unit; it does not record and communicate other relevant but non-monetary information. Accounting information is perceived as essentially monetary and quantified, and nonaccounting information is nonmonetary and nonquantified. The second limitation implied by the monetary-unit postulate concerns the limitation of the monetary unit itself as a unit of measure. The primary characteristic of the monetary unit—purchasing power of the quantity of goods or services that money can acquire—is of concern. Unlike the meter, which is invariably 100 centimeters long, the purchasing power of the monetary unit, which is the dollar, is subject to changes. Conventionally, accounting theory has dealt with this problem by stating that the unit-of-measure postulate is also "a stable monetary postulate" in that the postulate assumes either that the purchasing of the dollar is stable over time or that the changes are insignificant. This view is the subject of continuous and persistent criticisms.

The Accounting-Period Postulate

Although the going-concern postulate holds that the firm will exist for an indefinite time, a variety of information about the financial position and performance of a firm is needed by users for short-term decision making. In response to this constraint imposed by the user environment, the *accounting-period postulate* holds that the financial reports depicting the changes in the wealth of a firm should be disclosed periodically. Although the periods vary, income tax laws, which require income determination on an annual basis, and traditional business practice result in the period usually being a year. Although most companies use an accounting period that corresponds to the calendar year, some companies use a fiscal or "natural" business year.

By requiring the entity to provide periodic short-term financial reports, the accounting-period postulate imposes the use of accruals and deferrals, the application of which is the principal difference between accrual accounting and cash accounting.

9. THE THEORETICAL CONCEPTS OF ACCOUNTING

The *theoretical concepts of accounting* are self-evident statements or axioms, generally accepted by virtue of their conformity to the objectives of financial statements, that portray the nature of accounting entities operating in a free economy characterized by private ownership of property.

The three theoretical concepts of accounting are the proprietary theory, the entity theory, and the fund theory.

The Proprietary Theory

Under the *proprietary theory*, the entity is the agent, representative, or arrangement through which the individual entrepreneurs or shareholders operate. The primary objective of the proprietary theory is the determination and analysis of the proprietor's net worth. Accordingly, the accounting equation is viewed as:

$$Assets - Liabilities = Proprietor's\ Equity$$

The proprietor owns the assets and liabilities. If the liabilities may be considered negative assets, the proprietary theory may be said to be asset centered and, consequently, balance sheet oriented. Assets are valued, and balance sheets are prepared to measure the changes in the proprietary interest or wealth. *Revenues* and *expenses* are viewed as increases or decreases, respectively, in proprietorship not resulting from proprietary investments or capital withdrawals by the proprietor. Thus *net income* is an increase in the proprietor's wealth to be added to capital losses, interest on debt, and corporate income taxes, which are expenses, and *dividends* are withdrawals of capital.

Although the theory is generally held to be adapted best to closely held corporations such as proprietorships and partnerships, it has influenced some of the accounting techniques and terminology used by widely held corporations. For example, the *corporate concept of income*, which is arrived at after treating interest and income taxes as expenses, represents "net income to the stockholders" rather than to all providers of capital. Similarly, terms such as *earnings per share, book value per share*, and *dividend per share* connote a proprietary emphasis.

The Entity Theory

Under the *entity theory*, the entity is viewed as something separate and distinct from those who provided capital to it. Simply stated, the business unit rather than the proprietor is the center of accounting interest. It owns the resources of the enterprise and is liable to the claims of both owners and creditors. Accordingly, the accounting equation is as follows:

$$Assets = Equities$$
$$Assets = Liabilities + Stockholders\ Equity$$

Assets are rights accruing to the entity, and *equities* represent sources of the assets, consisting of liabilities and the stockholders' equity. Both the creditors and the stockholders are equity holders, although they have different rights with respect to income, risk, control, and liquidation. Thus income earned is the property of the entity until distributed as dividends to the shareholders. Because the business unit is held responsible for meeting the claims of the equity holders, the entity theory is said to be income centered and, consequently, income statement oriented. Accountability to the equity holders is accomplished by measuring the operating and financial performance of the firm. Accordingly, *income* is an increase in the stockholders' equity after the claims of other equity holders are met—for example, interest on long-term debt and income taxes. The increase in stockholders' equity is considered income to stockholders only if a dividend is declared. Similarly, undistributed profits remain the property of the entity, because they represent the corporation's proprietary equity in itself.

The entity theory is most applicable to the corporate form of business enterprise, which is separate and distinct from its owners. The impact of the entity theory may be found in most of the accounting techniques and terminology used in practice.

The Fund Theory

Under the *fund theory*, the basis of accounting is neither the proprietor nor the entity but is a group of assets and related obligations and restrictions governing the use of the assets called a "fund." Thus the fund theory views the business unit as consisting of economic resources (funds) and related obligations and restrictions in the use of the resources. The accounting equation as viewed as:

$$Assets = Restriction\ of\ Assets$$

The accounting unit is defined in terms of assets and the uses to which these assets are committed. *Liabilities* represent a series of legal and economic restrictions on the use of the assets. The fund theory is therefore asset centered in that it places primary focus on the administration and appropriate use of the assets. It is useful primarily to governments and nonprofit organizations. Hospitals, universities, cities, and governmental units, for example, are engaged in multifaceted operations that warrant separate funds. The fund theory is also relevant to profit-oriented organizations, which use funds for diverse activities such as sinking funds, accounting for bankruptcies and estates and trusts, branch or divisional accounting, segregation of assets between current and fixed assets, and in consolidation.

10. THE ACCOUNTING PRINCIPLES

The *accounting principles* are general decision rules, derived from both the objectives and the theoretical concepts of accounting, that govern the development of accounting techniques. They include the (a) cost principle, (b) revenue principle, (c) matching principle, (d) objectivity principle, (e) consistency principle, (f) full-disclosure principle, (g) conservatism principle, (h) materiality principle, and (i) comparability and uniformity principle.

The Cost Principle

According to the *cost principle*, the acquisition cost, or historical cost, is the appropriate valuation basis for the recognition of the acquisition of all goods and services, expenses, costs, and equities. In other words, an item is valued at the exchange price at the date of acquisition and shown in the financial statements at that value or an amortized portion of it. *Cost* represents the exchange price or monetary consideration given for the acquisition of goods or services. If the consideration comprises nonmonetary assets, the *exchange price* is the cash equivalent of the assets or services given up.

The cost principle may be justified by both its objectivity and by the going-concern postulate. First the acquisition cost is objective, verifiable information. Second, the going-concern postulate assumes that the entity will continue its activities indefinitely and, consequently, will eliminate the necessity of using current values or liquidation values for asset valuation.

The precarious validity of the unit-of-measure postulate, which assumes that the purchasing power of the dollar is stable, is a major limitation to the use of the cost principle. Historical cost valuation is bound to produce erroneous figures if changes in the values of assets over time are ignored.

The Revenue Principle

The *revenue principle* specifies the nature and components of revenue, the measurement of revenue, and the timing of revenue recognition. With regard to the nature and components of revenue, *revenue* may be interpreted as (a) an inflow of net assets resulting from the sales of goods or services, (b) an outflow of goods or services from the firm to its customers, and (c) a product of the firm resulting from the mere creation of goods or services by an enterprise during a given period. With regard to the measurement of revenue, revenue is measured by the value of the product or services exchanged in an arm's-length transaction. With regard to the timing-of-revenue recognition, accountants have relied on the realization principle to select a "critical event" in the cycle for the timing of revenue and the recognition of income. Under the critical-event approach, the recognition of revenue is triggered by a crucial event in the operating cycle. That event may be (a) the time of sale, (b) the completion of production, or (c) the receipt of payment subsequent to sale:

1. The sales basis for the recognition of revenue is justified because (a) the price of the product is then known with certainty, (b) the exchange has been finalized by delivery of goods, leading to an objective knowledge of the costs incurred; and (c) in terms of realization, a sale constitutes a crucial event.
2. The completion-of-production basis for the recognition of revenue is justified when a stable market and a stable price exist for a standard commodity. The production process rather than the sale, therefore, constitutes the crucial event for the recognition of revenue.
3. The cash basis for the recognition of revenue is justified when the sales will be made and when a reasonable accurate valuation cannot be placed on the product transferred. This method, which amounts to a mere deferral of revenues, is primarily identified with the "installment method" of recognized revenue.

The Matching Principle

The *matching principle* holds that expenses should be recognized in the same period as the associated revenues. That is, revenues are recognized in a given period according to the revenue principle, and then the related expenses are recognized. The association is best accomplished when it reflects the "cause and effect" relationship between costs and revenues. Operationally, it consists of a two-stage process for accounting for expenses. First, costs are capitalized as assets representing bundles of service potential or benefits. Second, these assets are written off as expenses to recognize the proportion of the asset's service potential that has expired in the generation of revenues during this period. Thus accrual rather than cash-basis accounting is implied by the matching principle in the form of capitalization and allocation.

The association between revenues and expenses depends on one of four criteria.

1. Direct matching or expired cost with a revenue (for example, cost of goods sold matched with related sale)
2. Direct matching of expired cost with the period (for example, president's salary for the period)
3. Allocation of costs over periods benefited (for example, depreciation expense)

4. Expensing of all other costs in the period incurred, unless it can be shown they have future benefit

Unexpired costs (that is, assets) not meeting one of the four criteria for expensing in the current period are chargeable to future periods and may be classified under different categories according to their different uses in the firm.

The Objectivity Principle

The usefulness of financial information depends heavily on the *reliability* of the measurement procedure used. Because ensuring maximum reliability is frequently difficult, accountants have employed the *principle of objectivity* to justify the choice of a measurement or measurement procedure. The principle of objectivity, however, has been subject to the following interpretations:

1. An objective measurement is an ''impersonal'' measure in that it is free from the personal bias of the measurers. In other words, *objectivity* refers to the external reality that is independent of the persons who perceive it.
2. An objective measurement is a verifiable measurement in that it is based on an evidence.
3. An objective measurement is the result of a consensus among a given group of observers or measurers. This view also implies that objectivity will depend on the given group of measurers.
4. The size of the dispersion of the measurement distribution may be used as an indicator of the degree of objectivity of a given measurement system.

The question still remains whether to opt for objectivity or reliability. The general consensus is that the accounting profession ought to find a trade-off between objectivity and bias that leads to acceptable levels of reliability. This is possible when a consensus exists on the alleged values to be measured.

The Consistency Principle

The *consistency principle* holds that similar economic events should be recorded and reported in a consistent manner from period to period. This principle implies that the same accounting procedures will be used for similar items over time. The application of consistency makes financial statement more comparable and more useful. Trends in accounting data and relationships with external factors are better revealed when similar measurement procedures are used. Similarly, distortion of income and balance-sheet amounts and possible manipulation of financial statements are avoided by consistency in the use of accounting procedures over time. Therefore, consistency is a user constraint intended to facilitate a user's decision by ensuring comparable presentation of financial statements of a given firm over time, thereby enhancing the statements' utility. Consistency is a major concern of accountants when auditing financial statements. In the standard opinion, the CPA recognizes the consistency principle by noting whether or not the financial statements were prepared in conformity with the generally accepted accounting principles applied on a basis "consistent with that of the preceding year."

The consistency principle does not preclude a firm's changing accounting procedures when justified by changing circumstances or if the alternative procedure is preferable (rule of preferability). According to APB Opinion No. 20, changes that justify a change in procedure are: (a) a change in accounting principle, (b) a change in accounting estimate, and (c) a change in reporting entity. These changes are to be reflected in the accounts and reported on the financial statements retroactively, for a change in accounting entity; prospectively, for a change in accounting estimate; and generally, currently for a change in accounting principles.

The Full-Disclosure Principle

There is a general consensus in accounting that there should be a "full," "fair," and "adequate" disclosure. *Full disclosure* requires that financial statements be designed and prepared to portray accurately the economic events that affected the firm for the period and to contain information sufficient to make them useful and not misleading to the average investor. More explicitly, the full-disclosure principle implies that no information of substance of interest to the average investor will be omitted or concealed. The principle is further reinforced by the various disclosure requirements set by the APB opinions, the FASB statements, and the SEC accounting releases and requirements. It is, however, a broad and open-ended construct, which leaves several questions unanswered or open to different interpretations.

First, what is meant by "full," "fair," and "adequate" disclosure? *Adequate* connotes a minimum set of information to be disclosed, *fair* implies an ethical constraint dictating an equitable treatment of users, and *full* refers to complete and comprehensive presentation of information. Another accepted position is to view "fairness" as the central objective and to trade off between full and adequate disclosure. Hence under the heading "Fair Presentation in Conformity with Generally Accepted Accounting Principles," APB Statement No. 4 states that fair presentation is met when "a proper balance has been achieved between the conflicting needs to disclose important aspects of financial positions and results of operations in accordance with conventional aspects and to summarize the voluminous underlying data into a limited number of financial statement captions and supporting notes."

Second, what data should be disclosed so that a "prudent average investor" will not be misled? Should they be essentially accounting information? Should they include novel information and additions such as human asset accounting, socio-economic accounting, inflation accounting, and segment reporting? The answers to these questions rest on a proper determination of the users, their needs, their level of sophistication, and, more importantly, their information-processing capabilities, given the risks of information overload caused by data expansion.

The Conservatism Principle

The *conservatism principle* is an exception or modifying principle in that it acts as a constraint to the presentation of relevant and reliable accounting data. The conservatism principle holds that when choosing among two or more acceptable accounting techniques, some preference is shown for the option that has the least favorable impact on stockholders' equity. More specifically, it implies that the lowest values of assets and revenues and the highest values of liabilities and expenses preferably should be reported. The conservatism principle, therefore, dictates a general pessimistic attitude from the accountant when choosing accounting techniques for financial reporting. To accomplish the objectives of understating current income and assets, the conservatism principle may lead to treatments that constitute a departure from acceptable or theoretical treatment. For example, the adoption of the "lower-of-cost-or-market" concept conflicts with the historical principle. Although last in-first out (LIFO) and accelerated depreciation are generally perceived as counterinflationary measures, they may be viewed as resulting from the adoption of the conservatism principle.

Conservatism has been used in the past as a way of dealing with uncertainty in the environment and the possible over-optimism of managers and owners and as a way of protecting creditors against an unwarranted distribution of the firm's assets as dividends. Conservatism was a more highly esteemed virtue in the past than it is today. It led to arbitrary and inconsistent treatment in the form of rapid asset write-offs or creation of excessive provisions for liabilities or both. In fact, conservatism is the most ancient and probably the most pervasive principle of accounting valuation.

Today, the emphasis on objective and fair presentation and the primacy of the investor as user has lessened the reliance on conservatism. It is perceived more as a guide for extraordinary situations than as a general rigid rule to apply in all circumstances. Conservatism is still applied in some situations that require an accountant's judgment, such as choosing the estimated useful life and residual value of an asset for depreciation accounting and the corollary rule of applying "lower of cost or market" in valuing inventories and marketable equity securities. Because it is essentially the manifestation of the accountant's intervention that may result in the introduction of bias, errors, possible distortions, and misleading statements, the present view of conservatism is bound to disappear as an accounting principle.

The Materiality Principle

Like conservatism, the *materiality principle* is an exception or modifying principle. The principle holds that transactions and events having an insignificant economic effect may be handled in the most expeditious manner, whether or not in conformity with the generally accepted accounting principles, and need not be disclosed. Materiality is an implicit guide for the accountant in deciding what should be disclosed in the financial reports. The accountant may decide, therefore, what is not important or what does not matter on the basis of record-keeping cost, accuracy of financial statements, and relevance to the user. In general, the accounting bodies have left the application of materiality to the accountant's judgment while stressing its importance.

The materiality principle lacks an operational definition. Most definitions of materiality stress the accountant's role in interpreting what is and what is not material. Guidelines or criteria to be used in determining materiality are urgently needed. Two basic criteria have been recommended. The first, referred to as the *size approach*, relates the size of the item to another relevant variable such as net income. For example, it has been suggested that a border zone of 10-15 percent of net income after taxes be used as the point of distinction between what is and what is not material. The second criterion, referred to as the *change criterion approach*, evaluates the impact of an item or trends or changes between periods. This approach contends that materiality criteria can be stated in terms of financial averages, trends, and ratios that express significant analytic relationships for accounting information.

The Uniformity and Comparability Principles

Whereas the consistency principle refers to the use of the same procedures for related items by a given firm over time, the *uniformity principle* refers to use of the same procedures by different firms. The desired objective is to reach comparability of financial statements by reducing the diversity created by the use of different accounting procedures by different firms. In fact, a constant debate has taken place over whether flexibility or uniformity should prevail in accounting and financial reporting.

The principal supports for uniformity are claims that: (a) it would reduce the diversity in the use of accounting procedures and the inadequacies and "horror stories" of accounting practices; (b) it would allow meaningful comparisons of the financial statements of different firms; (c) it would restore the confidence of users in the financial statements; and (d) it would lead to government intervention and regulation of accounting practice. The main supports for flexibility are the claims that: (a) uniformity in the use of accounting procedures for the same item occurring in many cases runs the risk of concealing important differences among cases; (b) comparability is a utopian goal; it cannot be achieved by the adoption of firm rules that do not take adequate account of different factual situations; and (c) differences in circumstances, or "circumstantial variables," call for different treatments so that corporate reporting can respond to circumstances in which transactions and events occur. The *circumstantial variables* may be defined as environmental conditions that vary among companies and that influence the feasibility of accounting methods and the objectivity of the measures resulting from applying the accounting methods.

The implicit objective of both uniformity and flexibility is to protect the user and present the user with meaningful data. Both fail because of their extreme positions on the issue of financial reporting. Uniformity per se does not lead to comparability—an admittedly unfeasible goal. Flexibility evidently leads to confusion and mistrust. A trade-off solution may be provided by encouraging uniformity by narrowing the diversity of accounting practices and, at the same time, allowing a proper recognition of market and economic events peculiar to a given firm and a given industry by a proper association of certain economic circumstances with related accounting techniques. This middle position calls for an operational definition of "differences in circumstances" and better guidelines for relating differences in circumstances to various accounting procedures.

11. FINANCIAL STATEMENTS OF BUSINESS ENTERPRISES

Annually, business enterprises produce a report. The financial statements included in the annual reports generally include a balance sheet, an income statement, a statement of changes in the financial position, notes to the financial statements, a reconciliation of retained earnings, an auditor's opinion, and supplementary information on the effects of changing prices.

The Balance Sheet

The *balance sheet*, or *statement of financial position*, expresses the financial position of a firm at the end of an accounting period, a moment in time. More precisely, it presents both the assets of a firm and claims on those assets (liabilities and owners' equity) at a specific time. Two major questions of interest to the reader are: which resources of a firm are recognized as assets, and which claims against the firm's assets are reorganized as liabilities? What valuations are placed on these assets and liabilities?

Assets

Four characteristics must be met for a resource (other than cases) to be recognized as an *asset*: (1) the resource must, singly or in combination with other resources, contribute directly or indirectly to future net cash inflows (or to obviating future net cash outflows); (2) the enterprise must be able to obtain the benefit from the resource and control the access of others to it; (3) the transaction or event giving rise to the enterprise's claim to or control of the benefit must already have occurred; and (4) the future benefit must be quantifiable or measurable in units of money. The assets are broken down into further, more specific, categories by order of decreasing liquidity.

Current assets is used to designate cash and other assets or resources commonly identified as those that are reasonably expected to be realized in cash or sold or consumed during the normal operating cycle of the business. Current assets consist generally of cash; marketable securities held as short-term investments; accounts and notes receivables net of allowance for uncollectible accounts; inventories or merchandise, raw materials, supplies, work in process, and finished goods; and prepared operating costs.

Investments is used to designate the investments in securities of other firms to be held for a long term and whose financial statements have not been consolidated with the parent or investor firm. Long-term investment of 50 percent of the voting stock of a corporation (subsidiary) calls for consolidation of the financial statements of the subsidiary with the parent firm.

Property, plant, and equipment designates the long-lived assets, generally called fixed assets, acquired for long-term use rather than resale, which usually include land, buildings, machinery and equipment, and various other equipment. With the exception of land, these assets are carried at original cost less accumulated depreciation.

Intangible assets designates resources that lack physical existence and includes copyrights, patents, trademarks, goodwill, organization costs, franchises, leaseholds, and similar items.

Liabilities

Four characteristics must be met before an obligation is recognized as a *liability*: (1) the obligation must involve a probable future sacrifice of resources—a future transfer of cash, goods, or services (or a foregoing of a future cash receipt); (2) the obligation must be one of the specific enterprise; (3) the transaction or event giving rise to the enterprise's obligation must already have occurred; and (4) the amount of the obligation and the time of its settlement must be measurable with reasonable accuracy. The liabilities are further broken down into specific categories.

Current liabilities is used principally to designate obligations whose liquidation is reasonably expected to require the use of existing resources properly classified as current assets or the creation of other current liabilities. It includes accounts payables, notes payables, accrued expenses, accrued taxes, and the current portion of long-term debt.

Long-term liabilities designates obligations having a due date or maturity of longer than a year. It includes bonds, mortgages, long-term leases, deferred income taxes, and deferred pension obligations.

Owner's Equity

Owner's equity represents the ownership interests in the firm and includes what was originally invested by them and whatever earnings are "plowed back" into the firm: It includes (1) *capital stock*, common or preferred, which is the portion of the capital specified in the articles of incorporation at par value; (2) *additional paid-in capital*, which is the portion paid in excess of the stated or par value; and (3) *retained earnings*, which represents earnings undistributed and "plowed back" into the firm.

Valuation of Assets and Liabilities

There are four possible valuation methods: (1) *acquisition cost*, or *historical cost*, which is the amount of cash or other payment made by the firm when it acquired specific assets; (2) *current entry value*, or *replacement cost*, which is the amount of cash or the equivalent necessary to replace one asset by a "similar" asset; (3) *current exit value*, or *net realizable value*, which is the amount assumed to be realized if the assets are sold in an orderly fashion; and (4) *capitalized value*, which is present value of future cash flows that can be generated by the asset.

Unfortunately, no single valuation base is used to value all of the assets and liabilities. All four valuation bases are used in the generally accepted accounting principles. Exhibit 3 presents a summary of valuation methods for various assets and liabilities. This situation presents an intellectual challenge to those investors who are not versed in the complexities and idiosyncrasies of accounting valuations.

The Income Statement

The *income statement* presents a measure of the financial performance of a firm during an accounting period. The net income is equal to the revenues and gains minus expenses and losses.

Revenues measure the inflow of net assets resulting from the sales of goods or services. Revenue may be recognized at the time of sale when (a) most of the services to be provided have been performed and (b) some measurable consideration has been received. Revenue may be recognized during the period of production for certain long-term contracts and special-order merchandise. Revenue also may be recognized at the time of cash collection for installment sales of merchandise, real estate, or franchises.

Expenses measure the outflow of net assets that have been used to generate the revenues. They are therefore recognized in the same period the revenues have been generated. Expenses are composed of cost of goods sold, selling, and administrative expenses. The value of the cost of goods sold depends on the cost-flow assumptions, either first in-first out (FIFO), last in-first out (LIFO), or weighted average. Under the *FIFO method*, the cost of goods sold is valued at the cost of the earliest units acquired. Under the *LIFO method*, the cost of goods sold is valued at the cost of the latest units acquired. Under the *weighted-average method*, the cost of goods sold is valued at the average of the costs of all goods available for sale use during the period. There is an important implication to the cost-flow assumptions. FIFO results in lower cost of goods sold and higher income than LIFO when prices are rising. This LIFO results in a cost-of-goods-sold figure that is close to current values and in lower cash outlays for income taxes.

Format and Classification within the Income Statement

In general, the income statement contains the following categories:

1. *Income from continuing operations*: It is equal to the revenues and gains from the operating areas of the business firm minus the corresponding expenses and losses.

2. *Income, gains, and losses from discontinued operations:* This section includes the income, gains, and losses resulting from the disposal of a segment of the firm.

3. *Extraordinary gains and losses*: This section includes all activities termed "extraordinary" if they meet all of the following criteria: they are (a) unusual, (b) infrequent, and (c) material (in amount).

4. *Adjustment for accounting changes*: This section includes four types of accounting changes, namely, (1) change in accounting estimate, (2) change in accounting principle, (3) change in reporting entity, and (4) correction of errors in prior years' financial statements. According to APB Opinion No. 20, these changes are to be reflected in the accounts and reported on the financial statements retroactively, for a change in accounting entity; prospectively, for a change in accounting estimate; and generally, currently for a change in accounting principle.

Earnings per Share

APB Opinion No. 15 recommends that earnings per share be included in the body of the income statement before receiving an auditor's unqualified opinion. Most firms have a complex capital structure that includes convertible bonds or convertible preferred stock. To warn about the dilutive effect of such a situation, a dual presentation of primary and fully diluted earnings per share is required. *Primary earnings per share* represents the earnings applicable to each share of outstanding common stock and common-stock equivalent. *Common-stock equivalents* are securities that are likely to be converted into, or exchanged for, common stock instead of their own periodic cash yields over time. *Fully diluted earnings per share*

*EXHIBIT 3 VALUATION BASES UNDER GENERALLY ACCEPTED
ACCOUNTING PRINCIPLES*

ACCOUNTS	*VALUATION BASE*
Cash	Face or curent exchange value (current cash equivalent)
Marketable Securities	The portfolio is valued at lower of cost or market (current exit value)
Accounts and notes receivable	Short-term accounts are valued at current cash equivalent, long-term accounts at the present value of the future cash flows (discounted at the historical market interest rate on date of issue)
Inventories	Lower of cost or market (current entry value)
Investments	Investments in bonds are valued at the present value of the future cash flows. Investments in stocks are valued at lower of cost or market where there is no significant influence and using the equity method where there is "significant influence"
Land	Acquisition cost
Depreciable assets	Acquisition cost (net of accumulated depreciation)
Patents, goodwill and intangibles	Stated at the amount payable if they are to be paid within the next year, if not, stated at the present value of future cash flows
Nonmonetary liabilities	If arising from transactions where revenues have already been recognized (warranties on product sold), they are stated at the estimated future cost of the warranty services; if arising from advances from customers for future goods or services, they are stated at the amount of cash received

represents the earnings applicable to each share if, besides outstanding common stock, all options, warrants, and convertible securities are exchanged for common stock.

The Statement of Changes in Financial Position

The *statement of changes in financial position* presents the inflows (sources) and outflows (uses) of funds for the accounting period. *Funds* are defined generally as working capital (current assets minus current liabilities). Other definitions of funds include cash only; cash and marketable securities; and cash, marketable securities, and accounts receivables net of current liabilities. Whatever the definition of funds, the statement of changes in financial position includes both the sources and uses of funds as follows:

1. *Sources—from operations*: Equal to income from continuing operations plus all expenses not requiring an outflow of funds
2. *Sources—proceeds from issuing noncurrent debt and capital stock*: Equal to funds generated from the issuance of stock and from long-term borrowing
3. *Sources—proceeds from the sale of net current assets*: Equal to funds generated from the sale of buildings, equipment, land, and other noncurrent assets
4. *Uses—for distributions to owners*: Equal to the dividends distributed to both common and preferred shareholders
5. *Uses—for redemption of long-term debt or capital stock*: Equal to the funds used for retiring noncurrent debt and acquiring capital stock (Treasury stock)
6. *Uses—for acquisition of noncurrent assets*: Equal to the funds used for the purchase of land, machinery, and equipment and other noncurrent assets

Notes to the Financial Statements

Given the complexity of the three major financial statements—the balance sheet, income statement, and statement of changes in the financial position—additional information may be needed to guide the annual-report user toward a better understanding of the accounting data. This additional information forms the major part of the notes to the financial statements. A high fluency in the accounting language is needed to comprehend the information conveyed by the notes.

The reconciliation of retained earnings section is used to reconcile the beginning and ending balances in retained earnings.

The auditor's opinion section is an important part of the annual report used to express the opinion of the independent certified public accountant on the financial statements, supporting schedules, and notes. The four types of opinion that may result from an independent audit of financial statements are:

1. *Unqualified opinion*: When the auditor states that the financial statements "present fairly" the position and activities of the firm.
2. *Qualified opinion*: When the auditor believes that the financial statements "present fairly" the position and activities of the firm but cannot make one or more of the statements necessary for an unqualified opinion. A qualified opinion is conveyed by the use of an "except for" or a "subject to" statement in the audit report. "Except for" is used to convey an objection about the financial statements being presented. "Subject to" is used to convey a contingency, uncertainty, or unresolved situations that may affect the financial statements.

3. *Disclaimer of opinion*: When the auditor has been so limited, or there is a serious and material departure from the GAAP, and as a result, the auditor expresses merely an inability to give an opinion.
4. *Adverse opinion*: When the auditor believes that the audit has shown some serious and material departures from the GAAP, and as a result, the financial statements do not present fairly the position and activities of the firm.

Supplementary Information on the Effects of Changing Prices

The Financial Accounting Standards Board Statement No. 33, "Financial Reporting and Changing Prices," requires that the company provide supplementary information concerning the effects of inflation on its financial statements. Required disclosures include selected financial information on a constant dollar basis (reflecting the effects of general inflation) as computed by use of the Consumer Price Index for All Urban Consumers (CPI) and on a current cost basis (reflecting specific price changes of goods and services). The FASB has provided flexibility and encouraged experimentation within the guidelines of the statement. Accordingly, users of annual reports should exercise discretion when considering the supplementary information on the effects of changing prices.

12. FUTURE SCOPE OF ACCOUNTING

The actual scope of financial accounting is limited to the recognition of only those transactions that are primarily the exchange of goods and services and do not include changes in human capital. Second, this definition limits the transactions to exchanges between two or more legal, economic entities; thus exchanges between a firm and its social environment are ignored for all practical purposes. Third, most transactions are actual or past events, so that the future financial postion and performance of a firm are not reflected in the financial statements. Finally, a need exists for some form of cash-flow reporting, employee reporting, and value-added reporting. All of these limitations are in the process of being corrected by new developments aimed at expanding the scope of accounting. These new developments include: (a) socio-economic accounting, (b) human-resource accounting, (c) public reporting of financial forecasts, (d) cash-flow reporting, (e) employee reporting, and (f) value-added reporting.

Socio-economic Accounting

The state of the world depends on a satisfactory resolution of all social issues: ecology, technology, pollution, urban blight, education, housing, crime, energy, urban congestion, poverty, population growth, monopoly power, consumer problems, discrimination, high national debt, and so forth. All sectors of the economy have moved at some time to tackle these issues and improve the quality of life. What is needed to secure a good result is some form of measurement of quality. What is needed is the development of an "arithmetic of quality" leading to an eventual "social report." Such a social report would identify, evaluate, and measure those aspects essential to maintain an adequate quality of life for all members of a nation as defined by social goals. This arithmetic of quality and the eventual production of social reports in conformity with social goals at both the firm and the national level is the purpose of socio-economic accounting. *Socio-economic accounting* is then a call for the measurement of the total performance of economic and government units and their contribution to the quality of life of all members of a nation. An exhaustive definition of socio-economic accounting goes as follows:

Socio-economic accounting results from the application of accounting in the social sciences; it refers to the ordering, measuring, analysis, and disclosure of the social and economic consequences of governmental and entrepreneurial behavior. It includes these activities at the macro and micro level. At the micro level, its purpose is the measurement and reporting of the impact of organizational behavior of firms on their environment. At the macro level, its purpose is the measurement and disclosure of the economic and social performance of a nation. At the micro level socio-economic accounting includes, therefore, financial and managerial social accounting and reporting and social auditing. At the macro level socio-economic accounting includes, therefore, social measurement, social accounting, and reporting.

Given this definition, the next objective is to rationalize and motivate the expansion of the scope of accounting and second to present the avenues for socio-economic accounting. The expansion of the scope of accounting to cover the goals of socio-economic accounting may be rationalized and motivated by some of the new paradigmatic thoughts in the social sciences, namely, the commitment to social welfare, the new environmental paradigm in sociology, the ecosystem perspective, and the sociologizing mode:

1. There is a commitment to social welfare. *Social welfare* includes all programs for meeting the basic social needs; it has its roots in religion, humanitarianism, and compassion. It calls for the creation of social structures or social agencies that have been appropriately described as the institutionalization of the philanthropic impulse and love of humankind.

2. The *human-exceptionalism paradigm* views humans as unique among earth's creatures. The *new environmental paradigm*, however, highlights the problems for human society that may arise from the limitations of the ecological world. It stipulates that human beings, as truly as other species, cannot ignore ecology and should perceive it as a factor that may influence and in turn be influenced by human behavior.

3. Given the limits to growth and the fragility of the ecosystem, a kind of ecosystem understanding and perspective is needed to protect human future.

4. Unlike the economizing mode, the *sociologizing mode* focuses on society's needs in a coordinated fashion and takes into account a notion of the public interest. The trend is clearly toward the sociologizing mode, mainly as a reaction to increasing criticism toward the corporation reinforced by the feeling that corporate-performance bias caused the quality of life in society to deteriorate.

Given these new paradigmatic thoughts, the avenues for socio-economic accounting include the need for an economic, a rectifying, and an ethical paradigm; a micro and macro social accounting; and social auditing:

1. The economic paradigm governing the relationships of a corporation and society need not be the role or importance of the market or the state as in libertarianism or the radical economics but a clear statement of national and social goals based on a commitment to social welfare and social justice and experimentation with institutional arrangements to solve economic and social problems.

2. The options open to the corporation are on a continuum from complete indifference to an active role in rectifying some of these social problems. Complete indifference would definitively be harmful to the long-term interests of the firm. Involvement in some form of rectification is a way of ensuring mutual acceptance of society and a role in securing social order and affluence.

3. An ethical paradigm of the corporate-society relationship is more favorable to and supportive of business's social involvement in general and socio-economic accounting in particular.

4. To accomplish these objectives, theories and techniques of social accounting need to be constructed, verified, and used by micro and macro economic and social units.

5. Public demand for socially oriented programs and for measurement and disclosure of the environment effects of organizational behavior will create pressure for a form of social auditing of the activities of the corporation.

Given these paradigmatic thoughts and the possible various avenues of implementation, socio-economic accounting is slowly emerging as a full-fledged accounting discipline.

Human-Resource Accounting

The objective of financial accounting is to provide information that is relevant to the decisions that users must make, including adequate information about one "neglected" asset of the firm—the human asset. More specifically, users may greatly benefit from a knowledge of the extent to which the human assets of an organization have increased or decreased during a given period. The conventional accounting treatment of human-resource outlays consists of expensing all human-capital formation expenditures and capitalizing similar outlays on physical capital. A more valid treatment would be to capitalize human-resource expenditures to yield future benefits and to reveal where such benefits can be measured. In fact, this treatment has created a new concern with the measurement of the cost or value of human resources to an organization and has led to the development of a new field of inquiry in accounting, known as human-resource accounting. A broad definition of *human-resource accounting* is the process of identifying, collecting, measuring, and disclosing data about human resources to interested users.

Monetary measures of human assets are historical cost, replacement cost, opportunity cost, and the compensation model. The principal nonmonetary measure is the "survey-of-organizations" model. Each of these methods has been explored in the accounting literature as a possible accounting measure of human assets. What is needed before there is an evaluation of these methods is their actual adoption by business firms and an examination of their usefulness for decision making. Three facts argue for the adoption of human-resource accounting by business firms:

1. Capitalizing human-resources costs is conceptually more valid than the expensing approach.
2. The information concerning "human assets" is likely to be relevant to a great variety of decisions made by external or internal users or both.
3. Accounting for human assets constitutes an explicit recognition of the premise that people are valuable organizational resources and an integral part of a mix of resources.

It is now up to the standard-setting agencies, the accounting profession, and the users to exert enough pressure to make human-resource accounting more of a reality than a good intellectual idea.

Public Reporting of Corporate Financial Forecasts

Faced with the challenge from diverse users to develop more relevant financial-reporting techniques, accountants and nonaccountants alike have recommended that forecasted information be incorporated into financial statements. Proposals vary from the suggestion that budgetary data be disclosed to the suggestion that public companies provide earnings forecasts in their annual or interim reports and prospectuses. From the point of view of the user, the disclosure of forecasts rather than budgets may be more relevant to his or her decision-making needs. In fact, the trend seems to be in favor of the disclosure of forecasts of specific accounts in general and earnings in particular. Assuming that adequate technology, experience, and competence are developed to ensure the accuracy of these forecasts, the users will be in a better position to assess the future profitability potential of the business firms.

Cash-Flow Accounting and Reporting

A dominant characteristic in early views of the purpose of financial statements is the *stewardship function*. According to this view, management is entrusted with control of the financial resources provided by capital suppliers. Accordingly, the purpose of financial statements is to report to concerned parties to facilitate the evaluation of management's stewardship. To accomplish this objective, the reporting system favored and deemed essential and superior to others is the *accrual system*. Simply stated, the *accrual basis of accounting* refers to a form of record-keeping that records not only transactions that result from the receipt and disbursement of cash but also amounts that the entity owes others and that others owe the entity. At the core of this system is the *matching* of revenues and expenses. Interest in the accrual method has generated a search for the "best" accrual method in general and the "ideal income" in particular. For a long time, this accounting paradigm governed the evaluation of accounting alternatives and the asset-valuation and income-determination proposals. However, this approach was constantly challenged by proponents of cash-flow accounting. The *cash-flow basis of accounting* may be defined as the recording not only of the cash receipts and disbursements of the period (the *cash* basis of accounting) but of the *future cash flows* owed to or by the firm as a result of selling and transferring the titles to certain goods (the *accrual* basis of accounting). The advocacy of cash-flow accounting is more evident in a questioning of the importance and efficacy of accrual accounting and a shift toward the cash-flow approach in security analysis.

The question of the superiority of accrual accounting over cash-flow accounting is central to the determination of the objectives and nature of financial reporting. Accrual accounting facilitates the evaluation of management's stewardship and is essential to the matching of revenues and expenses, which is required to align efforts and accomplishments properly. The efficacy of the accrual system has been questioned, however. All allocations are arbitrary and incorrigible, and the minimization of such allocations is recommended. A shift in security analysis from earnings-oriented valuation approaches to cash-flow-oriented valuation approaches is taking place. Most advocates of cash-flow accounting believe the problems of asset valuation and income determination are so formidable that they warrant the derivation of a separate accounting system and propose the inclusion of a comprehensive cash-flow statement in company reports.

Cash-flow accounting is viewed by supporters as superior to conventional accrual accounting because:

1. A system of cash-flow accounting might provide an analytic framework for linking past, present, and future financial performance.

2. For the perspective of investors, the projected cash flow would reflect both the company's ability to pay its way in the future and its planned financial policy.
3. A price-discounted flow ratio would be a more reliable investment indicator than the present price-earnings ratio, due to the numerous arbitrary allocations used to compute earnings per share.
4. Cash-flow accounting may be used to correct the gap in practice between the way in which an investment is made (generally based on cash flows) and the ways in which the results are evaluated (generally based on earnings).

Employee Reporting

The provision of financial and other relevant information to company employees and labor unions is a subject of growing interest. *The Corporate Report* is one of the first accounting documents to show concern for employees as users of published financial statements.[4] In fact, one of its primary recommendations, the *employment report*, is intended to show "the size and composition of the work force relying on the enterprise for its livelihood, the work contribution of employees, and the benefits earned."[5] The following data are recommended for inclusion in an employment report:

Number employed

Location of employment

Age distribution of permanent work force

Hours worked during year

Employee costs

Pension information

Education and training (including costs)

Recognized trade unions

Additional information (race relations, health and safety statistics, and so on)

Employment ratios[6]

As a result of the requirements of *The Corporate Report*, employee reporting is becoming more the rule than the exception in the United Kingdom. Other countries are demonstrating a growing awareness of information provision to company employees. These countries include: (a) the German Federal Republic, where, since 1972, employees have been considered the most important constituents to whom reports on the activities and performance of companies are addressed; (b) France, where, since 1979, companies have been required to conduct social audits and present social reports to the enterprise council, as well as to employees; and (c) Sweden, where the unions have free access to company information and the right to examine any company documents. In North America, the major disclosures in annual reports seem to occur in the areas of occupational safety and health in the United States and work stoppages in Canada.

Value-Added Reporting

Following favorable recommendations in *The Corporate Report*, a new form of accounting statement—the *value-added statement*—is gaining popularity in the corporate reports of the largest companies in the United Kingdom. This new statement may be viewed as a modified version of the income statement. Like the income statement, the value-added statement reports the operating performance of a company at a given time, using both accrual and matching procedures. Unlike the income statement, however, the value-added statement is interpreted not as a return to shareholders but as a return to a larger group of capital and labor providers. As a result, the value-added statement can be easily derived from the income statement, according to the following steps:

Step 1: The income statement can be expressed as :

$$R = S - B - DP - W - I - DD - T \qquad (1)$$

where

R = retained earnings
S = sales revenue
B = bought-in materials and services
DP = depreciation
W = wages
I = interest
DD = dividends
T = taxes

Equation (1) expresses the profit as a return to shareholders.

Step 2: The value statement may be obtained by rearranging equation (1) as:

$$S - B - DP = W + I + DD + T + R \qquad (2)$$

$$S - B = W + I + DD + T + DP + R \qquad (3)$$

Equation (2) expresses the *net* value added; equation (3) expresses the *gross* value added. In either case, the left part of the equation shares the value added (net or gross), and the right part of the equation divides the value added among the groups involved. Exhibit 4 shows how the value-added statement can be derived from a regular income statement.

EXHIBIT 4 DERIVING THE VALUE-ADDED STATEMENT

The conventional income statement of a company for 19X6 was:

Sales			$2,000,000
Less:	Materials Used	$100,000	
	Wages	200,000	
	Services Purchased	300,000	
	Interest Paid	60,000	
	Depreciation	40,000	
Profit Before Tax			$3,000,000
Income Tax (assume 50% tax rate)			150,000
Profit After Tax			$ 150,000
Less: Dividends Payable			50,000
	Retained Earnings for the Year		$ 100,000

A value-added statement for the same year would be:

Sales			$2,000,000
Less: Bought-in Materials and Services and Depreciation			440,000
Value Added Available for Distribution or Retention			$1,560,000
Applied as follows:			
To Employees			$ 200,000
To Providers of Capital			
Interest		$ 60,000	
Dividends		50,000	110,000
To Government			150,000
Retained Earnings			1,000,000
Value Added			$ 560,000

What are the advantages and disadvantages of such a report? Various advantages of including a value-added statement in the company's annual report have been cited:

1. It is generally believed that value added may be more favorable and acceptable to employees than profit and may motivate employees to work harder, because the value-added statement perceives them as responsible participators in a team effort with management.
2. The value-added statement is expected to facilitate the introduction of productivity incentives for employees—primarily in the form of the payment of incentives for the maximization of value-added-based ratios.
3. Value-added-based ratios are interpreted as more indicative and predictive of the strength of the company than conventional ratios.
4. Value-added measures are believed to constitute a better measure of the size and importance of companies.

Some disadvantages of including a value-added statement in the company's annual report have been cited:

1. Value added may be the wrong variable to maximize when making internal decisions pertaining to resource allocation.
2. Value added may lead to information overload and confusion, given the amount of information already included in the annual report and the small degree of familiarity with the concept of users.

13. LETTING THE ACCOUNTING TAIL WAG THE ECONOMIC DOG

The Income-Smoothing Hypothesis

As early as 1953 it was argued that management's objectives may not necessarily be to report maximum profits but to smooth the firm's income over the years. Generally, management will choose accounting principles that smooth the net income series.

Income smoothing is the intentional dampening of fluctuations about some level of earnings that is currently considered to be normal for a firm. The various empirical studies assumed various smoothing objects (operating income or ordinary income), various smoothing instruments (operating expenses, ordinary expenses, or extraordinary items), and various smoothing dimensions (accounting smoothing or real smoothing). Accounting smoothing affects income through accounting dimensions—namely, smoothing through the occurrence or recognition of events, smoothing through allocation overtime, and smoothing through classification. In other words, accountants can manage earnings through three broad classes: changing accounting methods, fiddling with manager's estimates of costs, and changing the period when expenses and revenues are included in results. Real smoothing affects income through the intentional changing of the operating decisions and their timing.

In general, two main motivations for smoothing are speculated in the literature: (1) to enhance the reliability of prediction based on the observed smoothed series of accounting numbers along a trend considered best or normal by management; (2) to reduce the uncertainty resulting from the fluctuations of income numbers in general and the reduction of systematic risk in particular by reducing the covariance of the firm's returns with the market returns. Both reasons of motivation result from a need felt by management to neutralize environmental uncertainty and dampen the wide fluctuations in the operating performance of the firm subject to an intermittent cycle of good and bad times. To do so management may resort to organizational slack behavior, budgeting slack behavior, or risk-avoiding behavior. Each of these behaviors necessitates decisions that affect the incurrence or allocation of discretionary expenses and results in income smoothing.

In addition to noting these behaviors intended to neutralize environmental uncertainty, it is also possible to identify organizational characterizations that differentiate along the extent of smoothing in different firms. One study examined the effects of the separation of ownership and control on income smoothing on the basis of the hypothesis that management-controlled firms are more likely to be engaged in smoothing as a manifestation of managerial discretion and budgetary slack.[7] Their results confirm that a majority of firms examined behave as if they were smoothers; a particularly strong majority is included among management-controlled firms with high barriers to entry.

Other organizational characterizations may exist to differentiate among firms according to the dimension of the attempt to smooth. One such characterization derived from the theories of economic dualism divides the industrial sector into two distinct *core* and *periphery* sectors. The study hypothesized that a higher degree of smoothing of income numbers will be exhibited by firms in the periphery sector than by firms in the core sector because of a reaction to different opportunity structures and experiences.[8] The results indicate that a majority of firms may be resorting to income smoothing and that a greater number of these income smoothers are firms in the periphery sector.

How Is It Really Done?

Managers do not really have to "cook the books" to manipulate earnings. The GAAP provides them with enough flexibility to be able to develop thousands of possible scenarios. That flexibility allows them to report earnings that follow a smooth, regular, upward path. That option suits most managers eager to avoid sharp fluctuations in their earnings. As a result, these managers give more attention to the accounting consequences of major decisions than to the economics. That is equivalent to letting the accounting tail wag the economic dog. It also shifts the objective function from the well-known maximization of shareholders' wealth to the maximization of management's wealth or welfare. To be more precise, most bonuses and other perquisites are tied to report earnings, providing managers with an excellent motivation to smooth earnings. A 1984 study by accounting professor Paul Healy of the Massachusetts Institute of Technology shows a relationship between bonus schemes and the accounting choices executives make. Healy found that executives whose bonus plans rewarded up to a ceiling tended to choose accounting options that minimized reported profits, and executives on bonus plans without upper limits chose profit-boosting options. To achieve any of their objectives toward maximizing their own welfare, managers have at their disposal various accepted accounting scenarios, including (a) changing accounting methods, (b) adjusting their cost estimates, and (c) allocating costs and revenues to whichever period is most beneficial, thus altering the timing of expenses and, to a much lesser degree, revenues. Most of this smoothing goes on in hard as well as good times. All of this "sugar bowling" is tolerated by auditors as long as it does not materially misrepresent earnings.

Is Defeasance an Example of Creative Accounting?

Defeasance of debt is a mechanism to wipe debt off the balance sheet providing the company secures the future repayment of the debt by irrevocably placing with an independent trustee essentially risk-free securities to be used solely for satisfying the debt service requirements. The company remains the primary obligor under the debt obligation. This practice was popular. The SEC in 1982 imposed a moratorium on the technique regarding an examination of the problem by the FASB. In November 1983 the FASB issued Statement No. 76, "Extinguishment of Debt," which provided guidance for when debt should be considered to be extinguished for financial-reporting purposes. The SEC concurred, rescinded its moratorium on in-substance defeasance, and even issued an interpretive release on the subject. Both the FASB and the SEC agreed that, first, the monetary assets placed in the trust should be risk free and, second, the trust should provide cash flows that approximately coincide, in timing and amount, with the scheduled interest and municipal payments on the debt that is being extinguished.

The situation became euphoric. Within a few months, the major public corporations wiped out as much as $5 billion debts through defeasance deals. *It was creative accounting at its best.* The situation got more interesting when the creative minds of Wall Street dealmakers got into the action and figured out how to "defease" and at the same time make money. Because U.S. corporations could borrow abroad cheaper than foreign governments, it was possible to create debt for themselves at a rate lower than the yield on foreign-government securities, buy the same government securities to be put in a trust, remove the debt from the balance sheet, and even make money in the deal. This in essence is simultaneous defeasance. The FASB failed to predict that corporations could use defeasance for international arbitrage. Some suggest that the FASB was ignorant of the arbitrage opportunity. It failed to assume that it is possible for multinationals to borrow at a lower rate than a risk-free university.

To try to correct the situation, the FASB issued on February 16, 1984, a proposed technical bulletin that did not agree with the accounting of a "simultaneous defeasance." First, it stated that the FASB never intended Statement No. 76 to apply to the issuance of new debt, without clarifying when a new debt became an old debt. Second, it reemphasized the requirements of the risk-free securities. The situation has prompted several questions:

1. Does this bulletin solve the problem? Will it be adopted or will enough pressure from Wall Street dealmakers lead to a "softened" version? If it is ever adopted, billions in dollar defeasances will have to be unwound and the assets and liabilities returned to corporate balance sheets (more to come on this issue).

2. In any case, assuming that the "simultaneous defeasance" is found unacceptable, and consequently billions of dollars in deals have to be undone, does the

extinguishment of debt in exchange for an irrevocable trust reflect the "real" capital structure of corporations?

3. What would happen to these trusts in case of bankruptcies? Would it be subject to an automatic stay that would prohibit distributions to bondholders, or might its assets be used to meet a payroll?

4. Who is going to evaluate the qualifications of the trustee, the nature of the trust, and the assets in the trust?

NOTES

1. Financial Accounting Standards Board, Structure Committee, *The Structure of Establishing Financial Accounting Standards* (Stamford, Conn.: Financial Accounting Foundation, April 1977), 15.

2. Financial Accounting Standards Board, *Financial Reporting by Private and Small Companies* (Stamford, Conn., 1981), 3-4.

3. Ibid.

4. Institute of Chartered Accountants in England and Wales, Accounting Standards Steering Committee, *The Corporate Report* (London, 1975).

5. Ibid., 48.

6. Ibid., 88-91.

7. J. W. Kamin and J. Ronen, "The Smoothing of Income Numbers: Some Empirical Evidence on Systematic Differences among Management-Controlled and Owner-Controlled Firms," *Accounting, Organizations, and Society,* October 1978, 141-53.

8. A. Belkaoui and R. Picur, "The Smoothing of Income Numbers: Some Empirical Evidence on Systematic Differences between Core and Periphery Industrial Sectors," *Journal of Business Finance and Accounting*, Fall 1984.

II

THE AMERICAN INSTITUTE OF CERTIFIED PUBLIC ACCOUNTANTS

---

1. THE AICPA: TOWARD LESS STANDARD SETTING AND MORE SELF-REGULATION

Less Standard Setting

Certified Public Accountant (CPA) is the major professional designation of those who practice public accounting. The American Institute of Certified Public Accountants (AICPA) is the professional coordinating organization of practicing Certified Public Accountants in the United States. One of its many functions is to prepare and grade a rigorous uniform examination that a person must satisfy before becoming a CPA. The examination consists of four parts: (1) accounting practice, (2) accounting theory, (3) auditing, and (4) business law.

Besides providing the uniform examination, the AICPA acts as the main spokesperson on all areas of interest to its members. Its two important senior technical committees—the Accounting Standards Executive Committee (AcSEC) and the Auditing Standards Committee (AuSEC)—are empowered to speak for the AICPA in the areas of financial and cost accounting and auditing, respectively. These committees issue *statements of positions* (SOPs) on accounting issues. These SOPs clarify and elaborate on controversial accounting issues and should be followed as guidelines if they do not contradict existing Financial Accounting Standards Board (FASB) pronouncements. Through its monthly publication *The Journal of Accountancy*, the AICPA communicates with its members on controversial accounting problems and solutions.

The AICPA was always interested in standard setting. In fact, since its inception in 1887, the AICPA has taken the lead in developing accounting principles. In 1938 it formed the Committee on Accounting Procedures (CAP) to narrow the areas of difference in corporate reporting by eliminating undesirable practices. Rather than develop a set of generally accepted accounting principles, the CAP adopted an ad hoc and pragmatic approach to controversial problems. During a period of twenty years, through 1958, the CAP issued 51 *accounting research bulletins* (ARBs), suggesting accounting treatments for various items and transactions. At the time, these ARBs were supported by the Securities and Exchange Commission and the stock exchanges and consequently represented the only source of the "generally accepted accounting principles" in the United States. After World War II the coexistence of many alternative accounting treatments; the new tax laws; financing techniques; and complex capital structure, such as business combinations, leasing, convertible debts, and investment tax credit, created the need for a new approach to the development of accounting principles. In 1959 the AICPA created a new body, the Accounting Principles Board (APB), to advance the written expression of what constitutes the generally accepted accounting principles. In addition, the AICPA appointed a director of accounting research and a permanent staff. Between 1959 and 1973 the APB issued opinions, intended to be used as guidelines for accounting practices. With the creation of the Financial Accounting Standards Board to replace the APB in 1973 as the standard-setting body, the AICPA issued Rule 203 of the AICPA's Code of Professional Ethics to define its new relationship with the FASB. Rule 203 constitutes an endorsement of the FASB as the standard-setting body. In spite of Rule 203, the AICPA does not seem comfortable in its new position. One evidence of such attitude is that the AICPA had begun, right after the FASB was formed, to issue through its Executive Committee statements of position. In effect, although the AcSEC does not establish generally accepted accounting principles and acts only as the institute's official spokesperson on all matters concerning financial accounting and reporting, one of its key responsibilities has been to respond to the proposals issued by the FASB and the Securities and Exchange Commission. To provide more guidance to the AICPA members, the AcSEC started issuing SOPs. Despite the perception that they are similar to standards, amendments, and interpretations issued by the FASB, SOP's are not enforceable under Rule 203 of the AICPA's Code of Professional Ethics. They merely provide guidance. In fact, each SOP includes a caveat similar to the following:

Statement[s] of position of the AICPA accounting standards division are issued for the general information of those interested in the subject. They present the conclusion of at least a majority of [the members of] the accounting standards['] executive committee, which is the senior technical body of the Institute, authorized to speak for the Institute in the areas of financial accounting and reporting and cost accounting.

The objective of statements of position is to influence the development of accounting and reporting standards in directions the division believes are in the public interest. It is intended that they should be considered, as deemed appropriately [*sic*], by bodies having authority to issue pronouncements on the subject. However, statements of position do not establish standards enforceable under the Institute's Code of Professional Ethics.

Although these caveats made clear that the SOPs are to be interpreted as primarily guidance, many public accountants attribute to them the status of the GAAP.

The AcSEC does not limit its guidance role to the issuance of SOPs. Except for special situations, AcSEC's recommendations on emerging problems may take the form of issue papers. They are intended to help the FASB in identifying accounting and financial accounting problems and suggest solutions to the FASB by adding a new topic to its agenda, by interpreting an existing standard, or by issuing a staff technical bulletin. These issue papers are uniformly and rigorously prepared. Typically, they include (a) a background section summarizing the problem; (2) an analysis of current service often based on research through the AICPA's National Automated Accounting Research System (NAARS); (c) a review of any relevant or analogous authoritative review; (d) a clear statement of the issues that need to be resolved, along with related subissues; and (e) the advisory conclusions of AcSEC and the committee or task force that developed the paper.[1]

Both the SOPs and the issue papers seem to contribute to mutual standard-setting efforts of the FASB and the AICPA, with the FASB still keeping the dominant policy role. In fact, one of the recommendations of the Financial Accounting Foundation (FAF) structure committee review was that in setting standards, the Financial Accounting Standards Board should rely more heavily on the work of others. As a result, the FASB has resorted to more "leveraging" as evidenced by a substantial increase in its use of task forces and the development of closer working relationships with AcSEC, the committee on corporate reporting of the Financial Executives Institute, and other outside groups. Leveraging has increased the board's activity without diminishing its primary role in the standard-setting process and without the possibility that an outside group like the AICPA would end up dictating its agenda.

More Self-Regulation

For a long time the accounting profession has been the subject of severe criticism as a result of numerous failures, improper payments, and other misdeeds by corporations. From everywhere in society came calls for more regulation. The question, however, was whether it should be private regulation, public regulation, or peer regulation. *Private regulation* takes place when firms prescribe and enforce operating policies and practices designed to ensure compliance with professional standards. *Public regulation* includes the laws, regulations, and court system meant to deal with fraud, gross negligence, or failure to comply with legally mandated standards governing independent audits of financial statements. *Peer regulation* takes place when firms agree to have their operations and procedures reviewed by other firms. The general consensus in the accounting profession is that private regulation is the most effective form of regulation. Control of employment and compensation permits immediate disciplinary measures that are highly effective. Peer and public regulation help to check on private regulation. As a result, the profession has come strongly in favor of a voluntary self-regulation program focusing on a mix of private and peer regulation. As part of this effort of the profession for a self-regulation program, the AICPA established in 1977 the Division for CPA Firms as a way of monitoring and improving the audit services provided by its members. The division is made up of two sections: (1) the SEC Practice Section (SECPS), and (2) the Private Companies Practice Section (PCPS). Both sections are very active in a peer-review program of each firm to be conducted by other practicing CPAs. An AICPA leaflet, *What Is Peer Review?* described peer review and the nine elements of quality control. It pointed out that the division's "aim is to maintain and improve the quality of the accounting of the accounting and auditing services performed by member firms."

A peer review provides reasonable assurance that the accounting and auditing work done by the firm is quality work—work that can be relied upon. . . . it means that a profession which plays an important role in the country's business and financial life is serious about self-regulation and actively pursues the goal of quality work by its members. The members . . . are willing to put their dedication to quality work to the challenge of a peer review every three years. Those who use financial statements and rely on a CPA's report reap the benefit of that dedication.

The objective is not only to evaluate each firm's audit policies and procedures but to improve the quality of the audit and accounting practices of members. The procedures to be used enable peer reviewers to determine whether a firm's policies and procedures are adequate to achieve the objective inherent in the nine basic elements of quality control for a CPA firm. They are:

1. Independence—to be free from financial, business, family, and other relationships involving a client when required by the profession's code of ethics

2. Assignment of personnel—to have people on the job with the technical training and competence required in the circumstances

3. Consultation—to have personnel seek assistance, when necessary, from competent authorities so that accounting or auditing issues may be properly resolved

4. Supervision—to determine that work is planned and carried out efficiently and in conformity with professional standards

5. Hiring—to have competent, properly motivated people of integrity

6. Continuing professional education—to provide staff with the training needed to fulfill their responsibilities and to keep them abreast of current developments

7. Advancement—to select for advancement people who are capable of handling the responsibilities involved

8. Client acceptance and continuance—to anticipate problems and minimize the likelihood of association with a client whose management lacks integrity

9. Inspection—to conduct a periodic internal review to be sure all other elements of the quality-control system are working

Under the SECPS, self-regulation is accomplished in a mandatory peer review, sanctions of firms for failure to meet the requirements of the section, mandatory rotation of all audit engagement partners, public reporting of certain firm information, and monitoring of all section activities by a public oversight board (POB). In effect the AICPA is intended to act as a neutral link or honest broker between the SEC and the profession. The POB gave teeth to the self-regulatory program, given its powers to monitor and evaluate the SECPS's performance. The POB is authorized to investigate any matter pertaining to the SECPS, report publicly on such matters, and make recommendations to the section's executive committee. It also serves as a "sounding board" for the public, Congress, and federal agencies in their interactions with the accounting profession. The board consists of knowledgeable and respected persons outside the public accounting profession who provide an objective review of the structure and operation of the self-regulatory effort. It also makes an annual report of its findings and comments.

Given this self-regulation program, efforts are continuously being made to encourage as many firms as possible to join one or both sections. In fact, early objections by the Executive Committee of the PCPS against publication of the Division for CPA Firms directory on the grounds that nonlisted firms would suffer serious competitive disadvantages were quickly dismissed. A directory for CPA firms is published annually.

Various criticisms have been raised against the self-regulation program of the profession. The primary target of criticism of the profession's self-disciplinary process seems to be the response to alleged audit failures. The accounting profession is criticized for being lax in investigating alleged audit failures and for not disciplining substandard performances. The answer to such criticism by D. R. Carmichael, then vice-president, technical services, of the AICPA, is stated as follows:

The disciplinary process often cannot cope with alleged audit failures because of the near impossibility of judging the degree of culpability of the auditor when financial statements are deficient.

There is a spectrum of conduct from honest mistakes to fraud, but along this spectrum it is extremely difficult to distinguish between an honest mistake and negligence. Even more extreme forms of conduct, such as recklessness and fraud, may be difficult to distinguish from negligence. This difficulty is caused by the necessary generality of professional standards, the complexities of professionals practice, and the nature of human failure.[2]

The structure of the division in two sections gave the erroneous perception that the profession consisted of two groups of members that provided different quality levels of service. To counter this criticism, a joint coordinating committee was formed to facilitate coordination between the two sections in identifying and dealing with common problems. However, a long-term solution would be to restructure the Division for CPA Firms into a more unified organization without sections. Such a unified structure would be able to provide an expanded range of services and ultimately make it feasible to attract all CPAs in public practice into the system.

John C. Burton, a former chief accountant at the SEC, challenged the AICPA's legal authority to achieve effective surveillance and discipline and proposed that legislation be enacted that would create a self-regulatory organization under direct SEC oversight, possibly patterned along the lines of the National Association of Securities Dealers. The governing body of this organization would be a board of directors, half of whose members would be from firms practicing before the SEC and half, public members drawn from the business, financial, professional, and academic communities.

Others have maintained that the AICPA program of self-regulation, if given a good chance, is a likely success and that the current frustrations with the limits of government involvement in regulation should make anyone hesitant to put another layer of regulation on any profession.

2. KNOWLEDGE, SKILLS, AND ABILITIES LIST

What knowledge, skills, and abilities might reasonably be required to perform work activities for planning and executing a professional engagement (audit, tax, compilation, review, or management advisory service) in accordance with the AICPA standards by people who are working toward, or who have already reached, such a level of responsibility? By *knowledge, skills, and abilities* (KSA) are meant the proficiency areas or human attributes required for minimum competency in the practice of public accounting. An AICPA task force developed a list of 269 KSA that might reasonably be required for competent performance by CPAs who have reached the level of responsibility for planning and executing a professional engagement in accordance with the AICPA standards:

PROFESSIONAL LITERATURE

   1. AICPA Code of Professional Ethics
   2. AICPA General, Field Work and Reporting Standards

3. AICPA Statements on Auditing Standards (SAS)
4. AICPA Statements on Standards for Accounting and Review Services
5. AICPA Statements on Quality Control Standards
6. AICPA Statements on Management Advisory Services
7. AICPA Statements on Responsibilities in Tax Practice
8. AICPA Audit Guides
9. Authoritative pronouncements of the FASB and predecessor organizations
10. Authoritative pronouncements of the SEC (Accounting Series Releases)
11. Authoritative pronouncements of the Cost Accounting Standards Board
12. Internal Revenue Code, regulations, and pronouncements of the IRS
13. Familiarity with topics covered in leading accounting publications
14. Authoritative pronouncements relative to governmental accounting (NCGA, OMB, GAO)

WORKING PAPERS

15. Design working papers format
16. Prepare or review working papers

FINANCIAL STATEMENTS GENERALLY

17. Purpose and format of balance sheet
18. Purpose and format of income statement
19. Purpose and format of statement of changes in financial position
20. Purpose and format of statement of owner's equity
21. Purpose and format of consolidated financial statements
22. Purpose and format of combined financial statements
23. Purpose and format of notes to the financial statements
24. Purpose and disclosure of accounting policies
25. Purpose and format of financial statements for not-for-profit organizations
26. Purpose and format of interim financial statements
27. Purpose and format of personal financial statements
28. Purpose and format of statement of charge and discharge
29. Purpose and format of statement of realization and liquidation
30. Purpose and format of statement of affairs
31. Purpose and format of bankruptcy deficiency account

AUDITING

32. Nature and evaluation of auditing risk
33. Nature and elements of the study and evaluation of internal control
34. Nature and elements of the study and evaluation of internal control in a computerized environment
35. Communication of material weaknesses in internal control
36. Content of reports on internal control
37. Effects of internal auditors' work on study of internal control
38. Familiarity with sales, receivables and cash cycles
39. Familiarity with purchases, payables, and cash disbursements cycles
40. Familiarity with inventories and production cycles
41. Familiarity with personnel and payroll cycles

42. Familiarity with property, plant, and equipment cycles
43. Preparation of flowchart
44. Planning and supervising the audit
45. Procedures to prepare the audit program
46. Procedures for time budgeting for field work
47. Procedures for tests of transactions
48. Procedures for tests of balances
49. Familiarity with client's business
50. Familiarity with legal environment of client's business
51. Auditor's responsibility for detection of errors or irregularities
52. Nature, competence, and sufficiency of audit evidence
53. Analytical review procedures
54. Client representations
55. Gathering and evaluating audit evidence
56. Related party transactions
57. Use of computers in performing the audit
58. Use of statistical sampling in performing the audit
59. Effect of subsequent events on financial statements
60. Operational auditing
61. Departures from generally accepted accounting principles
62. Consistency in applying generally accepted accounting principles
63. Reporting responsibilities
64. Audit opinions
65. Report on limited review of interim financial information
66. Association with special reports
67. Negative assurance
68. Supplementary information required by the FASB in financial reporting
69. Letters for underwriters
70. Part of examination made by other auditors
71. Past year's audits made by other auditors
72. Treatment of facts discovered after issuance of the auditor's report

ACCOUNTING AND REVIEW SERVICES

73. Compilation report
74. Review report

BUSINESS LAW

75. CPA liability to clients and third parties (statutory and common law)
76. Formation and termination of agency relationship
77. Authority and liability of principals, agents and undisclosed principals
78. Formation and operation of partnerships
79. Termination or dissolution of partnerships
80. Profit or loss distribution and other special allocations
81. Formation of corporations
82. Powers of corporations, stockholders, directors and officers
83. Financial structure, capital and dividends of corporations
84. Merger, consolidation and dissolution of corporations
85. Administration of trusts and estates

86. Joint ventures
87. Associations
88. Offer, acceptance and consideration for contracts
89. Defenses to enforcements of contracts
90. Rights and remedies upon discharge, breach or assignment of contracts
91. Leases of personality
92. Voluntary and involuntary bankruptcy
93. Effects of bankruptcy on debtor and creditors
94. Reorganizations in bankruptcy
95. Suretyship and guaranty
96. Bulk transfers (sales)
97. Consumer protection law
98. Administrative agency law
99. Antitrust law
100. Equal employment opportunity law
101. Federal Unemployment Tax Act
102. Workmen's Compensation
103. Federal Insurance Contributions Act
104. Fair Labor Standards Act
105. Federal securities registration and reporting requirements
106. Exempt securities and transactions
107. Insider information and antifraud provisions
108. Short-swing profits
109. Civil and criminal liabilities under Federal Securities Acts
110. Foreign Corrupt Practices Act
111. Proxy solicitations and tender offers
112. Types of negotiable instruments and requisites for negotiability
113. Transfer and negotiation of negotiable instruments
114. Liabilities, defenses and rights of parties to negotiable instruments
115. Contracts covering sales of goods
116. Warranties and product liability
117. Remedies and defenses of parties to a contract for sale of goods
118. Attachment and perfection of security interests
119. Rights of debtors, creditors and third parties in secured transactions
120. Documents of title and investment securities
121. Distinctions between real and personal property
122. Types of ownership of property
123. Easements and other nonpossessory interests
124. Landlord-tenant relationship
125. Deeds, recording, title defects and title insurance
126. Mortgage characteristics and recording requirements
127. Mortgage foreclosure and priorities
128. Fire and casualty insurance

FINANCIAL ACCOUNTING THEORY AND PRACTICE

129. Basic concepts, accounting terminology and accounting principles
130. Conceptual framework of accounting
131. Unique aspects of accounting for not-for-profit organizations

132. Nonmonetary transactions concepts
133. Analysis of financial statements
134. Constant dollar financial statements
135. Current cost financial statements
136. Measurement, valuation and presentation of cash
137. Measurement, valuation and presentation of marketable securities and investments
138. Measurement, valuation and presentation of receivables
139. Measurement, valuation and presentation of inventory
140. Measurement, valuation and presentation of property, plant and equipment
141. Measurement, valuation and presentation of leased assets
142. Measurement, valuation and presentation of intangible assets
143. Measurement, valuation and presentation of current liabilities
144. Measurement, valuation and presentation of of long-term liabilities
145. Measurement, valuation and presentation of issuance and retirement of long-term bonds
146. Measurement, valuation and presentation of lease liabilities
147. Measurement, valuation and presentation of contingent liabilities
148. Measurement, valuation and presentation of deferred revenue
149. Measurement, valuation and presentation of the elements of owner's equity
150. Measurement, valuation and presentation of treasury stock
151. Measurement, valuation and presentation of pension costs and liabilities
152. Cash, property and liquidating dividends
153. Stock dividends and splits
154. Stock options, warrants and rights
155. Quasi reorganizations
156. Realization, measurement and presentation of revenue
157. Measurement and presentation of cost of goods sold
158. Measurement, valuation and presentation of expenses
159. Recognition of gains or losses on sale, trade or involuntary conversion of fixed assets
160. Measurement, valuation and presentation of unusual gains and losses
161. Measurement, valuation and presentation of provisions for current and deferred income taxes
162. Measurement and presentation of discontinued operations
163. Measurement and presentation of extraordinary items
164. Measurement and presentation of accounting changes and corrections
165. Measurement and presentation of earnings per share
166. Business combinations and equity investments
167. Segments and lines of business
168. Gain or loss contingencies
169. Development stage enterprises
170. Percentage of completion and completed contract methods of revenue recognition
171. Installment method of revenue recognition
172. Foreign exchange
173. Research and development
174. Fund accounting

COST/MANAGERIAL ACCOUNTING THEORY AND PRACTICE

175. Cash flow analysis
176. Production costs
177. Computation and use of overhead rates
178. Job order cost accounting systems
179. Process cost accounting systems
180. Standard cost accounting systems
181. Variance analysis
182. Joint costing and by-product costing
183. Spoilage, waste and scrap
184. Absorption (full) costing
185. Direct (variable) costing
186. Product pricing
187. Transfer pricing
188. Budgeting for operations
189. Cost-volume-profit (breakeven) analysis
190. Gross profit analysis
191. Differential cost analysis
192. Capital budgeting
193. Return on investment
194. Responsibility accounting
195. Learning curves
196. Regression and correlation analysis
197. Inventory control (e.g., economic order quantity)
198. PERT/cost
199. Sensitivity analysis
200. Probability analysis
201. Linear programming
202. Behavioral implications of accounting data

FEDERAL TAXATION—INDIVIDUALS

203. Reporting basis of taxpayer
204. Business, investment alimony and other gross income
205. Capital gains and losses
206. Deductions from gross income
207. Exclusions from income
208. Basis for property
209. Character and recognition of gains or losses on property transactions
210. Itemized deductions
211. Zero Tax Bracket Amount
212. Filing status and exemptions
213. Tax computations including minimum tax, alternative minimum tax and income averaging
214. Tax credits
215. Claims for refunds
216. Assessments
217. Effect of gift and estate taxes on individuals

FEDERAL TAXATION—CORPORATIONS

218. Determination of gross income
219. Deductions from gross income
220. Capital gains and losses
221. Reconciliation of taxable income and book income
222. Reconciliation of opening and closing retained earnings
223. Tax computations
224. Tax credits
225. Controlled groups and consolidated tax returns
226. Subchapter S corporations
227. Personal Holding companies
228. Accumulated earnings tax
229. Tax-free incorporation
230. Reorganizations
231. Liquidation and dissolutions

FEDERAL TAXATION—PARTNERSHIPS

232. Contribution of capital or services in partnership formation
233. Basis and holding period of partner's interest
234. Basis of property contributed to partnership
235. Determination of partnership income and partners' distributive shares of income
236. Elections available to partners (different reporting methods)
237. Fiscal year end of partnership and partners
238. Guaranteed payments
239. Sales and exchanges between partner and partnership
240. Current distributions of partnership assets
241. Distribution of partnership assets in liquidation
242. Basis of assets distributed to partners
243. Sale or exchange of partnership interest
244. Payments to retired partner
245. Payments to deceased partner's successor
246. Determination of partnership income and partners' distributive shares of income from a limited partnership

FEDERAL TAXATION—ESTATE AND GIFT AND INCOME TAXATION OF ESTATES AND TRUSTS

247. Computation of taxable estate, estate tax and credits
248. Computation of taxable gifts, gift tax and credits
249. Exclusions from estate and gift tax
250. Computation of distributable net income of estates and trusts
251. Distributions deduction of estates and trusts
252. Computation of income tax and credits for estates and trusts
253. Trust throwback provisions

FEDERAL TAXATION—EXEMPT ORGANIZATIONS AND RETIREMENT PLANS

254. Types of exempt organizations and required information returns
255. Requirements for exemption from income tax
256. Foundations
257. Unrelated business income and tax
258. Reports required for cooperatives

OTHER

259. Computer programming
260. Commercial bank lending policies
261. Specialized industry applications (utilities, railroad companies, etc.)
262. Payroll rax returns
263. Time value of money—present value concepts
264. Actuarial concepts
265. Employment compensation and pension plans, including ERISA requirements

OTHER SKILLS

266. Writing skills
267. Oral skills
268. Research skills
269. Interpersonal skills*

3. WORK ACTIVITIES LIST

What are those work activities that are critical to competent professional performance in the accounting profession? By *work activities* is meant the functions performed by people in their roles as CPAs. An AICPA task force developed a list of 41 activities that describe the broad functions performed by CPAs in public accounting practice. They are grouped in six general work categories: engagement management and administration, auditing, tax practice, management advisory services, other professional services, and office and firm administration.

ENGAGEMENT MANAGEMENT AND ADMINISTRATION

PLANNING THE ENGAGEMENT. This work activity deals with preparing and reviewing engagement letters, new client reports or data sheets, time budgets, staff requirements, inquiring about current business developments affecting the entity, arranging with clients such matters as adequate work space for staff and access to records, etc.

---

*American Institute of Certified Public Accountants, Practice Analysis Task Force, *AICPA Report of the Practice Analysis Task Force* (New York, 1983), 119-25. Reprinted with permission. Copyright © 1983 by American Institute of Certified Public Accountants, Inc.

SUPERVISING THE PROFESSIONAL STAFF ON THE ENGAGEMENT

REVIEWING THE PROGRESS OF THE ENGAGEMENT. This work activity deals with reviewing work papers, meeting with staff and clients to discuss progress, deciding technical issues, presenting and explaining the final product to the client, etc.

ENGAGEMENT ADMINISTRATION. This work activity deals with comparing actual to budgeted time, modifying time schedules, modifying starting schedules, preparing and reviewing the final bill for the engagement, etc.

AUDIT WORK ACTIVITIES

STUDY AND EVALUATE INTERNAL CONTROL. Examples of this work activity include discussing accounting and control systems with client, examining documentation which explains client's systems, flow-charting transactions, performing compliance tests of the systems, using internal control checklist questionnaires, evaluating internal control, etc.

AUDIT PROCEDURES RELATING TO ASSERTIONS REGARDING EXISTENCE OR OCCURRENCE. This work activity deals with whether assets or liabilities of the entity exist at a given date and whether recorded transactions have occurred during a given period. For example, such procedures would include observing physical assets, obtaining confirmation of assets, etc.

AUDIT PROCEDURES RELATING TO ASSERTIONS REGARDING COMPLETENESS. This work activity deals with whether all transactions and accounts that should be presented in the financial statements are included. For example, such procedures would include testing shipping and receiving cutoff procedures, testing the clerical accuracy of asset listing, reconciling physical assets to general ledger and subsidiary ledger balances, etc.

AUDIT PROCEDURES RELATING TO ASSERTIONS REGARDING RIGHTS AND OBLIGATIONS. This work activity deals with whether assets are rights of the entity and liabilities are obligations of the entity at a given date. For example, such procedures would include examining leasing arrangements to determine that capitalized leases are properly recorded, examining loan agreements, etc.

AUDIT PROCEDURES RELATING TO ASSERTIONS REGARDING VALUATION OR ALLOCATION. This work activity deals with whether asset, liability, revenue, and expense components have been included in the financial statements at appropriate amounts. For example, such procedures would include obtaining current market value quotations of investments, analysing inventory turnover, analyzing receivables for adequacy of the allowance balance, etc.

AUDIT PROCEDURES TO DETERMINE IF INFORMATION ON THE FINANCIAL STATEMENTS IS PROPERLY PRESENTED AND ADEQUATELY DISCLOSED. This work activity deals with the form, arrangement, and content of the financial statements and appended notes. Examples of this work activity include determining that items in the statements are properly classified, determining if proper disclosure is made of any pledged, discounted or assigned receivables, determining that long-term debt is properly described and classified and determining that contingencies are adequately disclosed, etc.

AUDIT PROCEDURES RELATING TO PROGRAM AND PERFORMANCE AUDITS SUCH AS FOR GOVERNMENT AGENCIES. Examples of work activity include procedures designed to evaluate the operational efficiency and effectiveness of various government programs and compliance with federal regulations, etc.

PREPARE OR REVIEW AUDITORS' REPORT. Examples of this work activity include reviewing work papers, reviewing report format, writing report, discussing results of audit with client, etc.

PREPARE OR REVIEW REPORTS OR FILINGS FOR REGULATORY AGENCIES. This work activity deals with the preparation or review of financial statements, schedules, tables, statistics, and other financial information contained in registration statements or other documents filed with the Securities and Exchange Commission or other regulatory agency. Examples of work activity include conferring with clients, underwriters, and their respective counsel, meetings with the SEC and other regulatory agencies, issuing comfort letters, and reviewing compliance with rules and regulations governing accounting requirements in connection with such filings as forms 8-K, 10-Q, 10-K, S-1, etc.

PREPARE MANAGEMENT LETTER. This work activity deals with matters that the auditor had noted in the course of the engagement and wishes to call to the attention of management such as the communication of internal control weaknesses, etc.

TAX WORK ACTIVITIES

TAX CONSULTATION AND PLANNING. Examples of this work activity include advising clients of tax shelters, investigating tax consequences of contemplated business actions, advising clients of tax consequences of other contemplated actions, advising clients of taxpayer rights, testifying as an expert witness on tax matters, etc.

PREPARE OR REVIEW CORPORATE INCOME OR FRANCHISE TAX RETURNS. Examples of this work activity include tax research, review past years' returns and work papers, determine proper deductibility of expenses, determine which revenue items are taxable, determine if treatment of revenue and expense items is in the client's best interest, ascertain availability of tax credits, represent client before IRS, etc.

PREPARE OR REVIEW INDIVIDUAL INCOME TAX RETURNS. Examples of this work include tax research, review past years' returns and work papers, determine proper deductibility of expenses, determine which revenue items are taxable, determine if treatment of revenue and expense items is in the client's best interest, represent client before IRS, etc.

PREPARE OR REVIEW PARTNERSHIP INCOME TAX RETURNS. Examples of this work activity include tax research, review past years' returns and work papers, determine proper deductibility of expenses, determine which revenue items are taxable, determine if treatment of revenue and expense items is in the client's best interest, represent client before IRS, etc.

PREPARE OR REVIEW FIDUCIARY (ESTATE & TRUST) INCOME TAX RETURNS. Examples of this work activity include tax research, review past years' returns and work papers, determine proper deductibility of expenses, determine if treatment of revenue and expense items is in the client's best interest, represent client before IRS, etc.

PREPARE OR REVIEW ESTATE AND GIFT TAX RETURNS. Examples of this work activity include tax research, review past years' returns and work papers, determine proper deductibility of expenses and if treatment of expense items is in the client's best interest, represent client before IRS, etc.

PREPARE OR REVIEW INCOME TAX RETURNS FOR TAX-EXEMPT ENTITIES. Examples of this work activity include tax research, review past years' returns and work papers, determine if treatment of revenue and expense is in the client's best interest, represent client before the IRS, etc.

ESTATE PLANNING. Examples of this work activity include tax research, obtaining information about the assets and liabilities of the client and the client's testamentary objectives, computing tax consequences of various alternatives, meeting with clients and attorneys, etc.

MAS WORK ACTIVITIES

PERFORM FINANCIAL AND ECONOMIC ANALYSES. This work activity deals with capital requirements, structuring resource allocation, merger analysis, financial feasibility studies, insurance studies, projections, forecasts, etc.

MANAGERIAL INFORMATION AND CONTROL SYSTEMS. This work activity deals with identification of information requirements for planning, budgeting, reporting, order processing, inventory billing, and other management information and control systems, etc.

EDP SYSTEMS AND OPERATIONS. This work activity deals with evaluation, design, implementation of EDP systems, helping client use EDP effectively, etc.

INDUSTRIAL ENGINEERING AND OPERATIONS RESEARCH. This work activity deals with manufacturing methods, utilization of equipment, plant and office layout, production standards, quality control and methods, work flow, statistical, mathematical, and simulation methods for solving complex problems, etc.

PRODUCTION AND INVENTORY CONTROL. This work activity deals with systems for production planning, scheduling, control of material, product inventories, etc.

COST ACCOUNTING. This work activity deals with development and installation of cost accounting systems special purpose cost determination, etc.

ORGANIZATION AND PERSONNEL: EXECUTIVE AND MANAGEMENT RECRUITMENT. This work activity deals with organizational studies, manpower planning, personnel administration, job evaluation, personnel training, specifying, identifying, investigating and evaluating executive and managerial candidates, etc.

OTHER PROFESSIONAL SERVICES

PROVIDE COUNSEL ON GENERAL BUSINESS MATTERS. This work activity includes advice on diverse managerial questions not involving a special study.

PREPARE COMPILATIONS. This work activity deals with presenting in the form of financial statements information which constitutes the representation of management without undertaking to express any assurance on the statements.

PERFORM REVIEW OF FINANCIAL STATEMENTS. This work activity deals with performing inquiry and analytical procedures in order to provide a reasonable basis for expressing limited assurance that there are no material modifications that should be made to the statements in order for them to be in conformity with generally accepted accounting principles.

SPECIAL PROFESSIONAL SERVICES. This work activity deals with providing special professional sources such as forecasting and planning, reviewing financial forecasts, providing special inventory analysis, consolidations purchase acquisitions, insurance studies, etc.

MAINTAIN CLIENT ACCOUNTING RECORDS. This work activity deals with recording transactions, posting, preparing quarterly and annual payroll tax returns, preparing sales tax returns, etc.

PREPARE STATEMENTS AND ACCOUNTING FOR COURTS AND FIDUCIARIES. Examples of this work activity include the preparation of judicial and informal accountings for trustees of *intervivos* and testamentary trusts, executors of decedents' estates and trustees of bankrupt estates. This work activity might also include the preparation of a statement of charge and discharge, statement of realization and liquidation, statement of affairs, and deficiency account as well as financial statements for the fiduciaries.

OFFICE AND FIRM ADMINISTRATION

OFFICE OR FIRM MANAGEMENT. This work activity deals with office management, internal firm committee service, scheduling, etc.

DEVELOP HUMAN RESOURCES. This work activity deals with evaluation of professional staff, staff counseling and development, staff training, recruiting, etc.

QUALITY CONTROL (INCLUDING PEER REVIEW). This work activity deals with writing firm manuals, developing firm policy, maintaining technical competence within the firm, etc.

PROFESSIONAL AND CIVIC ACTIVITIES. This work activity deals with AICPA and state society committee service, participation in other professional associations, community service, etc.

CONTINUING PROFESSIONAL EDUCATION. This work activity deals wtih taking CPE courses, teaching CPE courses, preparing CPE courses, etc.

PRACTICE DEVELOPMENT. This work activity deals with marketing and selling professional services and related public relations activities.*

4. SUNSET REVIEW

State accountancy boards are essential to the efficient working of accountancy laws. In fact, state accountancy boards are responsible for the efficient conduct of accounting in each state. They are responsible for (a) the adoption of rules and promulgation of rules of conduct; (b) the administration of examinations; (c) the issuance of CPA certificates and permits to practice and licensing; and (d) the monitoring of all licensed practitioners to ensure ethical conduct. These items would be vital if one opted for self-regulation of the discipline and profession of accounting. It is then essential that their continued existence remain justified. The crucial time when their continued existence is called to question is when, periodically, they come for what is called *sunset review*. The result of such review determines the way the discipline and the profession will be organized in each state.

The sunset-review process resulted from the enactment of the first sunset law in Colorado in 1976. Since then most states have enacted some form of

---

*American Institute of Certified Public Accountants, Practice Analysis Task Force, *AICPA Report of the Practice Analysis Task Force* (New York, September 1983), 111-16. Reprinted with permission. Copyright © 1983 by the American Institute of Certified Public Accountants, Inc.

sunset law. A sunset law calls for the termination of governmental agencies, programs, and boards engaged in professional licensing on a specific date if their continued existence cannot be justified. When applied to state accountancy boards, a board is called on to justify its existence to a reviewing panel. Interested parties are also allowed to present their views. The panel proceeds with its review and recommendation to the legislature of either reestablishment, modification, or termination of the board. Although most recommendations, so far, have been either reestablishment or minor modification, such as the addition of a public member to a board, they may be more radical, such as a proposal, rejected by the New Hampshire legislature, to terminate the state accountancy board. In fact, the New Hampshire statute survived "sunset" and was reenacted with new features, including mandatory continuing professional education; a requirement that CPA candidates be of "good professional character" rather than of "good moral character"; a change in the composition of the state board to include three CPAs, one public accountant, and one public member; required biannual, rather than annual, renewals; and the establishment of fees by the board rather than by statute.

Given the possibility of the worst case—termination—the profession is risking high stakes and should be thoroughly prepared to survive the scrutiny of the sunset process. Otherwise the regulation of accounting will cease in those states where an accountancy board is eliminated under sunset. To ensure that the sunset review is favorable, the state accountancy board needs to ensure that the public interest is protected. Various questions need to be examined:

1. The review board needs to be reassured that the attest function is vital to the efficient conduct of business and is performed by qualified people who have met strict requirements for licensing.

2. The review board needs to be reassured that the entry requirements are not set too high and act as barriers to entry. Although the CPA examinations are difficult and the passing rates are low, the reason lies mainly in the less-than-stringent process that candidates must undergo before taking the exam. In effect in most states, the maximum requirement is an undergraduate degree in accounting. The review panel may inquire whether or not graduate education in accounting may be a better requirement for aspiring CPAs. This is in line with a trend for more graduate programs in accounting and more professional schools of accounting. This position is supported by the 1978 report of the Commission on Auditors' Responsibilities: "The importance of instilling in students an appropriate professional attitude and the need to expose them to the pressures and problems of public accounting practice during the formal educational process support the need for graduate professional schools of accounting similar to law schools" (p. 89).

3. The review board may need to be reassured again that the CPA exam and advisory-granting service, used by all jurisdictions, is not only fair and appropriate

but also well managed. One solution in this case has been devised by the AICPA and the National Association of State Boards of Accountancy (NASBA) in the form of a special CPA-examination review board appointed by the NASBA to conduct an ongoing review of the appropriateness of the CPA exam on behalf of all state boards of accountancy. A second solution, mainly with regard to the fairness of grading in the CPA program, is the critique program of the NASBA, whereby candidates who did not pass all parts of the CPA exams are allowed by the state boards to review their papers. This solution is unique among professions.

4. The review board may need to be reassured that the state accountancy boards are effectively handling the enforcement of technical and ethical standards through positive and continuous monitoring of performance and reactive responses to complaints.

Although the sunset-review process has definite merits as far as the protection of the public interest is concerned, its popularity is not shared by all. In fact, some states have either repealed it, like North Carolina in 1977, criticized it, like Arkansas and Maryland; or revamped it, like Kansas. In the Kansas case a new 1981 law required only the state-supported agencies to be subject to the sunset law. The other boards are just reviewed without the threat of termination by the house and senate governmental organization committees. The major complaints against the sunset-review process is that it is sometimes inefficient, duplicative, and not cost effective. In 1979 a report in the *Washington Monthly* claimed that sunset audits and hearings cost Colorado $212,300, and the result was the abolition of three agencies with a combined annual budget of $6,810. The repeal of the sunset process in North Carolina was based on the complaints that the Governmental Evaluation Commission had spent more than $200,000 a year since 1977 but had terminated only five agencies.

These criticisms may reflect the deregulatory outlook and mood at a given time. Nevertheless, the review process, with or without termination, is essential to the necessary protection of the public interest. To ensure its survival, the accounting profession should not only take the sunset process seriously but should be prepared for it.

5. PEER REVIEW: DOES IT WORK?

The question is how to regulate the activities of CPA firms and ensure that the quality of the services offered is adequate with the ultimate purpose of protecting the public from exploitation and inadequate service by accountants. Regulation may be exercised by the government (government regulation), the private sector (private regulation), or the profession itself (peer regulation).

Government regulation of accounting includes the laws, regulations, licensing requirements, courts, legislatures, commissions, and legal procedures used to protect the public from fraud. It has not been proved to be an effective deterrent of unacceptable behavior. *Private regulation* includes all of the professional requirements used to meet the profession's standards and to provide quality services as good as those provided by the competition. Private regulation uses the market factor as a guide and as a judge for the quality of services provided by the accounting professional. Finally, *peer regulation* includes voluntary rules established by the members of the accounting profession to improve the quality of services offered. It uses peers as a guide and as a judge of the quality of services provided by the accountants. In short, the quality of services offered by accounting professionals is either evaluated by the market in the case of private regulation or by peers in the case of peer regulation. It is affected by government regulation only in those cases where accountants have failed to meet the lowest standards acceptable to the community, are charged with wrongdoing, and are brought to trial. If they are found guilty, government regulations provide for various forms of punishment, including possible loss of the privilege to practice.

Some claim that peer and private regulation are not enough to ensure the quality of services provided by the accounting profession and that government regulation should be used. This threat came in 1978 with the introduction of HR.13175, the so-called Moss Bill (named after John E. Moss, former chairman of the House Commerce Committee's Subcommittee on Oversight and Investigations), which called mainly for the enactment of the National Organization of Securities and Exchange Commission Accountancy. The bill, officially titled the Public Accounting Regulatory Act, called for action: "To establish a National Organization of Securities and Exchange Commission Accountancy, to require that independent public accounting firms be registered with such an Organization in order to furnish audit reports with respect to financial statements filed with the Securities and Exchange Commission, to authorize disciplinary action against such accounting firms and principals in such firms." It claimed that the accounting profession has not established and appears unable to establish a self-regulatory environment. It also authorized the proposed Accountancy Commission to regulate the quality of services provided by accounting professionals and to impose various sanctions where necessary. Among its provisions were the following:

1. Only one member of the new agency's five-man board could be from a major accounting firm.
2. The Accountancy Commission would review the work of individual accounting firms every three years, checking for "acts or omissions" by such accounting firms or principals in such firms that are contrary to the interest of the investor public.
3. CPA firms' legal liability would be greatly increased, making them accountable for negligence even without evidence of fraud or intentional conduct.

Fortunately for the accounting profession, the Moss Bill never passed the house. The threat did not, however, go unnoticed. The AICPA decided to act to prove that self-regulation or peer regulation is a viable alternative. It first allowed CPAs, in addition to other individuals, to join the institute. More specifically, it created two sections: the Private Companies Practice Section (PCPS) for small accounting firms serving mostly private companies and the SEC Practice Section (SECPS) for those firms serving companies registered with the SEC. It also required that in the future all firms in both sections undergo independent peer reviews to be conducted every three years. In addition to establishing the system of peer reviews, the AICPA decided that the SECPS would be monitored by the Public Oversight Board (POB), comprised of people including, but not limited to, former public officials, lawyers, bankers, securities industry executives, educators, economists, and business executives.

Central to the AICPA innovation is the peer-review requirement, thus keeping the oversight of professional practice within the profession. The peer review is essentially a form of quality control by peers. In general, a firm is provided the name of available reviewers from a bank of reviewers from which it may select a review team. A firm may also choose a "firm-on-firm" review by selecting another CPA firm to review its quality control. In the latter case, a quality-control review panel, selected by the SEC Practice Section peer-review committee, is appointed to oversee the review.

The review itself is similar to an audit. In general, it consists of the following testing procedures:

1. A review of the firm's quality-control documents, manuals, checklists, and so on. In effect, the 1979 AICPA Statement on Quality Control Standards No. 1, "System of Quality Control for a CPA Firm," states that "to provide itself with reasonable assurance of meeting its responsibility to provide professional services that conform with professional standards, a firm shall have a system of quality control" (parag. 2).

2. A testing of the compliance with the documented policies and procedures by interviewing key and selected staff people; reviewing personnel files, administration files, and other evidential matter; or reviewing engagement work papers and reports.

3. An exit conference with the directors of the firm to discuss their findings and to report (a) any significant deficiencies in the quality-control procedures of the firm, (b) any noncompliance with the documented policies and procedures, and (c) any noncompliance with membership requirements of either SECPS or PCPS.

4. A written report and a letter of comments to be sent to the firm's managing partner and to the public file at the institute. The comments on quality-control system design and compliance that seem to attract the peer reviewers' attention focus on categories such as the following: (a) acceptance and continuance of clients, (b) independence, (c) hiring, (d) advancement, (e) professional development, (f) assignment of personnel, (g) consultation, (h) supervision in en-

gagement planning, (i) supervision in engagement performance, (j) supervision in engagement review, and (k) inspection. In all of these categories the reviewers rely on the profession's standards as a basis for evaluation. As an example, Price Waterhouse's letter to Touche Ross concerning its peer-review findings follows:

To the Partners of   October 10, 1979
Touche Ross & Co.

We have reviewed the system of quality control for the accounting and auditing practice of Touche Ross & Co. in effect for the year ended March 31, 1979, and have issued our report the ɔn dated October 10, 1979. This letter should be read in conjunction with that report.

Our review was for the purpose of reporting upon your system of quality control and your compliance with it and with the membership requirements of the SEC Practice Section of the AICPA Division for CPA Firms (the Section). Our review was performed in accordance with the standards promulgated by the peer review committee of the Section; however, our review would not necessarily disclose all weaknesses in the system or lack of compliance with it or with the membership requirements of the Section because our review was based on selective tests.

There are inherent limitations that should be recognized in considering the potential effectiveness of any system of quality control. In the performance of most control procedures, departures can result from misunderstanding of instructions, mistakes of judgment, carelessness, and other personal factors. Projection of any evaluation of a system of quality control to future periods is subject to the risk that the procedures may become inadequate because of changes in conditions or that the degree of compliance with the procedures may deteriorate.

During the course of our review, we noted the following areas which we believe could be improved to further strengthen your system of quality control:

Improved documentation of key issues considered and audit work performed

It is the firm's policy to require for every audit engagement a complete record of audit procedures performed and the facts and rationale for key judgments and conclusions. We believe documentation in the engagement record could be improved in the following areas:

—The facts, discussion of the issues considered, consultations, if any, with designated local office consultants and reviewers, and related reasoning for the conclusions reached on significant accounting, auditing and reporting matters.

—Procedures performed when using work of outside specialists and internal auditors.

—Effect of EDP control reviews on audit scope.

—Procedures followed in limited reviews of interim financial information.

—Communications between offices participating in a multi-office engagement.

We recommend that the importance of appropriate documentation procedures be re-emphasized to the professional staff.

Codify consultation policies

The firm's technical inquiry policy requires consultation with the Executive Office Accounting and Auditing Technical Staff in specific instances, as well as in cases where additional consultation outside the local office consultation process is considered necessary. We believe compliance with the firm's consultation policies could be improved by codifying in one firm publication the instances where such additional consulting is appropriate or required.

Improve compliance with firm policies on use of the work and reports of other auditors

The firm's written policies on the use of the work and reports of other auditors are reasonable and consistent with authoritative guidance. Firm policy requires timely approval of the National Director of Accounting and Auditing before accepting certain engagements involving other auditors and approval of the Executive Office Accounting and Auditing Technical Staff for exceptions from performing specified audit procedures concerned with the work of other auditors. Based on our review we recommend that the firm review its compliance with firm policy particularly in the areas of (1) acceptance of principal auditor responsibility, (2) reference in the firm's report to the work of other auditors, (3) the performance of appropriate procedures for supervising the work of other auditors, and (4) documentation of other auditor independence.

Improve compliance with firm policy on client representation letters

The firm's policy requires that representation letters obtained from clients conform with a model letter supplied as a part of the firm's reference material and that deletions, except in certain cases, from specified standard paragraphs be cleared with the Executive Office Accounting and Auditing Technical Staff. Firm guidance and professional literature also require consideration of additional representation paragraphs beyond those included in the model letter when unusual accounting or reporting requirements exist. Our review disclosed instances where letters of representation did not conform with firm policy. We recommend that the firm emphasize the importance of obtaining management's representations on all significant matters reflected in the financial statements and clarify the circumstances where deviations from the model letter are to be approved by the Executive Office Accounting and Auditing Technical Staff.

Emphasize importance of timely preparation of staff performance reports

Firm policy requires timely preparation of a formal written staff evaluation report for each staff member assigned to an engagement of appropriate length and complexity. We recommend that the firm emphasize to the appropriate responsible personnel the importance to the firm's overall quality procedures of timely evaluation of staff performance on qualifying engagements.

* * * * *

The foregoing matters were considered in determining our opinion set forth in our report dated October 10, 1979, and this letter does not change that report.

Price Waterhouse & Co.

When the review is not favorable, sanctions from the appropriate section may be imposed. The possible sanctions considered in the *1983 SECPS Manual* include:

1. Requiring corrective measures by the firm, including consideration by the firm of appropriate actions with respect to individual-firm personnel
2. Additional requirements for continuing professional education
3. Accelerated or special peer reviews
4. Admonishments, censures, or reprimands
5. Monetary fines
6. Suspension from memberships
7. Expulsion from membership

Whether the outcome is favorable or unfavorable, peer review provides various benefits besides the major benefit of keeping government regulation off the backs of CPA firms. Among the tangible benefits are the improvement of the quality control before or after the review itself; the educational process created before, and during, the review; and the improvement in the morale resulting from the discovery and correction of any material failure to perform in compliance with the firm's own quality-control document. In addition, the cost of a peer review is manageable. The SEC Practice Section's rates range from $35 to $90 an hour, depending on the size of the firm reviewed. The PCPS has set one rate for review captains, $45 an hour, and one rate for reviewers, $35 an hour. For a one-office firm with three partners and five professional staff, the total fee for the review would be roughly $2,400 to $3,300, which amounts to an additional cost to do business of only $800 to $1,100 and a guaranteed improvement in quality control.

Why then is the peer-review program being criticized? Some of the arguments follow:

1. Peer review might seem to be something that all public accountants would welcome to avoid the feared alternative of government regulation. However, although the large CPA firms have shown a high degree of acceptance and voluntarism, smaller CPA firms have reacted mostly with either apathy or hostility. Their response is based on the belief that, first, the peer review is going to lead to unnecessary additional expenses and new procedures that are most likely irrelevant to the nature of their practices, and that, second, the peer review is of more value to larger CPA firms. But the small practitioners need the peer-review system even more than the larger firms, and in most cases the benefits outweigh the costs.

2. Some small as well as large CPA firms are reluctant to let an outside observer, whether or not it is a competitor, evaluate the adequacy of their quality-control policies. One may wonder whether the threat is not the out-

side observer but the possibility of a qualified report. But these firms should realize that, with adequate preparation, a peer review is much easier to survive than a loss of clients or, in the worst case, a loss of privilege to practice as a result of an inadequate job. Besides, peer review is bound to inspire investors' confidence in the accountants' high professional standards and competency.

3. To date no official sanctions have been imposed by the AICPA SECPS Executive Committee. The most drastic step taken by the peer-review committee is to refuse to accept the review report until an appropriate response or modification has been made. What emerges from this behavior is that the SECPS and the PCPS appear to be avoiding tough actions. The whole peer-review exercise could easily be misinterpreted as mutual back scratching.

4. Membership in the SECPS and PCPS was not made mandatory by the AICPA. The argument most often used has been that such requirements should be imposed by the federal government and are not the province of a self-regulatory profession. Although the arguments may have some conceptual merits, the credibility of the peer-review system, the integrity of the profession, and the soundness of the quality control may rest on a mandatory membership. It is, however, appropriate to note that the AICPA is taking steps to ensure compliance with quality control. Although Statement on Quality Standards No. 1, "System of Quality Control for a CPA Firm," does not specifically refer to documentation of compliance, a proposed interpretation, "Documentation of Compliance with a System of Quality Control," advises CPA firms that documentation would ordinarily be required to demonstrate a firm's compliance with its policies and procedures for quality control. That is a very positive step toward making potential peer reviews more effective.

5. There is finally the issue of confidentiality, given that the peer-review committee's responses to unfavorable reports have been so far nonpublic. As a consequence, the credibility of the program is tarnished. The reason for confidentiality is generally supported by the complexity of the situation involving private rights, the public interest, the litigious nature of the American society, and the misconceptions about the role, rights, and responsibilities of auditors. Although this reason may be legitimate, there is an urgent need for the profession to find a means of publicizing its sanctions for the sake of the credibility of the peer-review program in general and self-regulation in particular.

6. PROFESSIONALISM VERSUS COMMERCIALISM IN ACCOUNTING

Professionalism in any field is a voluntary commitment to achieve excellence. The existence of soundly conceived or well-written rules of conduct may act as a check for professionalism in a profession. But it is the commitment more than the adherence to rules that defines professionalism. In accounting, professionalism is a commitment on the part of all accountants, preparers, and auditors to uphold both the technical and ethical standards of conduct characterized by a high degree of objectivity and integrity. The main result of professionalism is credible financial reporting. To ensure the maintenance of professionalism in the conduct of certified public accountants, the AICPA has devised a code of professional ethics that prescibes the desirable attitudes and conduct from its members.

Although professionalism is at the core of a credible profession, commercialism may be dictated by the nature of and the special conditions of the market forces. In effect, the changing environment in accounting has led the CPA firms toward more profitable commercial routes that may jeopardize their professionalism. The spectre of commercialism arises because of the following developments:

1. CPA firms are facing a competitive practice environment where the auditing segment of practice is either stabilizing or declining. To offset the declining revenues from the audit function, firms have expanded their areas of activities beyond those considered to be the traditional activities of the profession. By doing so they have risked their identity as professionals. The basic question is whether the CPA firms can offer a financial supermarket of services without sacrificing objectivity, independence, and ultimately their status as professionals.

2. Large CPA firms have begun absorbing smaller firms and expanding by opening operating offices in most U.S. cities and establishing affiliations on a worldwide basis. These firms have resorted to aggressive techniques to draw business in a very competitive environment. As a result, a wider gap has been created between them and the remainder of the profession; competitive rivalry rather than camaraderie has become the rule.

3. With the increase in size and the large scope of services offered, the larger firms do not operate any more as professional partnerships but more as any large, divisionalized corporate enterprises. New characteristics include central management, line divisional officers, a board of directors, and a chief executive. The small firms have remained as true partnerships managed by their partners. As a result of these new organizational and management structures, the large CPA firms have found themselves pursuing a continuous goal of increasing revenues and market share and turning the profession into a true commercial business. The main characteristic of a true profession, which is to put unselfish service to clients and the public ahead of income considerations, does not necessarily apply to large CPA firms.

4. With the increase in size and the larger scope of services offered, the larger firms have found themselves offering services and agreeing to financial arrangements that may violate those permissible under the rules of conduct. As an example, a CPA may be offered compensation in the form of commissions for the sale of products or services of others. As another

example, some CPAs found themselves implicated in abuses in the application of accounting principles. The result of these new attitudes and conduct of CPA firms is such an increase in lawsuits with monumental claims for damages that large CPA firms have begun building in-house legal departments to cope with all of the litigation. This situation has led in part to an erosion of the confidence that the public places in the independence and objectivity of the profession as a whole.

Given this state of affairs, the accounting profession finds itself grappling with the spectre of commercialism and yearning for a return to more professionalism. An ideal first step is a revision of the code of ethics to deal with all of the new issues facing the nature of accounting practice. The new rules of conduct should deal with those situations in which the CPA is performing nonattest, nonindependent financial services. The environment in which these services are performed is sufficiently different to warrant a specifically delineated code of conduct that represents a "professional" approach to performing these services. The revision of the code of ethics may not be enough, because the mere prohibition of practices such as advertising, competitive bidding, and contingent fees does not really establish barriers that will effectively deter CPA firms from competing for clients who need and want financial services in addition to an audit, a review, or a compilation. In fact, the profession understood this when it dropped its bans on advertising and solicitation.

The second step, then, is to ensure that those entering the profession possess high levels of skill and expertise. These new entrants have to be taught that their primary role is to protect the public from anything that may jeopardize credible financial reporting.

The third step is to ask each CPA firm to attest that it is following specific guidelines for matters such as:

1. Soliciting clients and bidding for audit engagements
2. Ensuring that adequate work is performed regardless of fee
3. Advising management, audit committees, and boards of directors on the most appropriate possibility from among reporting choices
4. Setting growth goals affecting the audit practice
5. Taking positions on FASB proposals independent of client viewpoints

The viability of the guidelines for each CPA firm will then be tested through the peer-review process. This last step was proposed in a 1984 address of FASB chairman Donald T. Kirk. Its main merit is that it calls for a voluntary commitment, which is the essence of professionalism.

7. SPECIALIZATION IN THE PROFESSION

Two questions in specialization are of prime importance to the profession: (a) Should the accounting profession follow the trend of medicine, law, and engineering and allow its practicing members to designate their specialities? (b) Should the non-CPA specialists used in the CPA firms be given an associate-membership classification in the AICPA?

Professional Specialization

The answer to the first question is a resounding yes. There is an information explosion in accounting, and no individual CPA can be fully competent in all areas of the accounting function. Specialization is unavoidable in most disciplines and particularly in accounting. Not only is there an information explosion but also an increase in the variety of services demanded from CPA firms. A de facto specialization is already taking place in most CPA firms. It takes the form of a natural segmentation of the typical, large CPA firm into audit, tax, and management-advisory-services departments. In fact, CPAs are specializing in two ways. One specialization is by type of service (audit, tax, or management-advisory services) or by type of client or industry. The next step is a recognition of specialists by officially accrediting them. On September 25, 1974, the Committee on Scope and Structure of the AICPA listed two important benefits or recognition of specialists.

The provision of such recognition would be an incentive to excellence. . . .[M]eeting a set of standards formulated by one's professional colleagues would be a source of personal satisfaction. . . . [It] would demand a vigorous pursuit of knowledge and that, in turn, should benefit the public by insuring an even higher quality of service.

Such recognition, . . . would underscore the point that the specialized areas are legitimately within the profession's scope of services. It would, in effect, validate what is presently being done in practice; . . . what is being done is what ought to be done if firms are to remain fully capable of meeting society's needs.[3]

So accreditation of specialists seems to be the next logical step in the professional evolutionary process.

The important question is what is meant by *accreditation*. It is the *public labeling*, by an official body, of the competence to practice in accounting. This type of labeling would be facilitated by the present classification of accounting in accepted separate activities. One proposed classification goes as follows:

ACCOUNTING AND AUDITING

1. Auditing and certifying financial reports for management, stockholders, and creditors
2. SEC registrations and regulatory agency reporting
3. Expert testimony in lawsuits

4. Discussions with creditors

5. Bankruptcies

TAXES

1. Preparation of tax returns

2. Defense of returns before the Treasury

3. Obtaining advance rulings

4. Income tax planning

5. Estate planning with attorneys

6. Allocation of taxes and their effect on profit and loss statements

MANAGEMENT SERVICES

1. Systems and work flow

2. EDP feasibility studies

3. Programming the computer

4. Internal reorganization

5. Analysis of material produced by EDP

6. Budgeting[4]

Although the list is not exhaustive, it suggests the type of specialization that may be given in the accounting profession. In fact, Justin Davidson, CPA and former dean of the Business School at Cornell University, proposed the following from labels to be added to the CPA designation:

1. CPE—Certified Public Examiner

2. CPTA—Certified Public Tax Adviser

3. CPC—Certified Public Consultant

4. CPG—Certified Public Generalist[5]

The CPE designation would mean that the CPA has chosen to practice primarily, but not exclusively, in the examination function: accounting, auditing, and attest. The CPTA designation would mean that the CPA is an expert in the tax function. The CPC designation would mean that the CPA has chosen to practice primarily, but not exclusively, in the management-services area. The CPG designation would mean that the CPA is a CPA generalist, the accounting equivalent of the family doctor. He or she has familiarity with and the ability to solve routine problems in all areas of accounting practice.

There are various advantages and disadvantages to specialization in the accounting profession. Among the advantages cited in the literature and in practice are the following:

1. Not accrediting specialists may lead anyone to claim to be a specialist.
2. Accrediting specialists confers status and motivates performance.
3. Accrediting specialists promotes cooperation within the profession.
4. Accrediting specialists protects the public.

Among the disadvantages cited in the literature and in practice are the following:

1. Accrediting specialists promotes narrowness.
2. Accrediting specialists is difficult and costs time and money.
3. Accrediting specialists is not accurate for all time.
4. Accrediting specialists creates many internal (within accounting firms) as well as external problems.
5. Accrediting specialists favors large firms that are in a better position to maintain a group of specialists and may tend to downgrade the small CPA firm.

The trend is for accreditation spurred by the demand of the public for some form of labeling. In fact, the drive toward accreditation has already made some material progress. Various new professional designations have emerged to meet the needs for specialization. Examples include (a) the Certificate in Management Accounting (CMA) designation administered by the Institute of Management Accounting of the National Association of Accountants, (b) the Certified Cost Analyst (CCA) designation administered by the Institute of Cost Analysis, (c) the Certified Internal Auditor (CCA) designation administered by the Institute of Internal Auditors, and (d) the Certificate in Data Processing (CDP) designation administered by the Data Processing Management Association.

If the trend is clearly in favor of accredited specialization, why doesn't it exist? The Code of Professional Ethics is the primary obstacle. It includes a no-specialization rule to prevent the untrained practitioner from designating himself with a specialty when no mechanism exists to test and accredit such practitioners. With the cry and the need for some form of specialization, the AICPA proposed in 1981 an interpretation of the ethics rule on specialist and expert designation. The AICPA members would be permitted to refer to themselves as experts or specialists in advertising or other forms of solicitation in a manner that is not false, misleading, or deceptive if the institute would modify an interpretation of a rule in its ethics code. More explicitly, under the proposed modification to Interpretation 502-4, "Self-Designation as Expert or Specialist," an AICPA member must be prepared to substantiate the basis for a specialist designation by presenting evidence of the appropriate mix of education and experience. The proposal did not draw sufficient support within the profession. In addition, legal counsel advised the AICPA that interpretation 502-4 probably violated federal antitrust laws and was therefore unenforceable. Consequently, interpretation 502-4 was withdrawn effective September 1981. *There are now no guidelines for substantiating a specialist self-designation.* The effort was another aborted action for the AICPA. But perhaps the AICPA was lucky; it avoided answering crucial questions:

What specialties would be recognized? How will specialists be certified or accredited? Who will certify the specialists? Will firms or individuals or both be certified? How will practitioners respond to the implementation of these programs? What will be the effect on state societies, on the structure of practice units, on the public and the profession?[6]

On the other side, the AICPA may not be that lucky, because this is going to open the floodgates to all sorts of dubious claims.

Non-CPA Associate Membership

The issue started when, in December 1969, the AICPA Board of Directors received a letter from a member requesting that it consider creating an associate-membership classification for non-CPAs serving on the professional staffs of CPA firms. Should these people be given an associate membership and be brought into a professional relationship with the institute? To the substantive ranks of CPAs practicing in small firms, the answer is no not only to professional specialization but *especially* to some form of affiliation for non-CPA specialists. To most large CPA firms, eager to meet the increasing demand for new services and the need for non-CPA specialists for these services, the answer may be a definite yes. This is especially important for the large CPA firms, since the Institute of Management Consultants, organized by the non-CPA consulting firms, had started a program to accredit "certified management consultants." This is expected to make it difficult for the CPA firms to attract and retain high-caliber non-CPA specialists unless the AICPA starts some form of accreditation of non-CPA specialists. It would be relatively easy to do so, according to the large CPA firms. The associate member would have to satisfy certain qualifications relating to education and experience and would have to pass an exam. The profession would consist of multiple subdisciplines, which in turn would affect preentry education and entry examination requirements. A useful proposal goes as follows: "to serve as test for entry into the profession, the CPA examination may have to be broadened to cover additional subjects, and postentry examinations might be necessary for the various specializations."[7]

These proposals are not acceptable to a large proportion of the accounting profession. In addition, the general public is silent on the question. There is practically no public cry for the accreditation of specialists, given that the issue is essentially an internal matter within the profession. What the outcome will be be in the future on both professional specialization and non-CPA associate membership is difficult to predict. Both issues are essentially political, affecting the revenues of both large and small CPA firms. The resolution will depend on which of the small or large firms will be dominating the future committees examining the questions.

8. ISSUES IDENTIFIED BY THE FUTURE ISSUES COMMITTEE

In the process of identifying, selecting, and assigning priorities to the fourteeen issues presented in their report, the Future Issues Committee considered more than 100 issues suggested by its members. A list of all of the issues considered in that process as an inventory of items for further consideration by the committee follows:

1. Changes in the composition of the Institute's membership
2. Increased specialization of accounts
3. Interstate-international expansion of the scope of practice
4. Improvement in the quality of practice by CPA firms
5. Expansion of nonaccounting and nonaudit services
6. Changes in the nature and extent of competition in the profession
7. Increase in the level of external competition
8. Replacement of accounting measures as the standard of corporate performance
9. Widespread computerization and automation of business operations
10. Need to adapt to the diverse disciplines used in the profession
11. Role of the Institute in defining the scope of and regulating the profession
12. Ability of the profession to increase its adaptability and to be in the forefront of change
13. Internationalization of auditing standards
14. Accounting standards overload
15. Non-CPAs in CPA firms
16. Possibility of broadening the scope of the attest function to include, for example, attestation on matters concerning product reliability and management efficiency
17. Fragmentation in the professional authority to regulate and set standards, among bodies such as state boards, NAA, FASB, and the Institute
18. Development of an effective measurement basis for financial reporting, for example, current value accounting versus historical cost accounting
19. Consideration of measures of social performance
20. Upward mobility of women

21. Possible simplification or elimination of income taxes

22. Ability of the Institute to form membership groups to serve the needs of segments of its membership specializing in particular areas

23. Maintenance of the CPA's preeminence in the tax field

24. Effects of changing human and social values on the accounting profession

25. Increase in the number of non-CPAs in CPA firms

26. Increase in the magnitude and significance of litigation against accounting firms

27. Increase in the concentration of audit practices

28. Maintenance of the usefulness and relevance of CPA firms' work

29. Maintenance of CPA firms' independence and objectivity

30. Maintenance of the economic viability of practice units

31. Decline in the relative importance of CPA firms of the function of attesting to financial statements

32. Identification of clients' needs for new products and services

33. Role of women in CPA partnerships—two-career families, number of hours, client relations, business development

34. Role of minorities in CPA partnerships—increasing their numbers, and opening up opportunities, business development, and client relations

35. Attacks on the independence of CPA firms and the need to define independence

36. Possible unionization of CPA firms' professional staffs

37. Increased competition among CPA firms

38. Conflicts between professionalism and commercialism in CPA firms

39. Management and control of non-CPA disciplines performed in CPA firms

40. Possible limitation of scope of service because of regulatory or legal constraints or because of rules established by professional associations

41. Pressures on CPA firms to perform a watchdog role, and contravening pressures from client expectations

42. Social responsibility of CPA firms

43. Ability of CPA firms to provide a variety of career paths and working conditions

44. Role of self-regulation

45. Mandatory membership of CPA firms in an organization concerned with self-regulation

46. Changing attitudes of CPA firms toward education

47. Adequacy of the supply of qualified entry-level accountants

48. Changing personnel mix toward relatively more senior people in CPA firms

49. Absorption of CPA firms into mega-financial organizations

50. International regulation of accounting and auditing

51. Effects of the proliferation of computerized tax packages on CPA firms

52. Effects of higher fees on the use of accounting services

53. Possibility of public accounting firms "going public"

54. Increase in the number of nonpracticing Institute members

55. Increase in the number of internal auditors and their efforts to attain professional designation

56. Continuing relevance of the CPA designation as a qualification for financial executives in industry

57. Effects on nonpracticing CPAs of the large number of agencies and bodies setting rules for accountants

58. Compliance of nonpracticing CPAs with ethical standards requiring independence

59. Identification of nonpracticing CPAs with the CPA profession

60. Identification of nonpracticing CPAs with professional associations other than the Institute

61. The Institute's identification of the needs of non-CPAs in CPA firms

62. Lack of standards in some nontraditional accounting areas, for example, forecasting and social accounting

63. Effects on the growing number of professional certifications other than the CPA designation

64. Possibility that financial statements of companies may be certified by their internal accountants

65. Increase in the prominence of management accounting

66. Availability of accounting services from unlicensed practitioners

67. Relationships of the client's financial management and internal auditors with the outside public accountant in an audit engagement

68. Status of nonpracticing CPAs in the profession

69. Diversity of interest among nonpracticing CPAs

70. Relations between the Institute and state societies

71. Need for more training and trainers because of the expanding body of knowledge required by the profession

72. Number and status of minorities in the profession

73. Assuring the availability of adequate qualified personnel for the profession

74. CPA's income potential relative to the income potential in other fields

75. Decline in the quality of general education and its effects on the profession

76. Diverse sources of accounting education

77. Professional development of non-CPA professionals in CPA firms

78. Possibility of broadening the scope of the CPA examination to include skills beyond theory, practice, auditing, and business law

79. Lags and leads between technology in practice and the contents of accounting education programs in colleges and universities

80. Shortage of doctoral candidates and accounting faculty

81. Comparative advantages of training in colleges and universities versus training in CPA firms

82. Diversity in CPA qualifications and performance requirements among jurisdictions

83. Specialist accreditation

84. Implications of a system of national certification for CPAs

85. International and national reciprocity in licensing CPAs

86. Development of licensing and training programs for reentry into public accounting

87. CPAs' need for training in human relations skills, for example, communication skills

88. Need to adopt the five-year education program as the minimum requirement for entry into the profession

89. Relevance of an experience requirement as a prerequisite for licensing

90. Accreditation of accounting programs

91. Possibility of retesting and relicensing to prevent professional obsolescence

92. Viability of CPE requirements

93. Possibility of broadening the scope of education for accountants to include, for example, international accounting and business practices

94. Competition for the Institute in the testing area from other testing bodies, for example, Educational Testing Service (ETS)

95. Effects of the high cost of general education on the supply of qualified entrants to the profession

96. Authority and effectiveness of state boards

97. Prospects of the public accounting profession being nationalized

98. Retention of standard setting in the private sector-survival of the FASB

99. Prospects of the replacement of the private audit function by government audits or the elimination of SEC's requirement for public companies to have audits

100. Viability of the AICPA division for CPA firms

101. Pressures on CPAs to accept responsibility for the discovery of fraud and illegal acts in audits of financial statements

102. Improvement in the public's understanding of CPA's function of attesting to financial statements

103. Differences in the level of emphasis on regulating the profession in the fifty-four licensing jurisdictions

104. Regulation overload and overlap

105. Level of congressional interest in the effectiveness of self-regulation

106. Advantages and disadvantages of active self-regulation versus free market (caveat emptor) regulation

107. Level of public understanding of the CPAs' work

108. Level of public recognition of the role and effectiveness of self-regulation in the profession

109. Effects on the profession of public pressures for greater corporate accountability

110. Implications of an enforceable versus an unenforceable code of ethics

111. Responsiveness of the code of ethics to the changing environment

112. Effects of government deregulation on the code of ethics

113. Extent of compliance with the code of ethics

114. Pressures for changes in the code of ethics

115. The profession's level of concern for the public interest

116. Effectiveness of the Institute's public relations program

117. Clarification of the Institute's mission, goals, and objectives

118. Decline in Institute membership relative to the total number of CPAs

119. Diversity of needs among the Institute's membership

120. Competition for the Institute from other organizations seeking to attract CPAs as members

121. Need to establish a long-range planning function within the Institute

122. Competition for the Institute's CPE division from other organizations that provide training for CPAs

123. Effects of special-interest organizations of CPAs on the Institute and the profession

124. Interactions of the Institute with government and regulatory authorities

125. Effects of other standard-setting bodies on the Institute

126. Level of Institute members' participation in its activities

127. Associate memberships in the Institute for non-CPAs in CPA firms

128. Implications for the profession of the increasing number of retired partners of CPA firms

129. Implications of interstate banking for the profession

130. Possible effects of an international financial crisis on accounting practice

131. Increase in demand for accounting as a result of changes in state and local financing practices

132. Possible increase in demand for audit services that would result from the adoption of a requirement that all local government entities be audited by CPAs

133. Control problems resulting from the increasing use of computer terminals in homes and offices to initiate and record business transactions

134. Ability of CPAs to take advantage of changing technology in providing services to clients*

---

*American Institute of Certified Public Accountants, *Major Issues for the CPA Profession and the AICPA: A Report by the AICPA Futures Issues Committee* (New York, 1984). Reprinted with permission. Copyright © 1984 by the American Institute of Certified Public Accountants, Inc.

NOTES

1. D. R. Beresford, "Emerging Problems: How the Profession Is Coping," *Journal of Accountancy*, February 1981, 59.

2. Lee Berton, "Arthur Young Professors' Roundtable: The 'Accounting Establishment' in Perspective," *Journal of Accountancy*, June 1978, 31.

3. American Institute of Certified Public Accountants, *Discussion Draft: Report on Committee on Scope and Structure* (New York, 1974).

4. R. S. Helstein, "Accounting: A Profession in Transition," *Journal of Accountancy,* September 1970, 74.

5. H. Justin Davidson, "Accreditation of CPA Specialists," *The New York Certified Public Accountant*, June 1970, 460.

6. G. Siegel, "Specialization and Segmentation in the Accounting Profession," *Journal of Accountancy*, November 1977, 75.

7. W. E. Olson, "Specialization: Search for a Solution," *Journal of Accountancy*, September 1982, 78.

III

CPA FIRMS AND INDIVIDUALS

1. SHOULD THE AUDITOR REVIEW AND EVALUATE INTERNAL ACCOUNTING CONTROL?

It is basic textbook knowledge and, in fact, a standard of fieldwork that a proper study and evaluation of internal accounting control should be a basis for the determination of the types and extent of substantive tests required by the auditors. That was, however, the exception rather than the rule until 1977. That year President Carter signed the Foreign Corrupt Practices Act (FCPA) into law in response to the disclosures of bribes to foreign government officials and falsification of books and records by major U.S. corporations. The law called specifically for the development and maintenance of adequate internal-control systems. As a result, auditors directed their attention to internal accounting control as a means of restricting their audit tests. At the same time, the AICPA issued a report (*Report of the Special Advisory Committee on Internal Accounting Control*) and a statement (Statement on Auditing Standards (SAS) No. 30: "Reporting on Internal Accounting Control") aimed at contributing to the efforts of improving internal-control systems. One important change in the audit program of large corporations is more reliance on a review and evaluation of internal-control systems. This resulted in less audit tests and reduced audit fees.

Five years later, 1982, Carter was in Plains, Georgia. The American Institute of Certified Public Accountants (AICPA) issued a new statement (Statement on Auditing Standards No. 43: "Omnibus Statement on Auditing Standards") that contained an amendment (Section 320) of the role of the auditor in evaluating internal control and seemed to relieve auditors of their responsibility to review and evaluate internal-control systems. It clarified the *minimum* study and evaluation of internal control required by auditors. The *minimum* is described as an understanding of the control environment and the flow of transactions. This new development meant that auditors would have less reliance on controls and more emphasis on substantive tests. One might wonder about the reason(s) for issuing this amendment.

1. Is it related to a weakening or an absence in the case of small companies of internal-control mechanisms and, therefore, the necessity to rely on more substantive tests?
2. Is it instead related to the desire to increase audit fees?
3. Is an understanding of the control environment and the flow of transactions enough to design substantive tests? Would not reliance on specific accounting controls be a better indicator of the substantive tests needed? Are some people in the profession getting greedy?

2. SHOULD AUDITORS JOIN THE PRIVILEGED FEW?

As part of the audit process, the accountant reviews *contingencies* that could affect the company's financial conditions as reflected in its financial statements. They are guided in their analysis by SFAS No. 5, "Accounting for Contingencies." One of the important contingencies examined is that the IRS will audit the company's tax return and make material adjustments to it. The auditor is assumed to estimate the probabilities of such adjustments and their magnitude. In the process, the auditor prepares a number of papers, including an audit program, reports to management, and tax accrual work papers. The tax accrual papers, which are the subject of a controversy, usually consist of (1) a summary analysis of the transactions recorded in the taxpayer's income tax accounts, (2) a computation of the tax provision for the current year, and (3) a memorandum discussing items reflected in the financial statements as income or expense, when the ultimate tax treatment is unclear.

The controversy is that the IRS policy states that its agents may seek access to both audit and tax work papers of independent accountants. Section 7602 of the Internal Revenue Code gives the commissioner of internal revenue sweeping authority to *summons* relevant documents in an investigation of income tax liability. In fact, the section gives the IRS the power to (a) examine any books, papers, records, or other data that may be relevant or material to such inquiry; (b) summon persons to produce such books, papers, records, or other data; and (c) give such testimony, under oath, as may be relevant or material to such inquiry.

Would the access of the IRS to the tax-accrual papers threaten the accountant's ability to perform an effective audit of company financial statements. Most concerned accountants would view the IRS review of their work papers as a fishing expedition and a mind-scam. Most would expect the courts to give them the same treatment as attorneys and reject the mind-scam of accountants. In effect, in *Hickman v. Taylor* (1947) the Supreme Court rejected a mind-scam of attorneys, because it destroys the mental privacy that a professional needs to work effectively. The accountants used the mind-scam argument to argue against the IRS's use of the auditor's work papers. The court's decisions, for some cases, were favorable to the accounting profession. This was true in *United States v. Humble Oil* (1974), *U.S. v. Powell* (1964), *SEC v. Arthur Young & Co.* (1979), *United States v. Matras* (1973), and *United States v. Coopers & Lybrand* (1977). Not all of the federal court's decisions were favorable to the accountants. This was true in *United States v. Arthur Young & Co.* (1981) and *United States v. Coopers & Lybrand* (1975). In fact, the Supreme Court in March 1984 overruled the Second Circuit of Appeals and said that the IRS was entitled to see the tax-accrual work papers of Arthur Young & Co. in the IRS's probe of Amerada Hess Corp. for 1972 through 1974. The company was accused of setting up a "slush fund" for political contributions and payments to foreign officials. Arthur Young and Amerada Hess argued that the work papers were irrelevant to any IRS investigation, because they were not used in preparing the tax returns. Moreover, they argued that accountants and clients are protected by the same *privilege of confidentiality* as lawyers. Both arguments were rejected. The court maintained that, first, the papers were relevant and, second, lawyers are "advocates" and "advisers" for their clients, but accountants play a "public watchdog" role as auditors. Chief Justice Burger wrote: "By certifying the public reports that collectively depict a corporation's financial status, the independent auditor assumes a public responsibility transcending any employment relationship with the client. . . . The independent public accountant performing this special function owes ultimate allegiance to the corporations' creditors and stockholders, as well as to the investing public."

The decision is not a cause for joy in the accounting profession in spite of assurance from the IRS that it will seek work papers only in unusual cases and when it cannot get the information from the taxpayer. But will the IRS stick to the policy in the future? The decision raises many questions:

1. Will the decision lead companies to be less candid with their outside auditors about their tax pictures?
2. Should not the accountants be protected from disclosure by the privilege of confidentiality that applies to work done by accountants in much the same way that it applies to lawyers' work?
3. Are the outside auditors "watchdogs" or "advocates and advisers" to their clients?
4. Will the relationship between the auditors and their clients change toward less communication and more distortion?
5. Will the companies continue to self-disclose if they know that the CPA may have to give the contents of the disclosure to the IRS? Will it lead to less forthright disclosure?
6. Will the discovery of tax-accrual work papers provide the IRS with a road map to the corporation's most aggressive interpretations of the Revenue Code?

7. Is the auditor's work-product privilege analogous to the attorney's work-product doctrine?

8. If candid communications between the taxpayer and the auditor are essential to ensure adequate reserves for tax contingencies, would it not be more appropriate that records of communications stating why a tax position was taken by the tax-payer and the settlement posture on that position should seldom, if ever, be discovered by the IRS?

9. Is the full disclosure of questionable positions required for effective revenue collection?

10. Why should corporations provide the IRS with the substance of the case against them?

11. Is the IRS at a disadvantage in its examination of tax returns because the tax-payer or his or her agent possesses the sources of information the IRS needs to audit the return?

12. Without client cooperation and self-disclosure, can the auditor review contingencies as required by FASB No. 5 and be able to give an unqualified opinion, or is the auditor limited now to give only a qualified, or adverse, opinion or a disclaimer?

3. WHAT ABOUT THE AUDIT COMMITTEES?

The increase in litigation related to corporate misconduct and frauds is clear evidence of the need for more responsible governance and reporting. As a result, boards of directors have established and developed audit committees with the objective of assisting the boards in their fiduciary responsibilities to the public at large. An *audit committee* is an oversight committee that reviews the company's operations, controls, and reports and recommends to the board any necessary measures. Over time the audit committee's role has expanded to include most activities deemed necessary to protect the integrity of the published financial information. In the process it provides public corporations with an opportunity to enhance their credibility with the public, protects the company's shareholders, and provides constructive guidance to management. What these committees do differs from one firm to another; they are, however, generally concerned with similar matters. Felix Pomeranz, a partner in the accounting firm of Coopers & Lybrand, in a *Journal of Accounting, Auditing and Finance* article identified the following matters:

1. As to independent auditors:
   - Selection of auditors.
   - Maintenance of an open channel of communication with them.
   - Review of the audit schedule reflected in the engagement letter.
   - Review of management letters, specifically findings not acted upon.
   - Post audit review.

2. As to Internal Auditors:
   - Approval of the internal audit department's "mandate" or "character."
   - Review of job description and position specifications for the chief auditing officer.
   - When appropriate, selection of a chief auditing officer.
   - Maintenance of an open channel of communication with the chief auditing officer.
   - Review and approval of the annual internal audit schedule; coordination of that schedule with that of the independent auditors.
   - Review and approval of long-range internal auditing goals.
   - Review of internal audit reports in summary form; consideration of matters remaining open and corrective actions not taken.

3. As to Annual Reports and SEC Filings:
   - Preissuance review with emphasis on financial statements.

4. As to Interim Reports:
   - Consideration of controls established over the process which generates interim information.
   - Preissuance review.

5. As to Illegal Acts:
   - Review of policies and techniques established to monitor compliance.

6. As to Emerging Accounting and Auditing Issues (examples):
   - Evaluation of the impact of new regulatory requirements on the company and its financial statements.
   - Effect of new technology on independent and internal auditors.
   - Review of EDP security.[1]

Various interest groups have expressed strong interest in and commitment to audit committees:

1. Those critical of corporate governance and independent auditing perceive audit committees as an ideal way of introducing substantive changes in the corporate structure and strengthening audit independence.

2. Those critical of corporate management perceive audit committees as an ideal way of controlling undesirable management practices.

3. The Securities and Exchange Commission (SEC) has expressed support in audit committees since the *McKesson & Robbins* case in the thirties. At that time it recommended in ASR No. 19 that a committee of the board nominate the auditors and arrange the details of their engagement.

Later the SEC specified the necessity of such a committee in decree, settling the litigation brought against V. Killearn Properties, Inc. More specifically, it directed that an audit committee be formed comprised of "at least three persons who shall be members of the board and outside directors" and that it have the following responsibilities:

i. It should review the engagement of the independent accountants, including the scope and general extent of their review, the audit procedures which will be utilized, and the compensation to be paid.

ii. It should review with the independent accountants and with the company's chief financial officer (as well as with other appropriate company personnel) the general policies and procedures utilized by the company with respect to internal auditing, accounting, and financial controls. The members of the committee should have at least general familiarity with the accounting and reporting principles and practices applied by the company in preparing its financial statements.

iii. It should review with the independent accountants, upon completion of their audit, (a) any report or opinion proposed to be rendered in connection therewith; (b) the independent accountants' perceptions of the company's financial and accounting personnel; (c) the cooperation which the independent accountants received during the course of their review; (d) the extent to which the resources of the company were and should be utilized to minimize time spent by the outside auditors; (e) any significant transactions which are not a normal part of the company's business; (f) any change in accounting principles; (g) all significant adjustments proposed by the auditor; (h) any recommendations which the independent accountants may have with respect to improving internal financial controls, choice of accounting principles, or management reporting systems.

iv. It should inquire of the appropriate company personnel and the independent auditors as to any instances of deviations from established codes of conduct of the company and periodically review such policies.

v. It should meet with the company's financial staff at least twice a year to review and discuss with them the scope of internal accounting and auditing procedures then in effect; and the extent to which recommendations made by the internal staff or by the independent accountants have been implemented.

vi. It should prepare and present to the company's board of directors a report summarizing its recommendation with respect to the retention (or discharge) of the independent accountants for the ensuing year.

vii. It should have the power to direct and supervise an investigation into any matter brought to its attention within the scope of its duties (including the power to retain outside counsel in connection with any such investigation).

In addition, the SEC specified that the Audit Committee shall have the following special duties, functions, and responsibilities:

viii. Review, either by the Committee as a whole or by a designated member, all releases and other information to be disseminated . . . [by the company] to press media, the public, or shareholders . . . which concern disclosure of financial conditions of and projections of financial conditions. . . .

ix. Review of the activities of the officers and directors of Killearn as to their future dealing with the company and take any action the Committee may deem appropriate with regard to such activities. . . .

x. Approve any settlement or disposition of any claims or actions from causes of action arising after the date hereof or any litigation now pending which Killearn may have against any past or present officers, directors, employees or controlling persons.

The SEC did not impose the requirements on all audit committees. SEC Release No. 34-15348 requires only that the assistance of an audit committee with a description of the functions it performs be disclosed. In March 1972 ASR No. 133 endorsed "the establishment of all publicly held companies of audit committees composed of outside directors." In 1974 ASR No. 165 amended item 8 of schedule 14A of the proxy rules to require disclosure of the existence or nonexistence of an audit committee of the board of directors and its composition.

1. The New York Stock Exchange (NYSE), in its November 1976 policy statement, argued that the audit committees are an important part of the "self-regulation scheme envisioned by Congress" in the securities laws. In April 1973 the NYSE in its white paper *Recommendations and Comments on Financial Reporting to Shareholders and Related Matters* stated that it "strongly recommends formation by each listed company of a corporate audit committee," consisting of three to five outside directors. Finally, on March 10, 1977, the SEC approved a rule proposed by the NYSE that requires all domestic companies listing common stock on the exchange to establish independent audit committees by July 1, 1978.

2. The *Report of the Commission on Auditors' Responsibilities*, known as the Cohen Report and published by the AICPA in 1977, urged a greater role of the audit committee in the auditor-management relationship: "an audit committee composed of outside, independent board members is potentially the most effective method for monitoring and achieving some balance in the relationship between the independent auditor and management. It can mitigate any management tendency to influence the independent auditor to depart from professional standards" (p. 103).

3. The AICPA expressed its strong interest in July 1967, when the AICPA Executive Committee statement on audit committees of boards of directors recommended that publicly owned corporations appoint committees of outside directors to nominate the independent auditors of a corporation's financial statements and to discuss the audit work with them. It further indicated that the auditors "communicate with the audit committee whenever any significant question having a material bearing on the company's financial statements has not been satisfactorily resolved at the management level." It also established a special committee to study the probability of an auditing or ethical standard that will make audit

committees mandatory. The special committee on advice by counsel concluded in December 1978 that it cannot legislate the creation of audit committees unless it exposes itself and the AICPA to a violation of antitrust principles. The AICPA indicated, however, that it "continues to support the establishment of audit committees and is prepared to support efforts by others having authority to require audit committees where such requirements give due recognition to a reasonable cost-benefit relationship."

4. The Metcalf Committee recommended the creation of audit committees in its 1977 report *Improving the Accountability of Publicly Owned Corporations and Their Auditors.* Its purpose should be to "handle relationships with the independent auditor, improve internal auditing controls and establish appropriate policies to prohibit unethical, management consulting, or major commercial relationship." In the view of the committee, "Audit committee members should be free of any significant involvement with the management of a corporation, such as commercial or investment banking relationships, outside legal counsel, management consulting, or major commercial relationship."

5. Even Congress got into the act with a bill introduced by Senator Howard Metzenbaum in April 1980. That bill (S.2567), The Protection of Shareholders' Act of 1980, was intended to establish federal minimum standards relating to the composition of corporate boards, duties of corporate directors, audit and nomination committees, shareholders' rights, and for other purposes. S.2567 sets down the duties of the audit committee as follows:

AUDIT COMMITTEE

Sec. 6 (a) The board of directors of an affected corporation shall establish and maintain an audit committee composed solely of persons who are not described in subsection (b) of section 5 of this Act.

(b) It shall be the function of the audit committee, in addition to any other functions agreed to by the board of directors, to—
    (1) review the arrangements and scope of the independent audit examination;
    (2) review, upon completion of the audit, the following items with the principal firm of independent auditors engaged by the affected corporation:
    (A) any report or opinion proposed to be rendered in connection with the audit;
    (B) the extent to which the resources of the affected corporation were and should be utilized to minimize the time spent by the independent auditors;
    (C) any significant transactions detected during the audit which were unrecorded, unauthorized, or not adequately supported;
    (D) any material change in the affected corporation's accounting principles;
    (E) all significant adjustments proposed by the auditor;
    (F) the scope of the auditor's examination; and
    (G) any recommendations which the independent auditors may have with respect to improving internal accounting controls and choice of accounting principles;

(3) investigate and make recommendations concerning the cooperation which the independent auditors received from officers and employees of the affected corporation during the conduct of the audit;

(4) subject to the approval of a majority of the outstanding shares of the affected corporation, hire and dismiss the independent auditors and determine the compensation which they shall be paid;

(5) inquire of appropriate company personnel and the independent auditors as to any instances of deviations from the affected corporation's established codes of conduct and periodically review such policies;

(6) meet with the affected corporation's chief financial officer and other appropriate personnel at least twice a year to review and discuss with them the general policies and procedures utilized or proposed to be utilized by the affected corporation with respect to internal accounting controls, including the internal audit function:

(7) direct and supervise an investigation into any matter brought to its attention with the scope of its duties;

(8) review executive perquisites;

(9) report on the committee's activities in the annual report to shareholders; and

(10) review, either as a committee of the whole or by a designated member, all releases and other information to be disseminated by the affected corporation to the press media, the public, or its shareholders which concern disclosures of financial condition and results of operation, or forecasts of such information, of the affected corporation and its subsidiaries.

(c) Pursuant to performing the function specified in paragraph (6), the audit committee shall have the power to retain outside counsel in connection with any investigation.

There are, however, serious challenges facing audit committees. First, given the increasing demands on audit committees, the question is whether they will be permitted to evolve in response to the real needs of business and in accordance with the abilities of their members or whether they will take on responsibilities and activities for which they are neither prepared nor knowledgeable and competent enough to solve.

Second, given the present functions of an audit committee, membership calls for significant technical competence, a substantial commitment of time, and the acceptance of important data and responsibilities.

Third, good judgment is needed in evaluating the influence on audit independence of a wide variety of management-advisory services. That judgment rests not only on technical competence but on a good familiarity with a company and its operations, personnel, and controls. This calls for commitment and performance of duties beyond those conventionally accepted for board-of-director membership.

Fourth, given this new scope of the duties of audit committee members, where will business find members not only qualified but willing to accept responsibilities and take on the additional time commitment? A survey of the audit committees of 200 of the Fortune 500 companies in 1976 reported that of the 767 members, 35 percent were executives of other companies, 27 percent were bankers, 15 percent were insiders (officers of the company), 6 percent were attorneys, 6 percent were academicians, with the balance distributed in other specialties. Although these members may be qualified people in their own disciplines, some proposals have suggested that the inclusion of a "qualified" CPA on the corporate board in general and on the audit committee in particular is likely to increase the competence of the committee. To avoid any conflict of interest, only nonpracticing CPAs may serve as members. In fact, Walter S. Holmes, Jr., CPA and then chairman and chief executive officer of C.I.T. Financial Corporation, made a similar suggestion in an interview with the *Journal of Accounting*: "We have a very good audit committee chaired by Leroy Layton, former AICPA chairman. I believe retired CPAs present a tremendous reservoir of talent and should be used by Corporate America in this regard. They have spent their whole lives being independent. Far from backscratching, audit committees staffed by retired CPAs present new challenges to the CPAs on the company's auditing firm's staff."[2] Another solution would be to invite the thousands of Ph.D.'s in accounting from academia to serve as members of audit committees. They are likely to bring to the audit committee not only their technical and conceptual expertise but also unique methodological and communication skills. (This last proposal will undoubtedly be interpreted by some readers as a strong personal bias, since I am a full-fledged academician.)

Fifth, there is some concern that audit committees tend to select larger independent accounting firms over smaller local or regional firms. This bias of audit committee members may be attributed to their familiarity and exposure to the larger, well-known CPA firms through their involvement as officers or directors of other public corporations that employ the largest firms. A more plausible explanation may be that audit committees select larger firms to avoid being blamed or criticized for the selection and to reduce the legal liabilities.

Sixth, there is a tendency for audit committees to feel obliged to discuss occasionally the change of auditors or to change auditors. That is in line with the accepted belief that the nomination and approval of independent auditors is one of the primary functions of audit committees. But frequent auditor changes create an additional cost to the firm, given the added cost needed to train and familiarize the new CPA firm with the business. In fact, Harold S. Geneen, CPA and then chairman of International Telephone and Telegraph Corporation, made a similar suggestion in an interview with the *Journal of Accounting*:

I think the audit committee helps ensure independence by performing a role that directors should perform—reviewing overall performance and protecting the integrity of the audit function. Audit committees also tend to raise the visibility of the internal audit function. However, I do not like discussions about changing audit firms every three or four years; it takes a long time for an auditor to become familiar with a company—to know which questions to ask and where to look for problems. Normal attrition and rotation of personnel within the CPA firm will ensure frequent fresh approaches to problems with the benefit of top-level audit continuity. We should not have to conduct a major training program every three or four years.

Seventh, with continuing changes in the economy, science and technology, government regulations, and foreign trade come new requirements for more effective financial reporting and disclosures made by the company and a need for the audit committee to anticipate or to react in a timely and constructive fashion to these changes and new requirements. The future holds various issues of importance to audit committee members. In 1984 Deloitte Haskins and Sells issued the booklet *Audit Committees 1984,* which summarizes some of the issues of importance to audit committee members. The topics include:

• Adequacy of financial disclosure

• Computer security

• Summary of annual reports as a more effective reporting format

• Major financial accounting and reporting issues such as pensions, income taxes, in-substance defeasance of debt, and future accounting issues

• Important SEC actions such as the pilot electronic filing system, the revised shelf-registration rule, the moratorium on capitalizing computer-software costs, and the new shareholder proposal rules

• Self-regulation of the accounting profession

• Internal controls review

• External review of the internal-audit function

• Looking ahead

Finally, the performance of audit committees has varied from one firm to another. Some audit committees have taken their responsibility seriously, but others have been "missing in action." For example, several major executives were asked in 1980 to repay in excess of $900,000 to Playboy Enterprises, Inc., based on an audit-committee request after failure to document properly the corporate purpose for certain benefits. During the same year the audit committee in California Life Corporation was found to be "missing in action" during a conflict between management and the independent auditor. In this case, the auditors found that the company had deferred many expenses, turning a $3.2 million loss into a $2.6 million profit. A stalemate arose with the auditors not allowing the deferral and the management not yielding to the auditors. The audit committee, in this case, was a mere rubber stamp that did not get involved in the serious conflict between the management and the auditors.

4. WHAT IS INDEPENDENCE AND IS IT POSSIBLE?

Independence is the cornerstone of the accounting profession. To lend credibility to financial assertions and representations made by management, auditors must not only be impartial but must be perceived to be independent by outside users of financial statements. The accounting profession has long recognized the need for auditor independence, both actual and perceived by third parties. Rule 101 of the AICPA Code of Professional Ethics explicitly states that a member or a firm of which the member is a partner or shareholder shall not express an opinion on the financial statements of an enterprise unless the member and his or her firm are independent in respect to such enterprise. The code even suggests that instances in which the CPA is virtually part of management or an employee under management's control would lead to situations in which actual or perceived independence might be impaired. What are those situations? First, one may argue that possible accounting treatments for the same or similar event had the most serious potential adverse effect on independence. Second, one may also argue that situations in which auditors perform nonaudit services for their audit clients may lead to a loss of independence. In fact, various studies indicate that:

1. Various users see a negative relationship between nonaudit services and independence.

2. The concern by the same users about the lack of independence decreases when a "separate" staff has the responsibility of performing the nonaudit services.

3. Financial executives seem less concerned over the "alleged" lack of independence than do chartered financial analysts.

4. Some people argue that before the external auditor decides how much to rely on the internal audit function, he or she should investigate the degree to which that function is independent of company management. Therefore, the internal auditor, like the external auditor, should also be independent. Some may wonder whether the internal auditor's objectivity is adversely affected when he or she recommends standards of control for systems or review procedures before they are implemented.

5. The client-auditor relationship is ill defined. Some authors have argued that it is one of mutual dependency, and others have contended that it is a power relationship. If it is the latter, the threat to independence is built into the structure of this professional role, and one may argue that pressures on auditors not to perform according to professional standards are constantly created. The question is whether the auditors can resist these pressures.

6. Potential causes of a lack of audit independence cited include inadequate educational preparation, providing to clients services incompatible with the attest function, litigation involving the auditor and the client, and client-related economic disincentives such as the threat of being fired, fee nonpayment, or litigation for nonperformance of an audit contract.

7. There are serious doubts that an auditor can maintain his or her independence when an actuary associated with the CPA firm has provided actuarial advice or calculations that are reflected in the audit client's management decisions. The report of the Subcommittee on Reports, Accounting and Management of the Senate Committee on Governmental Affairs, chaired by the late Senator Lee Metcalf, *Improving the Accountability of Publicly Owned Corporations and Their Auditors* (the Metcalf Report), recommended that "nonaccounting" management-advisory services of accounting firms, such as actuarial services, be discontinued. In fact, estimating the costs and liabilities of a pension plan and funding those obligations involve many matters of judgment. They should be made by the client. Most actuaries will contend that clients cannot have judgments as informed as the results produced by their actuaries. They must rely on their actuaries. Any connections between an actuary and an auditor are bound to create a problem of lack of independence.

This evidence about actual or perceived independence was bound to create new interest and cause some concerned debate. Congress got into the act first. Both the Metcalf Senate Hearings in 1977 and the Moss House Hearings in 1978 warned that auditor independence would be ensured by congressional action. In fact, the Metcalf Subcommittee charged explicitly that provision of nonaudit services creates a professional and financial interest by the auditor in the client's affairs that is inconsistent with the auditor's responsibility to remain independent in fact and in appearance. Congress, however, left it to its appropriate agency—the SEC—to take action.

Following the congressional interest, the AICPA's Commission on Auditors' Responsibilities (Cohen Commission) looked into the nonaudit-services debate and concluded in its 1978 report that too much fuss was being made and that there is no evidence that provision of services other than auditing has actually impaired the independence of auditors. Following the report of the Cohen Commission, the AICPA appointed in 1979 the Public Oversight Board (POB) to consider similar issues. The POB agreed with the Cohen Commission assertion that concern about potential conflicts between management-advisory services (MAS) and the audit function decreases as user knowledge and sophistication increase. The SEC at the time was not impressed with arguments. It adopted ASR No. 250 and No. 264 to emphasize the importance of auditor independence. But the SEC later rescinded both ASR No. 264 and No. 250 after it considered that the profession had made sufficient progress to regulate itself with the issue of independence.

The question remains to determine exactly what auditor independence is and what happens to it when the auditor performs nonaudit services. The real test of an auditor's independence is the perceived nature and extent of his or her relationship with the audit client. If the auditor is so heavily involved in the client's affairs that an outside observer would perceive that the auditor is almost an insider, independence is impaired. If the auditor is merely performing unrelated and acceptable services to the client, independence is not impaired, given that the auditor's skills are needed not only for audit services but for other essential nonaudit services. As long as these nonaudit services are not performed in a way that would cause the auditor to be, or seem to be, an insider, independence is not impaired. In fact, some argue that management would not permit its decision-making authority to be usurped by anyone, including those CPAs providing advisory services.

What really does happen when the auditor performs nonaudit services remains to be answered. The magnitude of nonaudit services is on the increase. Ernst Whitney conducted a survey of the ASR No. 250 disclosures in 4,319 proxy statements issued from October 1, 1978, through June 30, 1979. The average percentage of total nonaudit services disclosed in the proxy statements was 23 percent, and the average percentage of MAS fees to total audit fees was 8 percent. What is the effect of these activities on the auditor's independence? Most arguments and official positions taken so far imply that too much fuss is being made and that independence is still "safe."

First, for example, in 1983 the Association of Data Processing Service Organizations (ADAPSO) filed a petition requesting that the SEC propose a rule providing that an accounting firm would not be independent if it supplied computer products or services to its audit clients. The commission rejected the ADAPSO's petition, because the area of non-audit services had already rescinded ASR No. 250 and No. 264 and had left it to the accountants to ensure that their performance of nonaudit services did not adversely affect their independence. It is, however, important to note that the SEC has always maintained its position that performance of write-up and other bookkeeping services would adversely affect accountants' independence.

Second, some would argue that the nonaudit services provide the auditor with better insight to improve the efficiency and effectiveness of the client's operation as well as to comment on its reporting to outsiders. In fact, the 1975 report by the POB, *Scope of Services by the CPA Firms*, noted that for clients the following types of benefits accrue from auditor provision of nonaudit services:

1. The extensive knowledge of a client's business gained during the audit can translate into cost savings and quality improvements on the consulting side and vice versa.

2. MAS services will attract better candidates in the profession and make the CPA more responsive to the complex needs of today's organizations.

3. The CPA involvement in internal controls and design of information systems will enhance the quality of the statements and make the audit easier and less costly overall.

4. The firm will benefit from advice on not only the weaknesses and defects observed during the audit but from recommendations on the general management aspects of the organization.

Third, some people argue that an audit is a cooperative venture between management concerned by the economic success of the firm and the auditor concerned with fair reporting. The same people argue that the auditor cannot achieve any of these objectives if he or she is totally independent. In fact, total independence is impossible, given that the auditor depends on management for the fees, the information about the business, and access to the records and personnel.

Finally, some argue that the best guarantee of the auditor's independence is his or her concern for a good "reputation." Society imposes a heavy cost on the auditor whose reputation is damaged. Not only are the costs of litigation extremely high, but the auditor's ability to practice may be threatened. Furthermore, sanctions by state boards against the practitioner can result in the loss of license or suspension of license, which directly affects one's ability to practice. In short, sanctions and lawsuits against auditors for lack of independence may result in financial losses, loss of license, or damaged reputations.

But the question remains to determine what can be done to deal with possible lack of independence. Potential remedies for enhancing auditor independence, advanced by John K. Shank at the June 1978 Arthur Young & Co. Professors' Roundtable, include mandatory audit-firm or audit-personnel rotation, shareholder ratification of the audit firm, mandatory review of audit work papers by a partner unconnected with the audit, public disclosure of auditing-firm financial statements, and increased federal regulation of accounting and auditing.

The most interesting remedy was proposed by John C. Burton, a former chief accountant in the Securities and Exchange Commission, in the April 1980 *Journal of Accountancy* article "A Critical Look at Professionalism and Scope of Services." He suggested a new device to provide compensation to auditors by outside parties. It would consist of a statutory-mandated fee paid by all public companies to a governmental or an independent agency that has the responsibility for selecting and paying auditors. *The debate is wide open!*

5. ARE THE BIG EIGHT INVADING THE MIDDLE-MARKET TURF?

The Big Eight have for a long time specialized in servicing the Fortune 500 companies. The clients of the Big Eight are assumed to account for 94 percent of all sales, 94 percent of all profits, 90 percent of all income tax paid, 94 percent of all people involved, and 94 percent of all assets owned by firms in the New York Stock Exchange. In fact, there is fierce

competition among the Big Eight in securing the largest share of that
market. There is evidence that in 1982 Big Eight shares of NYSE companies
changing auditors increased from 78 to 92 percent, and their share of
American Stock Exchange (AMEX) companies changing auditors increased
from 11 to 72 percent. This market, known as the primary market, is,
however, private and not expanding, and sometimes the Big Eight end up
taking business away from one another. To maintain growth the Big Eight
have turned to the so-called middle market: privately held, often owner-
managed companies, with sales ranging from $1 million to $100 million.
With fewer companies going public and publicly held ones reluctant to
switch accountants, the only safety valve and the only road to growth for
the Big Eight are in the millions of smaller firms that, by the way, account for
97 percent of U.S. companies and 50 percent of the gross national product.
This is a market that in the past the Big Eight ignored totally. Now they are
invading it, creating in the process tough competition for the local firms. *It
promises to be a nasty fight.* These local firms have traditionally helped the
owner-managed business in most aspects of the business, including tax
planning, auditing, and even structuring of business deals. In response to
the threat by the Big Eight, these local firms have started expanding their
services by creating special consulting and tax departments. However, faced
with the sophisticated packages offered by the Big Eight and their advertising and soliciting capabilities, the local firms face a hard road. Moreover,
the Big Eight have developed small business divisions to cater to the middle
market, which can play the same role as the local small CPA firms. These
divisions have been given various names: Small Business Division (Arthur
Andersen & Co.), Private Business Advisory Services (Peat, Marwick,
Mitchell & Co.), Metropolitan Department (Price Waterhouse & Co.),
Privately Owned Business Group (Ernst & Whinney), Entrepreneurial
Services Group (Arthur Young & Co.), Emerging Business Services
(Coopers & Lybrand), Small Business Services Department (Deloitte
Haskins and Sells), and Private Company Advisory Services (Touche Ross
& Co.). With these special divisions the Big Eight are better prepared to
have "personal and comprehensive" relationships with the middle market.
In addition to these features, the Big Eight have two more weapons to make
their move on locals in the middle market effective. The first weapon is
price. The Big Eight not only can afford to offer lower prices, but they can
afford to "low ball" their bids to their clients in the middle market. A local
firm cannot afford to be a "loss leader" for as long as a Big Eight firm. The
second weapon is name recognition. A small company, engaged in its initial
public stock offerings to the market, will prefer to "dump" the local firm
and switch to a Big Eight firm, hoping that the switch will make the offering
more palatable to the SEC and to the public. The future offers more
puzzling questions:

1. Will the local firms merge to be able to compete with the Big Eight?

2. Will the local firms learn to fight back and offer better services to the middle market?

3. Will companies going public continue dumping the local accounting firms in favor of the better organized Big Eight firms?

4. Will the small business divisions of the Big Eight be able to play the role of a quasi-local accounting firm and effectively serve the middle market?

5. Will the local firms merge with one of the Big Eight to survive?

6. Will a Big Eight pay as much attention to a small company as to a large company?

7. Will small business run the risk of losing the attention it gets from local CPA firms for the prestige of having a Big Eight accountant?

6. CONSULTING FOR LAW FIRMS

One new development in the area of consulting by the CPA firms is to fill the law firms' growing need for better organization, computer systems, and marketing efforts. Because of the dramatic changes in the legal system, law firms are becoming more aware of the need for long-range planning for which lawyers are neither prepared nor inclined to. The environmental situation has changed for law firms. The big firms are not money makers anymore. In 1983 Foreman & Dyess, Houston's seventh largest law firm, billed about $17 million—a fourfold increase in just six years—and the top partners drew $280,000 each in salary. In March 1983 the lawyers, who specialized in oil, gas, and bankruptcy matters, did not want to subsidize the firm's other departments any more. The firm went out of business, and the business-rich partners re-formed as a new firm. As an article in *Newsweek* of April 16, 1984, put it, competition and greed took over a once genteel profession that is facing the iron law of the marketplace. According to the annual Price Waterhouse survey of 24 law firms with more than 200 lawyers, fees grew by nearly 75 percent in the five years beginning in 1978, while operating expenses doubled. After inflation, the partners' take fell 9 percent. Add to that the statistical facts that, first, the number of U.S. lawyers has increased by 16 percent in the past three years; second, there is a decline in the median age of lawyers by about four years to 40; and, third, law-school graduates command $47,000 a year in New York—a 50 percent jump in fifteen years. All of these facts tend to exacerbate management conflicts within the law firms. Given this situation and the imbalance in the demand and supply of lawyers and the surplus of lawyers, law firms will be competing for less business, which makes them a lucrative opportunity for consultants. The CPA firms, aware of this situation, have not lost time in trying to set some of the action. Most CPA firms now have a law-firm consulting group to offer services in at least three areas: organizational issues, computer systems, and marketing. The future offers more puzzling questions:

1. Will the collaboration lead to the merging of law and CPA firms?
2. Will this venture into consulting for law firms lead to consulting for other service-oriented firms such as medical or engineering firms?
3. Will these ventures continue to increase the importance of the MAS branches of CPA firms at the expense of the more traditional branches such as accounting systems, tax planning, and auditing?

7. "LOW BALLING": A POPULAR STRATEGY

CPA firms, large and small, are competing for a finite number of firms to whom they are offering, respectively, the same services. As a result, fee competition is common and increasing. One way of beating the competition is through the practice of *"low balling"*, setting audit fees below total current costs. "Low balling" may be taking place on initial audit engagements. It may also be taking place when large firms compete with smaller firms for local engagements. Casual evidence on "low balling" is on the increase. Few companies reported to the Cohen Commission (the AICPA Commission on Auditors' Responsibilities) that in their recent negotiations, the new auditors indicated willingness to offer competitive prices, to make bids with fees guaranteed for several years, to renegotiate prices after receipt of competitive offers, and to set billing rates at as much as 50 percent below normal. Similarly, a 1979 article in the New Orleans *Times-Picayune* reported on the practice of "low balling" in conjunction with the audit of the city of Shidell:

Leonard Brooke of Deloitte Haskins and Sells said his firm expected just to break even on the first audit at a charge of $16,000. "I'd be amazed if it can be done for $25,000," said Brooke, who admitted his firm was submitting a low proposal the first year in order to do business with the city in succeeding years. . . .
    A fee of $15,000—lowest of the four—was proposed by Wally Giles and Eugene Fremaux of Price Waterhouse. "In reality, that fee does not constitute what our full rate would be if we didn't absorb the first year's start-up cost," said Giles.[4]

Another example may be used to suggest the possibility of "low balling." In 1984 the City of Chicago switched auditors from Peat Marwick Mitchell & Co. to Arthur Andersen & Co. In the process it saved $37,500 by switching auditors. Peat Marwick was receiving $375,000 for auditing the city's corporate and special funds. Arthur Andersen is charging $337,500 for the same service. But "low balling" is also observed in diverse environments such as bidding for franchise contracts, cable-television monopolies, and input contracts. Among CPA firms, however, "low balling" takes two new dimensions. First, it is anticompetitive and unfair to small firms. Second, and more importantly, "low balling" is alleged to impair auditor independence by creating a receivable from the client similar to an unpaid audit fee. The Cohen Commission agreed with this last statement (p. 121):

"We believe that accepting an audit engagement with the expectation of offsetting early losses or lower revenues with fees to be charged in future audits creates the same threat to independence [as an unpaid audit fee]." Therefore, these questions arise:

1. Does "low balling" by auditors impair their independence?
2. Is "low balling" a natural way to react to the fierce competition among CPA firms?
3. Should "low balling" be the subject of regulation? Should it be curtailed?

8. ACCOUNTANTS ARE WORKING ON A NEW IMAGE

According to the February 1968 issue of the *Journal of Accountancy*, a diatribe of Elbert Hubbard, an American author who died in 1915, referred to accountants as "cold, passive, noncommital, with eyes like a codfish, polite in contact but at the same time unresponsive, cool, calm, and as damnably composed as a concrete post or a plaster-of-paris cat, a human petrification with a heart of feldspar."

In an address to the American Association of University Instructors in Accounting on December 29, 1923, Henry Rand Hatfield described the situation of accounting academicians as follows:

I am sure that all of us who teach accounting in the universities suffer from the implied contempt of our colleagues, who look upon accounting as an intruder, a Saul among the prophets, a pariah whose very presence detracts somewhat from the sanctity of the academic halls. It is true that we ourselves speak of the science of accounts, or of the art of accounting, even of the philosophy of accounts. But accounting is, alas, only a pseudo-science unrecognized by J. McKeen Cattle: its products are displayed neither in the salon nor in the national academy; one finds it discussed by neither realist, idealist, nor phenomenalist. The humanists look down upon us as beings who dabble in the sordid figures of dollars and cents instead of toying with infinities and searching for the elusive soul of things; the scientists and technologists despise us as able only to record rather than perform deeds.

More recently, an article by Jacques Barzun in *Harper's* magazine in October 1978 depicted the professions under siege and the situation of the accountant as follows: "Latest on the carpet, the austere, unfathomable accountant is shown up as a master of misrepresentation, a cordon bleu at cooking the books. With this fall, the idea of 'the professional man' is near to being swallowed in contempt."

Accountants suffered then and now a less-than-glamourous image. Accountants do not dominate the headlines on television. There are no accounting heros known to the general public for their bravery, public service, or good deeds. The two most familiar accountants on television today are Bob Newhart, who was a Chicago CPA before becoming a comedian, and Norm, a character on "Cheers" known for his drinking, shyness, and low self-esteem. It is still too soon for a show depicting teams of adventure-hungry CPAs solving social cases and saving lives.

Accountants, aware of this public perception, are working hard behind the scenes on a new image. For example, because of the lack of success experienced by accountants in selling their new image, the AICPA published the *Public Relations Guide for CPAs*, a booklet for CPA practitioners planning public relations programs. It is a guide that includes step-by-step procedures for arranging interviews by newspaper reporters, writing news releases, appearing on radio and television talk shows, and speaking before community and professional groups. The AICPA chairman Bernard Z. Lee observed in the November 1983 *Journal of Accountancy* that "the accounting profession has matured and is no longer obscure, and that development brings with it considerable hazards and opportunities."[5] Through the number and scope of their services, they are communicating the image of a learned and complex profession. They are called upon by everybody including the government to examine the soundness and integrity of all sorts of economic endeavors from the proposal to save Chrysler to the annual "Oscars" presentation on television. Each year, we are told solemnly that the secret ballots for the "Academy Awards" show have been tabulated and are known only to the firm of Price Waterhouse & Co. In fact, the Academy of Motion Picture Arts and Science was at one time losing credibility with its "Oscars" ceremony and called on Price Waterhouse & Co. to restore it. A shot of respectability and integrity was needed for the process of tabulating votes for the awards.

Accountants are more and more perceived to be the guardians of the nation's investors, checking corporate financial reports to ensure that they are not misleading. To justify this important title of guardian of the integrity of the financial data disclosed to the market, the profession has set rigid requirements for entry into the profession. The licensing examination for CPAs, a demanding and complex endurance test, lasts three full days, and most candidates have to take it more than once. No more than 10 percent are believed to pass all four parts the first time. The accounting profession is also responding to an ethnically diversified society and to the gender gap as more ethnics and women are joining the ranks of CPAs.

As a result of the importance of accountants in the corporate structure, many are taking charge as chief executive officers (CEOs). In fact, in 1977 a CPA drew one of the largest paychecks among all U.S. CEOs. That CPA was Harold S. Geneen, chairman and then chief executive officer of International Telephone and Telegraph Corporation. His salary and bonuses, excluding deferred compensation, amounted to $986,000. Corporations are continuously seeking accounting professionals who can help a corporation get where it wants to go financially. This situation is reinforced by the ever-increasing reporting and auditing requirements being placed on U.S.

businesses by the Internal Revenue Service, the Securities and Exchange Commission, and other government regulatory bodies, as well as by the accounting profession itself.

It is not surprising that the accountant is constantly recognized as the right person to help rebuild the financial base, strengthen the financial structure, implement cost controls, and promote well-managed growth. The accounting profession is serving not only various functions but also various public-business leaders, stockholders, bankers, managers, and executives in the nonprofit and governmental fields, as well as individual taxpayers. From all of these publics, the accounting profession has gained recognition, stature, and status. But it has kept its image of attracting rational, practical, and technically oriented people willing to work behind the scenes.

9. BIAS AND BIAS LAW APPLY TO PARTNERSHIPS

"The paramount destiny and mission of women are to fulfill the nobel and benign offices of wife and mother. This is the law of the Creator."
Justice Joseph P. Bradley, U.S. Supreme Court, 1873

The Bradley quotation from a century ago refers to one of the most infamous opinions of the Supeme Court that denied Myra Bradwell, an Illinois woman, entry into the practice of law. Times have changed. In the last decade, women have been moving into most professions, including engineering, medicine, and architecture. Of all people enrolled in law school, 38 percent are women; of those enrolled in accounting classes, 50 percent are women. The most dramatic increase in women members is in the field of accounting. At many academic institutions the accounting student body and the accounting honorary organizations are predominantly female. As a result, the accounting profession is fast becoming a female-oriented profession. An editorial in the April 1984 issue of the *Practical Accountant* predicted that by 1990, with the economy on the upside, there is a distinct possibility that the staffs of accounting firms overall will be predominantly female. The editorial suggested that sabbaticals (such as for maternity and child rearing) and increased costs may follow, presenting a serious challenge to the accounting practice in the 1990s.

Although that is a concern, a more important question is whether the situation will affect the selection of partners in CPA firms with a bias against women. A partner shares directly in the profits of a firm, and the position is not only the richest in terms of income, but it also represents the peak of prestige in the profession. Female lawyers and accountants have long complained that getting those coveted partnerships is stymied by the "old boys' " network, in which male partners pick other males to join their rank at the top. A recent study by the National Law Journal of 151 of the largest law firms shows that only 8.3 percent of the partners are women.

Studies of certified public accounting firms show only 37 partners among the 5,985 partners in the country's Big Eight accounting firms. *A priori*, one would think that bias applied to partnerships would be difficult to uphold, given that Title VII of the 1964 U.S. Civil Rights Act bans discrimination in hiring and firing or in any "terms, conditions or privileges of employment" because of a person's race, sex, religion, or national origin. Besides, past court decisions have made clear that Title VII applies to most hiring, firing, and promotion decisions and to many employee benefits. Law and accounting firms have long disagreed with this rationale. First, they argue that advancement to a partnership is a change of status from employee to employer and, therefore, outside the scope of Title VII. Second, they argue that the selection of partners is a business decision rather than an employer-employee relationship, and as such it is not covered by federal civil rights law. Finally, they argue that a partnership is comparable to marriage and therefore to coerce a mismatched or unwanted partnership too closely resembles a statute for the enforcement of shotgun weddings.

Fortunately, a partnership's decision about whether promoting an employee must comply with the anti-discrimination provisions of federal law came to the Supreme Court in 1984 in *Elizabeth Hishon v. King & Spaulding*. Hishon was facing an "up-or-out" policy that law and accounting firms have, stipulating that if you are not made a partner within a specified time, you must leave the firm. Hishon's suit, brought under Title VII of the 1964 Civil Rights Act, had been dismissed by the Eleventh U.S. Circuit Court of Appeals. The law firm had argued that application of the law to the partnership-selection process infringed on constitutional rights of free association and free expression. On May 4, 1984, the Supreme Court rejected the argument and ordered the reinstatement of Hishon's suit. (She still must prove at a trial that she was the victim of discrimination, a charge the law firm denies.) It unanimously declared that law firms may not deny partnerships to women solely on the basis of sex. Basically, the court affirmed that law firms cannot discriminate between males and females in selecting partners, and all such promotions must be done on a sex-blind basis. The decision exposes a variety of partnerships to job-bias lawsuits for refusing to promote women, or men for that matter, to partner status. Besides affecting law firms, the decision affects the securities, accounting, advertising, consulting, and public relations industries. With regard to the accounting profession, the ruling means that Title VII of the 1964 Civil Rights Act requires that women be considered on an equal basis with men in the selection of accounting partners, a *professional niche traditionally dominated by white males.* In effect, the history of the job-bias law does not contain any evidence that Congress meant to exempt partnership-selection decisions. This may lead to a flood of sex-discrimination cases against accounting firms for refusing to promote women to partnership as long as partnership may be proven in court to be a *term, condition, or privilege of employment.* The fact that the Supreme Court decision was unanimous will give additional weight to such lawsuits, because unanimous decisions by the courts are rare. This partnership decision follows an earlier Supreme Court decision in *Gunther v. the State of Washington,* puts employers on notice that they can be sued under Title VII for claims by women of less pay for comparable work, and legitimizes the concept of pay equity. The two civil rights rulings give women accountants a good opportunity for equal pay and partnerships and may shatter the "up-or-out" policy that most accounting firms have.

10. AUDITOR SWITCH: GET THE RIGHT ACCOUNTING FIRM AND YOU GET THE OPINION YOU WANT

Is it true that a firm can get the opinion it wants by changing auditors? Actual cases suggest that it is:

1. Deloitte Haskins qualified the opinion of Wespercorp's results for fiscal 1983, ended June 30, 1983, citing potential claims resulting from adjustments to previously reported quarterly data. One disagreement acknowledged by Wespercorp was Deloitte Haskins' questioning of the practice of recognizing revenue upon shipment of computer systems, which Wespercorp considered to have met the GAAP. In 1984 Wespercorp dismissed Deloitte Haskins and retained Touche Ross & Co. Was the disagreement the deciding factor in the switch?

2. Peat Marwick was appointed by the Byrne administration in 1979 to be auditors of Chicago. During the 1983 primaries, ads appeared in the two major daily newspapers signed by concerned Chicago leaders praising the financial health of the city. Anthony M. Mandolini, the partner at Peat Marwick who handled the city account, was one of the signatories. Arthur Andersen was reported to have refused to sign the ads. Following the election, the new mayor, Harold Washington, appointed a task force that reported a potential budget-deficit problem for 1983. As expected, the City Council Finance Committee, which is given the power by the city code to appoint the city's auditor, in 1984 dumped Peat Marwick Mitchell & Co. as the city's auditors in favor of Arthur Andersen & Co. and Coopers & Lybrand. Was politics the deciding factor in the switch?

3. Arthur Andersen & Co. was an auditor to both Northwest Industries and Pogo Producing Co. In 1981 Northwest acquired 20 percent of Pogo's stock and used the equity method to show 20 percent of Pogo's earnings on its income statement. Northwest paid some $77 million over the book value for the Pogo holdings. For oil and gas acquisition, the acceptable procedure is to allocate the $77 million to proved and unproved oil and gas properties and then use depreciation changes for the proved properties. Thus the more proved properties, the better for Northwest. At that time Pogo was resisting

a takeover by Northwest. So it claimed that only $10 million of the $77 million were in proved reserves, while Northwest claimed $32 million. Besides, Pogo claimed that Northwest had overstated the value of proved reserves by $38 million and that it should reduce its earnings by $38 million in write-offs. Arthur Andersen & Co. was understandably reluctant to take the side of Pogo. So Pogo hired Coopers & Lybrand to take its side in court. Is this another case where the right accounting firm will give you the opinion you want?

4. Broadview Financial Corp., the Cleveland-based savings and loan association, wanted to take immediate gains in its 1982 annual report from some real estate investments while its auditor, Peat Marwick, preferred that the profits be spread over the life of the project. So Broadview Financial Corp. switched auditors and hired Deloitte Haskins and Sells. It also went ahead with the gain recognition and reported a loss of $16.8 million for 1982. Deloitte, however, took the same stand as Peat Marwick by forcing Broadview to revise its loss to $25.4 million and by including in its opinion an emphasis paragraph about the net-worth problem. The switch of auditors in this case did not work to the firm's advantage.

5. *Public Accounting Report*, an industry newsletter, reported that in 1982 the number of publicly held firms firing their auditors jumped 48 percent to 442 from 298 the year before. It also reported that 92 came directly because auditors qualified the companies' reports, and 122 were the result of "accounting disagreements" or "personality conflicts," which is equivalent to disputes over qualifications. The newsletter failed to report whether the qualified firms that switched auditors tended subsequently to receive more clean opinions or fewer qualified opinions.

11. CHECKLIST: SELECTING CPA SERVICES

The selection of a public accounting firm is not to be taken lightly. The accounting professional can play a major role in the success of your business or personal affairs. The following checklist is by no means comprehensive; however, it is a reference to some of the more important considerations when making this critical choice.

TYPES OF SERVICE PROVIDED BY CPAs

Audits of financial statements.

Compilations of financial statements.

Financial statement reviews.

Prepare business tax returns.

Assistance in preparing this service list was provided by CPA William Gifford Jr., CPA Earl Goldberg, management consultant Deborah Bricker, the Illinois CPA Society, the American Institute of Certified Public Accountants, and the Conference Board.

Prepare tax returns for individuals.

Prepare tax returns for Subchapter S corporations.

Recommend tax savings procedures.

Preparation of financial reports.

Provide assistance in securing loans.

Design accounting systems for individuals.

Consult on accounting aspects of business problems.

Professional advice on management aspects of business.

Conduct special studies on financing, credits, costs.

Conduct special studies on inventories, collections.

Forecast cash flow.

Cost control systems development.

Manual accounting systems development.

Assist in mergers and expansion programs.

Liaison with bankers and other professionals.

Help individuals in estate tax planning.

Advise on deferred compensation arrangements.

Advise and organize trust arrangements.

Prepare statistical reports.

Prepare research reports.

Audit research and statistical reports.

Organize and evaluate the use of economic resources.

WHEN DOES A PRIVATELY HELD COMPANY REQUIRE AN AUDIT?

For a review by an absentee owner with professional managers.

When required by a lender as part of a loan agreement.

If owner/manager is not financially oriented.

If the company is likely to be sold within a few years.

When major suppliers require it prior to honoring an order.

If a major customer requires proof of performance ability.

If the management of an employee-owned company wishes to prove performance.

When the management wishes to have the CPA available for confidential discussion.

CONSIDERATIONS IN SELECTING AN ACCOUNTING FIRM

Professional standing/memberships.

Hourly rates and other fees to be charged.

Will partner or professional staff member handle the account?

All required services available? In-house or outside consultant?

Good rapport between you and account people?

Good reputation. References from other clients.

Experience in your service area.

Agreement on an engagement letter.

Size of firm relative to your needs.

Range of services available if needed.

Location of firm if proximity required.

Previous experience in your field or industry.

SELF-ANALYSIS OF ACCOUNTING NEEDS

Compilation of financial information needed?

Help with preparation of financial statements required?

Will auditing be important to you?

Will tax service and advice be important to you?

Will management services be required?

Will accounting services be the most important?

Does your company have several locations?

Do you have facilities in other states/countries?

Will you require special reports for government agencies?

Is there any need for preparing business loan applications?

Are there any mergers/acquisitions likely in the future?

Will you require personal financial help?

HOW TO HELP KEEP ACCOUNTING AND AUDITING COSTS DOWN

Compile information requiring business decisions in advance.

Explain goals and objectives.

Be explicit on what you expect from the accounting firm.

Inform CPA of changes in business directions and procedures.

Keep good records to avoid charges for routine work.

Use professional regularly to keep him involved in the firm.

CONTENTS OF AN ENGAGEMENT LETTER

Detailed description of services to be rendered.

Specific time frame for special projects.

General time frames for long-term engagements.

Specifics on fee or hourly rates.

Billing procedures.

Terms and conditions of accounting firm.

TYPES OF MANAGEMENT ADVISORY SERVICES (MAS)

Computer system design.

Computer system installation.

Actuarial consulting.

Feasibility studies.

Compensation and employee benefit programs.

Merger and acquisition analysis.

Executive recruiting.

Organization planning.

Inventory and production controls.

Office systems development.

Litigation support.

Assistance with divestitures and liquidations.

Special studies.

Insurance claim services.

CONSIDERATIONS IN SELECTING AN ACCOUNTING FIRM FOR MAS WORK

Areas of MAS experience.

Length of MAS experience.

Is MAS planning available?

Is MAS implementation available?

Is MAS control and analysis available?

Is plan compatible with your philosophy?

Is plan compatible with your daily operation?

What is the consultants accountability to you?

How will progress and results be reported?

Are standard procedures used where possible?

What is the control for on time completion?

What is the control for completion in budget?

Do individuals on consultant staff meet experience and professional standards touted by consultant firm?

References of other clients.

Were other jobs finished on time? In budget?

Do references demonstrate independence?

What distinguishes consultant from others?

What skills are special?

What is fee for the project? How does it compare?

SUGGESTED CONTENT OF MAS PROPOSAL

Objectives and scope of the project.

Detailed approach to conduct the project.

Detailed phasing of the project.

Results or final product of the project.

Estimated fees and/or hours for completion of project.

Specific work tasks to be completed.

The purpose of each task.

Persons responsible for each task.

Hours required for each task.

Completion date for each task and entire project.

Budget controls.

Controls for completion date.*

12. EX-JEWEL CHIEF PROFILES IDEAL ACCOUNTING FIRM

What do the heads of major corporations look for when selecting a CPA firm? If they are like Donald S. Perkins, retired chairman and CEO of Jewel Companies, Inc., they expect a great many things from their accountants. Perkins described the qualities of an ideal public auditing firm at a recent Arthur Andersen & Co. partners' meeting. He said that in selecting an accounting firm, he would look for the firm that came closest to his ideals.

Each time a new auditing blunder hit the headlines your first thought may be related to the damage to the finances and the reputation of the partners. My first thought is about damage to the credibility of corporations or institutions which exist only as long as the public suffers their existence and which depend on you for assurance to the public of their integrity.

When I was invited to join you at this meeting I was asked to be candid about your profession as it appears to a former purchaser and current observer and monitor of your services. My credentials as current observer and monitor include the patience to serve on nine audit committees and to chair three of them. You are a better judge of your profession and of Arthur Andersen than I could ever be, so rather than criticize, it occurred to me that I might put my interests in a positive light . . . by telling you what my ideal public auditing firm would be like.

1. My ideal firm would develop people who have the training and the self-confidence to "tell it like it is" to top management and to directors. They would refuse to work for a client whose CEO wasn't interested in at least an annual private review by the auditors of the company's accounting practices and talent . . . and they would

---

*Reprinted with permission from the September 26, 1983, issue of *Crain's Chicago Business*. Copyright 1983 by Crain Communications Inc.

request of each client an annual evaluation of the quality of their work and their service.

2. My ideal firm would have as partners, well-rounded business people. I don't think that proficiency at the entry level jobs at Jewel, such as stocking shelves, develops any more breadth than do entry level jobs in accounting. But through both inside the firm and outside activities my firm would acknowledge that the only process more expensive than developing broad-gauged partners is the process of not developing them.

3. My ideal firm would have as partners well-rounded family men and women. It is difficult enough in retailing to differentiate between quality and quantity of hours. . . . I can imagine how much more difficult it is when you bill by the hour. However, of all the speeches and words I delivered in my 30 years at Jewel, one message stands out above all the rest. Amidst a price-war in the mid '70s when the Jewel Food Store profit had been cut by 70%, I said at a Jewel Food Store officer meeting, "I'm worried that you are trying to make up with hours what this environment will not permit to happen. Do not lose sight of the fact that your health and your family are more important than Jewel."

4. My ideal firm would require success in external volunteer activity as well as accounting proficiency for evaluation and retention as a partner. Not only would such a requirement help to develop an acting partner of broader scope, it also would help to develop a retired partner who is likely to remain a happy and contributing person.

5. My ideal firm would get the best candidates to join the firm because of the special training and development offered for a career, not because more salary was offered initially.

6. My ideal firm would recognize that the 20th time you sign off on an audit it may not be as stimulating as the first time it is done. They would recognize that, as for airline pilots, repetition becomes boring and boring becomes dangerous. They would regularly evaluate partners as carefully as they do candidates for partnership.

7. My ideal firm would know that it is only as strong as its weakest office and its weakest partner, and it would be constantly up-grading.

8. My ideal firm would view size as a threat to quality. It would have learned from its corporate clients that acquisitions are seldom as worthwhile as internally, and often slowly, developed growth.

9. My deal firm would be as proud of a resigned account as an account added. In resigning an account it would use the same key criterion an independent director might use, a loss of confidence in top management.

10. My ideal firm would communicate to management and directors in simple English.

11. My ideal firm would communicate with candor to a client's management and to its board. I appreciated a line which I quote from an Audit Committee Report by one of your competitors. They said, "Although this accounting change is unquestionably permissible, it does make the financial statements less conservative than in the past."

12. My ideal firm would write audit reports and plans creatively and thoughtfully. One year's report or plan would not read like a word processing reprint of the report or plan of the previous year.

13. My ideal firm probably would not do systems consulting work. If they did, they would pride themselves on working more for nonauditing than for auditing

clients. They would understand that although increasing the range of services need not inhibit independence, it does nothing to enhance independence.

14. My ideal firm would display the same cost concern as independent auditors that they would show if they were employees. They would teach managements how to train, develop and deploy internal auditors for the fullest possible use of external auditing fees.

15. My ideal firm would spend more time and charge more to audit clients whose internal controls were acceptable than those whose internal controls were outstanding.

16. My ideal firm would not discount its fees to obtain a new client. They would recognize that other clients would assume that they were paying for that discount.

17. My ideal firm would make it clear that they did not take any client for granted . . . just as they would expect that they should not be taken for granted. They would know that the best way to be certain that they are not taken for granted is to have contact with the chief executive officer. Their partners would be rare in your industry. They would know how to talk to chief executives and would have developed a breadth of skills that made them as comfortable in contacts with the chief executives as they are with the controller.

18. And finally, my ideal firm might even charge more because they would be worth it. They would have differentiated their services and their people from their competitors. They would make it very clear to their clients that they understood that it was not the central purpose of the client enterprise to support accountants.*

13. DIRECT UNINVITED SOLICITATION:
CLIENT CHASING BY CPAs

One of the major barriers to competition in the accounting profession is the prohibition against one accountant soliciting another's client without the client's invitation. The definition of direct uninvited solicitation is, however, far from clear. A survey of CPAs showed that the respondents believe that the act of handing a potential client a business card does not constitute direct uninvited solicitation. But the respondents believe that writing letters or placing telephone calls to potential clients definitely constitutes direct uninvited solicitation. The survey found also that there are some ambiguities in CPA thinking about what constitutes direct uninvited solicitation. In spite of the difficulties of definition, there are two divergent arguments about whether or not direct uninvited solicitation should be banned.

Supporters of the ban, consisting mainly of small CPA firms, argue that it protects them from the unfair competition from large national firms. They also view acts of direct uninvited solicitation as manifestations of a trend away from professionalism to commercialism. Others argue for the ban, using the support of the theories that the CPAs (a) are not independent

---

*Reprinted with permission from the September 26, 1983, issue of *Crain's Chicago Business.* Copyright 1983 by Crain Communications Inc.

of clients obtained by direct uninvited solicitation or (b) do not maintain their independence in mental attitude toward those clients subjected to direct uninvited solicitation by another CPA. This last theory was advanced by Philip L. Defliese as follows:

The independent auditor's position is unique in that he has two clients—the company he is auditing and the person relying on his opinion on the financial statement: the prospective investor or general public. Only through an independent approach to his task can the reliability of his opinion be assured. The threat of a loss of an engagement or the need to lower his fee (and possibly impair quality), while he is so engaged may consciously or subconsciously affect his independent attitude toward the management he is auditing. This can insure the public interest.[6]

Opponents of the ban, consisting mainly of large CPA firms, argue that it creates a barrier to free competition, to an efficient market for accounting services, and to "fair" fees. This position is also supported by the Justice Department and the Supreme Court. In 1976 the Supreme Court struck down a National Society of Professional Engineers ban on competitive bidding. The Justice Department does not look favorably on any ban on competitive bidding. This attitude was explicitly expressed in September 1979, when the chief of the antitrust division's special litigation section stated that, in the Justice Department's view, a blanket ban on written and oral solicitation by accountants "substantially impedes the ordinary give and take of the marketplace and under cases like [*Professional Engineers, Texas State Board of Public Accountancy*, and *American Institute of Architects*] would be illegal under the antitrust laws absent the state-action exemption.[7] (The *state-action exemption* is a doctrine that confers immunity from antitrust law for a restraint of trade that is clearly articulated and affirmatively expressed as state policy and is actively supervised by the state itself.) As a result, the Justice Department tried first to convince accountants' national organizations and most state boards to drop the bans. The results were successful with the AICPA and some of the state boards. On March 31, 1975, the AICPA, following a mail ballot of the membership, changed the wording of Rule 502 as follows:

Previous Version: Advertising and Other Forms of Solicitation. A member shall not seek to obtain clients in a manner that is false, misleading, or deceptive. A direct uninvited solicitation of a specific potential client is prohibited.

New Version: Advertising and Other Forms of Solicitation. A member shall not seek to obtain clients in a manner that is false, misleading, or deceptive.

The AICPA dropped the second sentence of the rule that prohibited direct uninvited solicitation.

In 1981 the AICPA special committee on solicitation concluded in its report that:

1. A prohibition against unscrupulous solicitation should be added to the current solicitation rule.

2. The AICPA Board of Directors should issue a policy statement that members who choose to engage in the commercial practices of solicitation and advertising should exercise appropriate restraint.

3. The AICPA should not influence state legislators to adopt more stringent solicitation bans than the institute itself can impose.

4. The institute should not require its members to submit copies of all direct uninvited promotional literature for simultaneous or subsequent review.

At the same time, a member of the AICPA Special Committee on Solicitation, Louis W. Donner, remarked that an adverse court decision on a re-imposed ban on direct uninvited solicitation not only would likely result in loss of the ban but would enjoin the AICPA from having any rule or making any statement that solicitation for services is unethical, unprofessional, or contrary to AICPA policy.

In 1982 the state boards in Kentucky and West Virginia dropped the bans following inquiries and threats of action by the Justice Department. In most other states, however, the bans exist, leading to admonishment or revoking of licenses of those accountants caught soliciting. To resolve this problem, the Justice Department has filed a lawsuit against the Louisiana State Board of Accountancy for prohibiting "direct uninvited solicitation." If the Justice Department wins in Louisiana, the bans will disappear in the other states as well, and an interesting "open warfare-client chasing" situation may result.

To avoid any possible warfare, the Board of Directors of the AICPA adopted in December 1982 a policy statement urging members who engage in advertising and solicitation to avoid excesses that could jeopardize adherence to technical and ethical standards. The statement urged members to exercise "common sense, good taste, moderation and individual responsibility" in advertising and solicitation. This statement is in conformity with Rule 502 of the AICPA Rules of Conduct, which deals with prohibition against false, misleading, or deceptive solicitation.

14. WHEN ACCOUNTANTS MISS THE MARK

Touche Ross

November 1983—The S.E.C. censures Touche Ross for failing to use "generally accepted auditing standards" in its examination in the mid-1970's of the financial statements of Litton Industries, a big defense contractor. The agency also censures the firm for accounting irregularities in its 1978 audit of the Gelco Corporation. Touche Ross neither admits nor denies the charges.

Coopers & Lybrand

August 1983—The S.E.C. charges both a partner and a manager at Coopers & Lybrand with conducting a deficient 1979 audit of the Security America Corporation, a Chicago insurance holding company. Later, Security's chief subsidiary is forced into liquidation. Without admitting or denying the charge, the two accountants settle the case with the S.E.C.

Arthur Andersen

July 1983—Wareen Essner . . . , a former senior partner at Arthur Andersen, is indicted for having issued a false financial statement about the bankrupt Drysdale Government Securities Corporation. He had reported that Drysdale was formed with a net value of $20.8 million—a statement the Justice Department's lawsuit contradicts. The Government case says Drysdale had been begun with $150 million in liabilities. Chase, which lost $270 million in the Drysdale collapse, sues the accounting firm, charging it "knew or recklessly disregarded the facts" in its audit.

Fox & Company

June 1983—The S.E.C. files a civil court action and an administrative action against Fox, charging that the firm's audits of Saxon Industries, Flight Transportation and Alpex Computer were not conducted in accordance with accepted auditing standards. The commission says Fox "aided and abetted," Saxon—which later filed for bankruptcy—in missing financial statements. The court orders a review of Fox's auditing practices of public companies.

Ernst & Whinney

January 1983—Ernst & Whinney's accountants give United American Bank of Knoxville, Tenn., a favorable auditing report. One month later, the bank, owned by Jake Butcher, fails. Ernst & Whinney contends its auditors could not have detected that the bank was shifting bad loans to other Butcher-controlled banks.

Peat Marwick

July 1982—Penn Square Bank collapses from bad energy loans and Peat Marwick comes under criticism for not having audited enough of the bank's loan portfolio. The Comptroller of the Currency concludes that Peat Marwick's audit was "unacceptable." Peat Marwick claims it followed generally accepted accounting procedures.

Fourteen months later, the Michigan National Bank of Detroit files suit against Peat Marwick, asking $41 million in damages for energy loans it bought from Penn Square. In all, five Penn Square creditors sue the accounting firm.

May 1982—Datapoint, a computer maker, surprises investors by reporting a huge third-quarter loss and revealing that company officials inflated sales and earnings figures. Peat Marwick is named in several shareholder suits for lax auditing practices.*

15. ACCOUNTANTS' LIABILITY

The U.S. society is a litigious society. The price tag is enormous with evidence showing that many civil cases that go to trial—with or without a jury—can easily cost the taxpayers more money than is at stake for any of the litigants. In a speech to the American Bar Association on February 12, 1984, Chief Justice Warren Burger observed: "Our system is too costly, too painful, too destructive, too inefficient for a truly civilized people." As a result the accountants find themselves affected in many ways by the litigation explosion.

What is affecting accountants started with the prudent liability and the notion of strict liability, whereby "strict liability means that whenever a particular product emerges from an assembly line in a defective condition, the manufacturer will be liable for any injury that the defect causes."[8] The notion of strict product liability was later expanded to the area of professional liability affecting in the process architects, doctors, lawyers, accountants, and so on. In the case of the accountants, it meant that they should be held responsible for a business that does not function properly. This has generated a flood of lawsuits against accountants. Each time a company fails, its independent auditors become one of the few potential defendants that are solvent and, therefore, likely target for a suit. Given this situation, the first step is to identify the many potential sources of legal liability of accountants.

1. The first source of legal liability is the common liability to clients. This involves contractual liability, negligence liability, and problems of independence.

With respect to contractual liability, the auditor is bound by a contract with the client and an engagement letter specifying the scope of the audit and that his or her audit examination is to be performed with due care and in accordance with professional standards and that an opinion is to be issued regarding the quality of the client's financial statement. Without this, the accountant would be subjected to legal liability.

With respect to negligence liability, it would arise not only from a breach of contract but from a failure to observe professional standards and from lapses such as the following: (a) inadequate preparation by failing to pre-

---

New York Times, May 13, 1984. Copyright © 1984 by The New York Times Company. Reprinted by permission.

pare or revise the audit program for a client to take into account internal or external changes, (b) lapses in examination by omission or misapplication of a procedure required by the generally accepted standards, (c) inadequate supervision, review, and training of the audit staff, (d) shortcomings of evaluation and judgment, and (e) failure in reporting the right opinion. The accountant can avoid negligent liability if he or she can prove that (a) the client's own negligence contributed to the problem in the company; (b) the client failed to supervise its personnel, which contributed to the accountant's failure to perform his or her contract and to report the truth; (c) the client disregarded the auditor's recommendations; and (d) the client knew that reliance on the auditor's opinion is unjustified and that such reliance is a form of contributory negligence.

With respect to problems of independence, they arise when the auditor issues an opinion on the financial statements while acting as an advocate for the client or as unjustifiably differential to the client management's judgment. It usually happens when the accountant is also performing nonaudit accounting services for the client.

2. The second source of liability for accountants is the common liability to third parties. For a long time accountants were liable at common law for negligence in the performance of their professional engagements only to their clients. That is known as the *privity-of-contract doctrine.* The test of the privity-of-contract doctrine involving auditors came in *Ultramares Corp.* v. *Touche.*[9] In that case, the defendant certified the accounts of a firm knowing that banks and other lenders were guilty of negligence and fraudulent misrepresentation in not detecting fictitious amounts included in accounts receivable and accounts payable. In his opinion, Justice Cardozo drew a sharp distinction between fraudulent conduct and merely negligent conduct, holding that the auditor would not be liable to third parties for the latter:

If liability for negligence exists, a thoughtless slip or blunder, the failure to detect a theft or forgery beneath the cover of deceptive entries, may expose accountants to a liability in an indeterminate amount for an indeterminate time to an indeterminate class. The hazards of a business conducted on these terms are so extreme as to rekindle doubt whether a flaw may not exist in an implication of a duty that espouses to these consequences. The court also stated, however, that if the degree of negligence is so gross as to amount to "constructive fraud," accountants' liability extends to third parties.

Then the defense of lack of privity eroded as the work of the auditors became more and more the subject of lawsuits by nonclient plaintiffs.

An accountant may be liable for ordinary negligence to third parties, for whom the accountant knows the client has specifically engaged him or her to produce the accounting product. This type of third party is known as the *primary beneficiary.* An accountant may also be liable for ordinary negligence to third parties, those known or reasonably foreseen by the accountant, as well as those the accountant knows will rely on his or her work product in making a particular business decision. This type of third party is known as the *foreseen party*. This liability may extend to all third parties, including merely foreseeable third parties. In other words, users of financial statements beyond those actually foreseen could hold a CPA liable.

In addition, accountants may be found liable to third parties for actual or constructive fraud that is inferred from evidence of gross negligence. The plaintiff is required in this case to prove that the auditor knew the falsity (or its equivalent) of a representation. This knowledge is known as the *scienter* and the requirement of its proof as the *scienter requirement*. In any case, fraud consists of the following elements: (a) false representation, (b) knowledge of a wrong and acting with the intent to deceive, (c) intent to induce action in reliance, (d) justifiable reliance, and (e) resulting damage.

3. The third source of liability for accountants arises under the Federal Securities laws. Everybody relies on the accountants to play a role in producing accurate information. This main responsibility lies in making an independent verification of a company's financial statements. The SEC perceives the purpose of an audit as a public accountant's examination intended to be an independent check upon management's accounting of its stewardships. Thus the accountant has a direct and unavoidable responsibility, particularly where his or her engagement relates to a company that makes filings with the commission or in which there is a substantial public interest. That audit responsibility is exactly the reason for the potential legal liability of a certified public accountant under the Federal Securities laws; specifically under (a) Section 11 of the Securities Act of 1933, (b) Section 10 (b) of the Securities Exchange Act of 1934 and related Rule 10b-5, (c) Section 12(2) of the 1933 act, (d) Section 9 and 18 of the 1934 act, (e) Section 17(a) of the 1933 act, and (f) Section 14 of the 1934 act.

Section 11 of the 1933 act defines the rights of third parties and auditors as follows:

In case any part of the registration statement . . . contained an untrue statement of a material fact or omitted to state a material fact required to be stated therein or necessary to make the statements therein not misleading, any person acquiring such security . . . may . . . sue . . . every accountant . . . who has with his consent been named as having . . . certified any part of the registration statement . . . with respect to the statement in such registration . . . which purports to have been . . . certified by him.

Section 11 lists among potential defendants every accountant who helps prepare any part of the registration statement or any financial statement used in it. It imposes a civil liability on accountants for misrepresentations or omissions of material facts in a registration statement. The leading Section

11 case, *Escott v. Barchris Construction Corp.,*[10] was a class action against a bowling-alley construction corporation that had issued debentures and subsequently declared bankruptcy and against its accountants. The court ruled that the accountants were liable for not meeting the minimum standard of "due diligence" in their review for subsequent events occurring to the effective date of the registration statement.

Section 10b of the 1934 act states:

It shall be unlawful for any person directly or indirectly, by the use of any means or instrumentality of interstate commerce, or of the mails or of any facility of any national securities exchange, a) to employ any device, scheme, or artifice to defraud, b) to make any untrue statement of a material fact or omit to state a material fact necessary in order to make the statements made, in the light of the circumstances under which they are made, not misleading, or c) to engage in any act, practice, or course of business which operates or would operate as a fraud or deceit upon any person in connection with the purchase or sale of any security.[11]

The elements of Section 10(b) violations are therefore (a) a manipulative or deceptive practice, (b) in connection with a purchase or sale, (c) which results in a loss to plaintiff. Unlike the case in Section 11 of the 1933 act, here the plaintiff carries the burden of proof under Section 10(b). For a while the courts disagreed on the standard of performance to enforce against an accountant under Rule 10b-5. Then in 1976 the Supreme Court resolved the controversy in *Ernst & Ernst v. Hochfelder.*[12] It ruled that some knowledge and intent to deceive are required before accountants can be held liable for violation of Rule 10b-5. In other words, the private suit must require the allegation of a scienter. Most lower courts have held that "recklessness" by a dependent is sufficient to satisfy the scienter requirement of Section 10(b), although mere negligence is not.

Section 12(2) of the 1933 act provides that any person offering or selling a security by means of a prospectus or oral statements that contain untrue statements or misleading opinions shall be liable to the purchases for the damages sustained. Some courts have taken a broad view by implicating accountants as liable for aiding and abetting section 12(2) violations.

Section 18(a) of the 1934 act imposes civil liability on accountants for filing a false or misleading statement. To escape liability, the defendent must prove that "he acted in good faith and had no knowledge that such statement was false or misleading."

Section 17(a) of the 1933 act states that it should be unlawful for any person in the offer or sale of securities (a) to defraud, (b) to obtain money or property by means of an untrue statement or misleading omission, or (c) to engage in any transaction, practice, or course of business that deceives a purchaser. This section does not state, however, if a party violating the law is liable. The issue remains to be solved by the Supreme Court.

Section 14 of the 1934 act sets forth a comprehensive scheme governing solicitation of proxies. Rule 14 a-9 outlaws proxy solicitation by use of false statements or misleading omissions.

4. The fourth source of liability for accountants arises under the Foreign Corrupt Practices Act of 1977. It makes it illegal to offer a bribe to an official of a foreign country. It also requires SEC registrants under the 1934 act to maintain reasonably complete and accurate records and an adequate system of internal control to prevent bribery. Until now the SEC has refused to take any action against perceived violations of the accounting provisions of the FCPA unless those violations are linked to breaches of other securities.

5. The fifth source of liability is the criminal liability under both federal and state laws. The criminal provisions are in the Uniform Mail Fraud Statute and the Federal False Statements Statute. All of these statutes make it a criminal offense to defraud another person through knowingly being involved with false financial statements. Four of the most widely publicized criminal prosecutions were the *Continental Vending*, *Four Seasons*, *National Student Marketing*, and *Equity Funding* cases, where errors of judgment on the parts of the auditors resulted in criminal liabilities. The SEC position on bringing criminal charges against auditors was once stated as follows:

While virtually all Commission cases are civil in character, on rare occasions it is concluded that a case is sufficiently serious that it should be referred to the department of Justice for consideration of criminal prosecution. Referrals in regard to accountants have only been made when the Commission and the staff believed that the evidence indicated that a professional accountant certified financial statements that he knew to be false when he reported on them. The Commission does not make criminal references in cases that it believes are simply matters of professional judgment even if the judgments appear to be bad ones.[13]

16. WHAT'S BEHIND THE CPA-CLIENT RELATIONSHIP?

Judging the performance of an accounting firm requires some basic knowledge about the role of the accountant and appropriate relationships with the client. Unfortunately, this is not common knowledge.

A lawyer-columnist for Crain Communications recently received a letter with a number of questions about areas basic to CPA-client understanding.

Q. Should an accounting firm be responsible for explaining the mechanics of the financial data or is it the client's responsibility?

A. Financial statements (profit and loss, the balance sheet and changes in working capital) are reflections of the financial performance of a company. It is extremely important to understand how your accountant comes up with the figures on those statements to make certain they fairly present the financial position of the company. You may not have the experience yourself to do this. As a result, your accountant should be willing to spend the time to educate you or someone in your company on proper accounting techniques, how to read a financial statement and how the numbers in the financial statement got there.

Your accountant is not at your place every day, although it may sometimes seem like it. Thus, it is important that you can point out mistakes in the way some transactions have been recorded. For this to occur, however, requires a strong effort up front by the accountant to educate you in how the numbers come together. Many accounting firms, including the Big Eight, often have special personnel to help smaller companies in the procedure.

If you don't understand something, ask. If the answer is unclear, evasive or non-existent, it may be time to look for another accounting firm. The firm should be responsive to your needs.

Q. Where does bookkeeping end and accounting begin?

A. Bookkeeping is accounting. However, there is a large difference between posting entries, knowing where to post the right amount at the right time and determining whether or not the results of those postings accurately reflect the financial performance of your company. This requires an understanding of the company, where it is going, its sales activity, the normal financial performance of the company and those in the same field.

The postings may be right, but there may be an improper matching of income with expense. Knowing how to handle transactions in accordance with generally accepted accounting principles may be the difference between bookkeeping and accounting.

A number of small, one-person firms may be good bookkeepers but not good accountants. Bookkeeping firms provide a reliable service and can handle large companies, but they require a certain amount of knowledge on the part of the client.

If the client is not alert, bookkeeping can result in "garbage-in-garbage-out" conditions. Larger firms can often resolve this by monitoring bookkeeping to assure that the records reflect the proper financial position of the company.

Q. Is it the accountant's responsibility when serving as a consultant to notify the client of all options, or is it to offer the singular option deemed most suitable and disregard the others?

A. Your accountant, attorney, insurance agent and any other person consulting you about your business could literally inundate you with options on any particular topic. Unless that is your expressed preference, you probably will not get all options.

What you should get is a list of several options the professional feels are most suited for the facts and circumstances in your company. From that list, there should be a preference selected by the professional and an explanation given why that option best fits the situation.

The ultimate decision, however, is always up to you. If the preferred option does not fit with your overall operation, you should discuss that and determine whether or not one of the other options explained in the list might fit better.

Some executives prefer to get only one answer to a question. They are of the opinion that the professional is being paid to do the job and is in the best position to make the decision. The professional may be in the best position to select from a group of options in a particular matter; however, you should be made aware of appropriate alternatives so that you can make the ultimate intelligent decision for your company.

Q. Is it necessary for the accountant to have a working knowledge of the particulars of a client's field, or are all types of business basically accounted for in the same manner?

A. Like snowflakes, no two businesses are exactly alike. However, there are similarities within the same industry or type of business. Your accountant should have experience in handling manufacturing if you are a manufacturer or in international transactions if you import and export.

You know your company better than anyone else and your accountant should have a good understanding of the company, but not as if he or she were there on a daily basis. That is why you should receive options and a preference by the accountant on various matters. You will have to live with what you decide. Relying constantly on a consultant's decision may not result in what you can live with or what is best.

Q. How does one go about locating a new accounting firm? What is to be expected in service from a prospective accounting firm?

A. If you are seriously interested in changing accounting firms, you should look for an accounting firm as you would any other professional service. Ask your attorney, your banker and other professionals who use accounting firms or need to review their work (their financial statements) for their recommendation.

The key is comfort. Do you feel comfortable that the accounting firms have the personnel, experience and ability to assist you in your accounting, auditing and tax needs now and in the future?

They should be willing to take time to understand your business, provide information about the accounting and auditing process, and come tax time, provide an understanding of how the tax return came together and what to do in the future to reduce your tax liability.*

NOTES

1. Felix Pomeranz, "How the Audit Committee Should Work," *Journal of Accounting, Auditing and Finance*, Fall 1977, 45-52.

2. John R. Linden, "Rising Corporate Stars: The Accountant as Chief Executive Officers," *Journal of Accounting* (September 1978): 64-71.

3. Ibid., 65.

4. *Times-Picayune*, March 23, 1979.

5. Bernard Z. Lee, Rholan E. Larson and Philip B. Chenok, "Issues Confronting the Accounting Profession," *Journal of Accountancy* (November 1983): 78-85.

6. Letter, Philip L. Defliese to State Board for Public Accountancy, The University of the State of New York, November 26, 1980.

7. Letter, J. W. Poole to P. M. Bluhm, Vermont legislation draftsman, September 7, 1979.

8. Jethro Lieberman, *The Litigious Society* (New York: Basic Books, 1981), 42.

9. Ultramares Corp. v. Touche, 255 N.Y. 170, 174, N.E. 441 (1931).

10. Escott v. Barchris Construction Corp., 283 F. Supp. 643 (S.D.N.Y. 1968).

11. Securities Act of 1934, 17 C.F.R. Section 240.10b-5 (1971).

---

12. 12. Ernst & Ernst v. Hochfelder, 425 U.S. 185, 96 S. Ct. 1375, 47 L. Ed. 2d 668 (1976).

13. J. C. Burton, "SEC Enforcement and Professional Accountants: Philosophy, Objectives, and Approach," *Vanderbilt Law Review* 78 (January 1975): 28.

IV

THE FINANCIAL ACCOUNTING STANDARDS BOARD

1. THE FASB: STRUCTURE AND FUNCTIONING

Creation of the FASB

Accounting standards dominate the accountant's work. Those standards are being constantly changed, deleted, or added both in the United States and abroad. They provide the accountant with practical and handy rules for the conduct of his or her work. They are generally accepted as firm rules backed by sanctions for nonconformity.

Accounting standards usually consist of three parts: (1) a description of the problem to be tackled; (2) a reasoned discussion (possibly exploring fundamental theory) of ways of solving the problem; and (3) in line of decision or theory, the prescribed solution. In general, accounting and auditing standards have been restricted to point 3, which has generated a lot of controversies about the absence of supporting theories and the use of an ad hoc formulating approach. In fact, accounting standards have come a long way from the situation in the 1930s. The first six standards were produced in the mid-1930s to eliminate certain accounting abuses that were assumed to be linked to the crash of the stock market. The six standards are very informative of the primitive stage of accounting at the time.

1. Do not recognize revenue until a sale is made, and do not defer current-period expenses in anticipation of future sales.
2. Do not charge expenses to capital surplus; rather, deduct them in measuring earnings.
3. Dividends paid by a subsidiary to its parent out of retained earnings arising before acquisition are not income to the parent. They are a return of capital.
4. Dividends paid to you on treasury stock are not income.
5. Do not bury significant receivables from officers and employees with trade receivables.

6. When property is acquired by issuing stock, the property should be recorded at fair value, not at the par value of the stock issued.

Good accounting practice has evolved beyond these six standards through the works of both the Committee on Accounting Procedures (CAP) and the Accounting Principles Board (APB). Both standard-setting bodies used nontheoretical approaches to the standard-setting process, generating a crisis of confidence in the profession. As a result the Financial Accounting Standards Board (FASB) replaced the APB in 1973 as the body responsible for establishing accounting standards. The demise of the APB was due mainly to the following factors:

1. The continuous existence of alternative, accounting treatments that allowed companies to show higher earnings per share, especially as a result of corporate mergers and acquisitions.
2. The lack of adequate accounting treatments for new accounting treatments such as the investment-tax credit, accounting for the franchising industries, the land-development business, and long-term leases.
3. A number of cases of fraud and lawsuits implicating the accounting methods where there is a failure to disclose relevant information. Examples include the cases of *Wester*, *Mill Factors*, *Equity Funding*, *Student Marketing*, *Penn Central*, *Four Seasons Nursing Homes*, *Continental Vending*, *Revenue Properties*, *Black Watch Farms*, and *Investors Overseas Services*.
4. The failure of the APB to develop a conceptual framework.

After investigating the situation, a committee appointed by the American Institute of Certified Public Accountants (AICPA) known as the Wheat Committee proposed a new structure for establishing standards. The proposed new structure consisted of a nonprofit organization, the Financial Accounting Foundation (FAF), that would operate the FASB and would be cosponsored by five interest groups: The Financial Executive Institute, the National Association of Accountants, the American Accounting Association, the Financial Analysts Federation, and the Security Industry Association. Exhibit 5 illustrates the FASB structure adopted in 1973.

The FASB is the authoritative, independent body charged with establishing and improving financial accounting and reporting standards; these standards are concerned with meaningful information about economic events and transactions in a useful manner in financial statements. The members of the FASB are assumed to represent most parties interested in financial accounting. More specifically, four members are CPAs in public practice and three members are from areas related to accounting (government, industry, and education). Although APB members have been permitted to retain their positions with firms, companies, and institutions, FASB members must sever all such ties. In addition the FASB members are

EXHIBIT 5 STRUCTURE OF THE FINANCIAL ACCOUNTING STANDARDS
           BOARD (FASB)

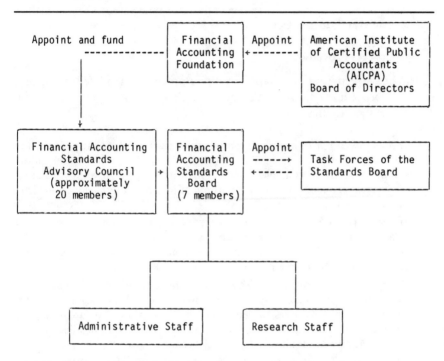

not required to be CPAs. Both features reduce the possibility of actual or
apparent conflicts of interest. The five-year terms of standards board
members are staggered, so that the terms of no more than two members end
in a single year. Finally, the FASB members are well-paid, full-time
members appointed for renewable five-year terms. The broader representation increased independence, and, in addition, smaller full-time renumer-
ated memberships should make the FASB more successful than the APB. In
fact, since creation in 1973, the annual budget of the FASB has tripled to
almost $10 million, and its staff has grown to 125. Its chairman earns
$225,000 a year, with the other six board members getting $185,000 each.

The mission of the FASB is to establish and improve the standards of
financial accounting and reporting for the guidance and education of the
public, including issues, auditors, and users of financial information.

To accomplish its mission the FASB is assumed to act to:

1. Improve the usefulness of financial reporting by focusing on the primary characteristics of relevance and reliability and on the qualities of comparability and
   consistency

2. Keep standards current to reflect changes in methods of doing business and
   changes in the economic environment

3. Consider promptly any significant areas of deficiency in financial reporting that might be improved through the standard-setting process
4. Improve the common understanding of the nature and purposes of information contained in financial reports

Due-Process Procedure

The board activities are shaped by "due process" mandated by formal rules of procedure. In fact, the board follows certain precepts in the conduct of its activities:

1. *To be objective in its decision making* and to ensure, insofar as possible, the neutrality of information resulting from its standards. To be neutral, information must report economic activity as faithfully as possible without coloring the image it communicates for the purpose of influencing behavior in any particular decision.
2. *To weigh carefully the views of its constituents* in developing concepts and standards. The ultimate determinant of concepts and standards, however, must be the board's judgment, based on research, public input, and careful deliberation, about the usefulness of the resulting information.
3. *To promulgate standards only when the expected benefits exceed the perceived costs.* Although reliable quantitative cost-benefit calculations are seldom possible, the board strives to determine that a proposed standard will fill a significant need and that the costs it imposes, compared with possible alternatives, are justified in relation to the overall benefits.
4. *To bring about needed changes in ways that minimize disruption to the continuity of reporting practice.* Reasonable effective dates and transition provisions are established when new standards are introduced. The board considers it desirable that change be evolutionary to the extent that it can be accommodated by the need for relevance, reliability, comparability, and consistency.
5. *To review the effects of past decisions* and interpret, amend, or replace standards in a timely fashion when such action is indicated.[1]

To implement these precepts, the FASB adopted the following due-process procedure:

1. A reporting problem is identified and placed on the board's agenda.
2. A task force composed of a group of knowledgeable individuals in the accounting and business community is appointed. The technical staff of the FASB, in consultation with the task force, prepares a discussion memorandum (DM) on the reporting problem. The DM exposes the principal questions and alternatives to be considered by the board.
3. The DM is made available to the public for examination for a period of at least 60 days.

4. A public hearing is staged, during which viewpoints regarding the merits and limitations of various possible positions are presented to the board.

5. Based on the oral and written comments received, the board issues an exposure draft (ED) of a proposed statement of financial accounting standards. Unlike the DM, the ED sets forth the definite position of the board on the reporting problem.

6. The ED is made available to the public for examination for a period of at least 30 days.

7. Another public hearing is staged, during which viewpoints regarding the merits and limitations of the positions set forth in the ED are presented to the board.

8. Based on the oral and written comments received following the issuance of the ED, the board may take any of the following actions:
   a. Adopt the Proposed Standard as an official statement of financial accounting standards (SFAS)
   b. Propose a revision of the proposed standard, again following the due-process procedure
   c. Postpone the issuance of a standard and keep the problem on the agenda
   d. Not issue a standard and eliminate the issue from the agenda

Public participation in the due process procedure does not alter the fact that the actual decisions regarding accounting standards are made by the members of the FASB. In fact, an affirmative vote of four of the seven members of the FASB is needed to approve a pronouncement. This simple majority rule adopted by the FASB is sharply different from the two-thirds vote that the predecessor committees required. The FASB rule allows it to deal with reducing the number of undesirable compromises that often are necessary to get a two-thirds vote.

Types of Pronouncements

The FASB issues four types of pronouncements:

1. *Statements of financial accounting standards* (SFAS): These statements create or change existing rules within the general body of accounting rules, known as the generally accepted accounting principles (GAAP).

2. *Interpretations.* These pronouncements also become integral parts of the GAAP. They are intended to correct existing SFAS, APBs, or ARBs.

3. *Statements of financial accounting concepts* (SFAC): These statements are part of the elements of a conceptual framework being developed by the FASB. They include the SFAC on objectives, elements, qualitative characteristics, and measurement and reporting. (More is said about the conceptual framework in the next chapters).

4. *Technical bulletins*: These pronouncements provide guidance for applying standards in accounting research bulletins, APB opinions, and FASB statements and interpretations and for resolving accounting issues not directly ad-

dressed in those standards. In 1984 the FASB issued Technical Bulletin No. 79-1 (revised), which expands the scope of FASB technical bulletins to allow them to address more emerging problems and implementation issues and modifies the procedures involved in issuing the bulletins. Under the new FASB procedures guidance provided in a technical bulletin may (a) clarify, explain, or elaborate upon an underlying standard; (b) specify that the standard does not apply to enterprises in a particular industry or provide for a deferral of the effective date of a standard for that industry; or (c) address areas not directly covered by existing standards. If a major change in accounting practice is necessary, an FASB statement or interpretation generally would be more appropriate to provide guidance than a technical bulletin.

Relationships with the SEC and the AICPA

The relationship of the FASB with both the AICPA and the Securities and Exchange Commission (SEC) is at best uneven. The relationship of the FASB to the accounting profession was clarified by Rule 203 of the AICPA's Code of Professional Ethics, adopted early in 1973, which stated:

A member shall not express an opinion that financial statements are presented in conformity with generally accepted accounting principles if such statements contain any departure from an accounting principle promulgated by the body designated by Council to establish such principles which has a material effect on the statements taken as a whole, unless the member can demonstrate that due to unusual circumstances the financial statements would otherwise have been misleading. In such cases his report must describe the departure, the approximate effects thereof, if practicable, and the reasons why compliance with the principle would result in a misleading statement.

As authorized by Rule 203, the council passed a resolution at its May 1973 meeting designating the FASB as the body to establish such principles. Rule 203 constitutes an endorsement of the FASB, with the reservation that recognizes that, in unusual circumstances, literal compliance with presumptively binding, generally accepted accounting principles issued by a recognized standard-setting body may not invariably ensure that financial statements are presented fairly. In spite of Rule 203, the AICPA does not seem pleased with the transfer of standard setting. One evidence of this attitude is the fact that the AICPA started, after the FASB was formed, to issue through its Executive Committee statements of position (SOPs) to which many public accountants attributed the status of the GAAP.

The relationship of the FASB with the SEC was clarified when the SEC issued, on December 20, 1973, Accounting Series Release No. 150, which reaffirmed the SEC's policy of reliance on the private sector.

The Commission intends to continue its policy of looking to the private sector for leadership in establishing and improving accounting principles and standards through the FASB with the expectation that the body's conclusions will promote the interests of investors.

In Accounting Series Release No. 4 (1938) the Commission stated its policy that financial statements prepared in accordance with accounting practices for which there was no substantial authoritative support were presumed to be misleading and that footnote or other disclosure would not avoid this presumption. It also stated that, where there was a difference of opinion between the Commission and a registrant as to the proper accounting to be followed in a particular case, disclosure would be accepted in lieu of correction of the financial statements themselves only if substantial support existed for the accounting practices followed by the registrant and the position of the Commission had not been expressed in rules, regulations or other official releases. For purposes of this policy, principles, standards and practices promulgated by the FASB in its statements and interpretations will be considered by the Commission as having substantial support, and those contrary to such FASB pronouncements will be considered to have no such support.

ASR No. 150 also states, however, that, "the Commission will continue to identify and will determine the appropriate methods of disclosure to meet these needs." The SEC continues to permit the establishment of accounting standards by the private sector, and the commission's intervention as the federal government's major participant in the accounting standard-setting process is in the form of cooperation, advice, and occasional pressure, rather than in the form of rigid controls. In other words, the SEC endorses the FASB with some reservations, in that it has not delegated any of its authority or given up any right to reject, modify, or supersede FASB pronouncements through its own rule-making procedures.

2. IS THE BOARD DOING A GOOD JOB?

One may ask whether the Board is doing a good job. Questions and suggested answers follow:

1. Is the board spending too much time on the balance sheet at the expense of the income statement? Although the criticism may hold, we cannot help but think that it is time to correct all of the previous abuses that lead the balance sheet to become a repository for residual debits and credits that were not resources or obligations. It is definitely time to come up with correct definitions of assets and liabilities and give the balance sheet the credibility and the usefulness it is assumed to have. The time spent on the balance sheet is not lost.

2. Is the board focusing on narrow pieces of issues instead of complete questions? Although the criticism holds, one cannot help agreeing that the FASB needs to address day-to-day problems confronting the profession and in need of solutions and at the same time address the general picture in the form of a conceptual framework. The conceptual framework, once

completed, will eliminate the need for rigid, detailed, and narrow standards in the future.

3. Is the board basing its decisions on the wrong economic theories as the foundations of standard setting? Unfortunately, the board is not following the precepts of any right or wrong economic or accounting theory. Its main objective is simple and straightforward. Hence the conceptual framework starts with usefulness for investor and creditor decision making as the primary objective of financial reporting. It also recognizes users' needs for information about a firm's resources and obligations and its performance, liquidity, funds flow, and management's stewardship. Some may argue that these objectives are too general to serve as effective guides. Some others may argue that the public interest should be the primary objective.

4. Is the due process too lengthy, costly, and cumbersome? Some may argue that a dictatorship in accounting standards would move a lot more quickly. But the question remains whether that would solve any problems and whether the public would accept standards that are arrived at hastily or arbitrarily, as the obvious result of internal "horse trading." Most likely, the "dictatorial" approach or a legislative-deadline approach would not be as acceptable as the present judicial approach.

5. Is the conceptual problem a panacea for all future accounting problems? Some people in effect are expecting the framework to give the right answer every time an accounting problem comes up. Others dismiss completely its usefulness, arguing either that it is a quest for a Rosetta stone that does not exist or that assuming that a few board members could develop an accounting constitution shows the variety of ignorance. The FASB is more realistic by viewing the conceptual framework as a sort of constitution for providing guidance in resolving new or emerging problems in accounting.

6. Is the affected constituency participating in the standard-setting process? The due-process procedure implies that the setting of accounting standards must involve all elements of the affected constituency. The board then has a positive obligation to do everything it can to encourage response from the constituency. Unfortunately, five groups have been identified as unresponsive: (a) small businesses; (b) security analysts, investment advisors, and others in the securities industry; (c) bank credit officers; (d) individual academicians; and (e) nonfinancial executives (for example, corporate chief executive officers). Many of these groups cannot maintain an extensive research staff and therefore cannot analyze and respond to complex and voluminous discussion memos. One way to solve this problem may be for the FASB to discuss the issues in the discussion memorandum in layman's language and to indicate the board's tentative thinking on those issues.

7. Finally, what are the main characteristics of the history of the FASB? According to John C. Biegler, former chairman of the FASB, the board has

clearly gone through a "honeymoon stage" (1973-75), a "reorientation stage" (1976-77), and the latest "consolidation and development stage" (1978 and after). What is needed for the future is an "innovation stage" on both the conceptual framework front and the "standards" front. Both projects have to be accepted by the constituency for the FASB to survive and maintain its credibility. The innovation stage should include timely guidance on all issues, past and emerging issues, in addition to broad standards of accounting and reporting. Although some observers have urged the board to delegate much of the implementation guidance to the AcSEC (AICPA Accounting Standards Executive Committee), this view is countered by others who may be concerned with the unfortunate creation of two standard-setting bodies in the private sector.

3. ACCOUNTING STANDARDS OVERLOAD: A HANGMAN'S NOOSE

> When I first encountered the subject, "standards overload" looked like the legendary Gordian know, so intricate it couldn't be untied by any ordinary mortal. After five years of wrestling with the problem, however, I think maybe it isn't a Gordian knot after all—it looks more like a hangman's noose.
>
> David Moss, "Standards Overload—No Simple Solution," *Journal of Accounting*, November 1983, 120.

The Nature and Causes of Accounting Standards Overload

The accounting standards overload is not really new. In 1952 a report by a group of accountants, lawyers, and businesspeople headed by George O. May stated that "there is no public interest which calls for applying to the hundreds of thousands of small corporations, whose management and ownership are closely combined, requirements deemed appropriate for the guidance of investors in the few large corporations whose securities are widely distributed." The same message was conveyed in the 1980 report of the AICPA Special Committee on Small and Medium-Sized Firms, which also identified accounting standards overload as one of the many problems confronting such firms and recommended that the AICPA consider alternate means of providing additional relief from accounting standards that are not cost effective for small businesses.

The accounting standards overload is generally associated with the proliferation of accounting standards. The following situations have also been identified with accounting standards overload.

1. Too many standards

2. Too detailed standards

3. No rigid standards, making selectivity of application difficult

4. General-purpose standards failing to provide for differences in the needs of pre-parers, users, and CPAs

5. General-purpose standards failing to provide for differences between (a) public and nonpublic entities, (b) annual and interim financial statements, (c) large and small enterprises, and (d) audited and unaudited financial statements

6. Excessive disclosures, complex measurements, or both

The situation took years to develop to the state of becoming a serious problem. Various factors contributed to the standards-overload problem. First, with the numerous questions raised about what to disclose and what not to disclose, accountants began to issue a greater number of standards, which tended to leave less to judgment and to reduce the amount of litigation involving accounting principles. Second, the need to protect the public interest and to assist the individual investor generated various and numerous governmental and professional regulations and disclosures. Finally, the desire to satisfy the needs of many users required more detailed standards and disclosures.

What resulted is a complex and cumbersome situation. Mandated GAAP increased in number, complexity, and specificity, affecting the costs of pre-paring financial statements for both small and large firms. Some believe the GAAP are becoming intolerable to some firms, their auditors, and the users of information. Others think that the new and detailed GAAP requirements are more designed to serve the informational needs of investors and creditors at the expense of the particular users of financial statements of small or closely held businesses. This is in direct conflict with the accepted agreement that serving the needs of users of financial statements is, or should be, the primary objective of financial reporting. In effect, that is exactly the main emphasis of FASB's Statement of Financial Accounting Concepts No. 1, "Objectives of Financial Reporting by Business Enter-prises": "Financial reporting should provide information that is useful to present and potential investors and creditors and other users in making rational investment, credit, and similar decisions. The information should be comprehensible to those who have a reasonable understanding of business and economic activities and are willing to study the information with reasonable diligence."

The problem of overload is aggravated by the proliferation of standard-setting bodies. In addition to the FASB, the development of the GAAP and related disclosures are influenced by other bodies such as the SEC; the AICPA, including the Accounting Standards Executive Committee (AcSEC) and the Auditing Standards Board (ASB); and to some extent Congress. Examples of congressional actions having accounting conse-quences are the investment tax credit and the enactment of the Foreign Corrupt Practices Act. In addition, the standards themselves are not only excessive in number but too narrow in their application to cover all possible situations and requiring too much detailed guidance.

Effects of Accounting Standards Overload

The large number, narrowness, and rigidity of accounting standards can have serious effects on the work performed by accountants, the value of financial information to users, and business decisions made by management. The accountants may lose sight of their real jobs because of the excessive data required when complying with existing standards. Audit failures may result because the accountant may lose the focus of the audit and may forget to perform basic audit procedures. The proliferation of complex accounting regulations may lead to noncompliance with those regulations by business with the tacit agreement of CPAs. The embattled practitioner is in fact caught in the middle between the demands of professional standards and the discontent of small business clients with the burden these standards impose on them. This situation will, undoubtedly, have serious implications for legal liability, erosion of professional ethics, loss of public support, and dissonance within the accounting profession. One way out for practitioners faced with the GAAP departures is to give a modified opinion. Most CPAs, however, resist a modified opinion for the GAAP omissions in audited financial statements, because they think the negative connotation is not acceptable. What may be needed is an education of the public to greater acceptance of CPA reports that take note of omitted GAAP requirements.

The users may also be confused by the number and complexity of the notes used to explain the requirements under the existing standards. Users of financial reports of small businesses generally are concerned with the complexity introduced by the Financial Accounting Standards Board pronouncements. The jargon used in the notes can be understood only by accountants and other financial persons. Consider, for example, the following note from the 1981 United Leasing Corporation's Form 10-K, describing the company's method of recognizing revenue from a lease used to finance an asset.

Direct financial leases—At the time of closing a direct financing lease, the company records on its balance sheet the gross sales receivable, estimated residual valuation of the leased equipment, and unearned lease income. The unearned income represents the excess of the gross lease receivable plus the estimated residual valuation over the cost of the equipment leased. A portion of the unearned income equal to the initial direct costs incurred in consumating the lease plus an amount equal to the provision for losses is recognized as revenue at the time the lease is closed. Commencing with the second month of the lease, the remainder of the unearned lease income is recorded as revenue over the lease term so as to approximate a constant rate of return on the net investment in the lease.

The note can be understood only by a seasoned veteran familiar with the accounting jargon and body of knowledge.

The managers may also be overwhelmed by the number and complexity of the standards. In fact, they may be tempted to rewrite contracts and change business practices so as not to have to comply with some of the accounting standards. It is possible to restructure the terms of leases to avoid capitalization and the intricate requirements of Statement of Financial Accounting Standards No. 13 on leases. The major motivation for the restructuring of transactions by managers of small businesses is to avoid not only the detailed requirements of some accounting standards but the excessive costs of preparing and verifying the information. Besides, the costs of complying with the standards may outweigh the benefits, given that users of financial reports of small businesses may be more interested in cash-flow projections than in the other financial-statement information. In fact, because users of financial reports of small businesses have more immediate contact with management they do not need to rely on financial reports as much as users of reports or large businesses.

Solutions to Standards-Overload Problem

The gravity of the standards-overload problem led various interest groups to address the problem and suggest solutions. The AICPA Special Committee on Accounting Standards Overload evaluated the following possible approaches to dealing with accounting standards overload:

1. No change; retain status quo
2. A change from the present concept of a set of unitary GAAP for all business enterprises to two sets of GAAP, thus creating a separate set of GAAP for certain entities, such as small nonpublic businesses
3. Changes in GAAP to simplify application to all business enterprises
4. Establishing differential disclosure and measurement alternatives
5. A change in CPA's standards for reporting on financial statements
6. An alternative to the GAAP as an optional basis for presenting financial statements

Of all of these approaches, the committee recommended either establishing different disclosure and measurement alternatives or adopting an alternative to the GAAP.

The approach based on differential disclosure and measurement alternatives for small nonpublic enterprises is a good solution to the standards-overload problem in that it considers relevance to users and cost-benefit considerations with respect to small nonpublic entities. This is in line with the FASB's Statement of Financial Accounting Concepts No. 2, which states: "The optimal information for one user will not be optimal for another. Consequently, the Board which must try to cater to many different users while considering the burdens placed on those who have to provide information, constantly treads a fine line between requiring disclosure of too much information and requiring too little."

The approach calls for a flexible concept of the GAAP with differential measurement alternatives to serve the specialized needs of small nonpublic companies. One way of implementing this approach would be for the standard-setting body to adopt a basis for exemption from the detailed requirements of each standard. The basis might be public versus private or a size test based on asset values.

The approach that relies on an alternative to the GAAP rests on three possibilities: (1) a new basis accounting method (BAM), (2) the cash or modified cash basis, or (3) the income tax basis.

A BAM is out of the question, because it would create more costs than benefits. Some of the conclusions of the committee include the following:

1. BAM will contain the essentials of the GAAP and allow significant departures from the measurement principles of the GAAP. As such, it would confuse everybody and undermine the GAAP in the process.
2. BAM will add rather than reduce the overload problem, given that it will create new requirements in addition to the GAAP.
3. BAM will require a position on each of the GAAP issues, which will be costly and time consuming.
4. BAM will need to be prepared by a new standard-setting body.
5. BAM will be perceived not as a subset of the GAAP but as a search set of the GAAP for special entities.

Given these constraints, the committee suggested that the issuance, in accordance with existing reporting standards, of compiled, reviewed, or audited other-comprehensive-bases-of-accounting (OCBOA) financial statements, including income tax-basis financial statements, can help alleviate the burden of accounting standards overload for small nonpublic entities.

Following the publication in February 1983 of the reports of the Special Committee on Accounting Overload, which recommends ways to provide relief from standards that are not perceived to be cost effective, particularly for small closely held businesses, the AICPA Board of Directors made three basic recommendations and asked for a response from the FASB regarding its "intentions and proposed course of action." The AICPA recommendations and the November 1983 FASB responses follow:

Recommendation 1: The FASB should promptly reconsider and act on certain standards that are widely perceived to be unnecessarily burdensome and costly, particularly for small nonpublic entities.

These standards include the following: accounting for leases, accounting for income taxes, the pro forma disclosures required for business combinations by APB Opinion 16, and capitalization of interest cost. The FASB responded that it is re-examining each of these standards.

Recommendation 2: In reconsidering existing standards and in developing new standards, the FASB's objective should be to simplify standards by avoiding complex and detailed rules for all entities to the extent feasible.

The FASB agreed with the simplification objective. It pointed out, however, that some complex economic activity requires by definition complex accounting standards. In addition, the following characteristics of standards may be unavoidable in some cases:

- Some standards require assumptions about future events.
- Some standards require application of specific criteria to determine the treatment of particular circumstances.
- Some standards require present value calculations.
- Some standards result in differences between book and tax treatments.
- Some standards are applied to small companies that do not have extensive in-house staffs.

The solution is for more guidance by the FASB aimed a) at ensuring timely, consistent application of general standards in the face of pressures for alternative treatments and b) at a better understanding of how general standards are meant to be applied. With regard to the first objective the FASB is considering two changes to the FASB procedures to enable it to deal more effectively with the application issues:

- The scope of the FASB Technical Bulletins may be broadened to permit time to address more of the narrow implementation, and clarification issues that the Board has dealt with in the past through FASB statements and interpretations.
- An advisory group drawn from both public accounting and industry may be established to help in early identification and definition of financial reporting issues.

In fact, the FASB decided in 1984 to expand the scope of its Technical bulletins. Accordingly, in addition to interpretive matters, Technical bulletins will a) address areas not directly covered by existing pronouncements and b) provide guidance that, for a particular situation, differs from the general application required by an existing pronouncement.

With regard to the second objective, the FASB is considering two goals: (1) better organization of accounting standards and increased explanations, and 2) additional communication between the Board and those who need to understand its standards.

Recommendation 3: To the extent that simplicity and flexibility are not feasible, the FASB should explicitly and specifically consider the information needs of the users of the financial statements of small nonpublic entities and the costs and benefits of developing the information with the objective of providing, within the framework of a unified set of generally accepted accounting principles, differential disclosure alternatives as well as differential measurement alternatives for such entities.

Although the FASB has already established differential disclosures requirements based on a company's size or ownership, it does not consider differential measurement as a generally effective solution to standards overload.

Besides the AICPA and the FASB, other groups are concerned with the standards-overload problem. For example, corporate America worries that it is not getting its message through to average shareholders because of the overwhelming avalanche of financial data required by present rules. The solution is to allow the firms to simplify and send shorter, simpler annual reports. That is exactly the promise behind a 1984 research report, "Summary Reporting of Financial Information," prepared by Deloitte Haskins & Sells for the Financial Executives Research Foundation and based on experimental summary reports submitted by the nineteen major corporations participating in the study. The shorter reports would tell shareholders who want more information that they can request a copy of the 10K form the company files each year with the SEC. The major stumbling blocks to issuing summary annual reports may be the SEC and the FASB. The proposal thrusts deep into territory where the SEC and FASB reign supreme and runs against standing rules for auditor reporting. The SEC needs to approve the idea. A special waiver of the proxy rules may be needed to conduct an initial experiment. Similarly, the FASB would have to decide whether it would set rules to cover the summary reports.

4. THE FASB'S CONCEPTUAL FRAMEWORK

Of vital importance to the accounting discipline is the idea that the accounting profession and other interest groups accept their concepts, principles, and techniques. To guarantee such a consensus, the general belief is that the techniques should be derived from a vigorous conceptual framework of financial accounting. Since its inception, the FASB has recognized the importance of such an established body of concepts and objectives. The board quickly acknowledged the erosion of the credibility of financial reporting and criticized the following situations:

- Two or more methods of accounting are accepted for the same facts.
- Less conservative accounting methods are being used rather than the earlier, more conservative methods.
- Reserves are used to artifically smooth earnings fluctuations.
- Financial statements fail to warn of impending liquidity crunches.
- Deferrals are followed by "big bath" write-offs.
- Unjustified optimism exists in estimates of recoverability.
- Off balance sheet financing (that is, disclosure in the notes to the financial statements) is common.
- An unwanted assertion of immateriality has been used to justify nondisclosure of unfavorable information or departures from standards.
- Form is elevated over substance.[2]

To correct some of these limitations and provide a more vigorous way of setting standards and increasing financial statement users' understanding and confidence in financial reporting, the FASB has instituted a conceptual framework project. The board described the project as follows:

A conceptual framework is a constitution, a coherent system of interrelated *objectives* and *fundamentals* that can lead to consistent standards and that prescribed the nature, function and limits of financial accounting and financial statements. The *objectives* identify the goals and the purposes of accounting. The *fundamentals* are the underlying concepts of accounting—concepts that guide the selection of events to be accounted for, the measurement of those events, and the means of summarizing and communicating to interested parties. Concepts of that type are fundamental in the sense that other concepts flow from them and repeated references to them will be necessary in establishing, interpreting, and applying accounting and reporting standards.[3]

The conceptual framework, therefore, is intended to act as a constitution for the standard-setting process. Its purpose is to guide in resolving disputes that arise during the standard-setting process by narrowing the question to whether or not specific standards conform to the conceptual framework. In fact, the FASB identified four benefits that will result from a conceptual framework. It will, when completed:

1. Guide the FASB in establishing accounting standards
2. Provide a frame of reference for resolving accounting questions in the absence of specific promulgated standards
3. Determine the bounds of judgment in preparing financial statements
4. Enhance comparability by decreasing the number of alternative accounting methods

Exhibit 6 illustrates the overall scope of the conceptual framework and lists the related documents issued thus far by the FASB.

1. At the first level, the *objectives* identify the goals and purposes of accounting. Statement of Financial Accounting Concepts No. 1 ("Objectives of Reporting by Business Enterprises") presents the goals and purposes of accounting for business enterprises. Statement of Financial Accounting Concepts No. 4 ("Objectives of Financial Reporting by Nonbusiness Organizations") presents the goals and purposes of accounting for nonbusiness organizations.
2. At the second level, the *fundamentals* include the *qualitative characteristics* of accounting information (Statement of Financial Accounting Concepts No. 2) and the definitions of the *elements* of financial statements (Statement of Financial Accounting Concepts No. 3).
3. At the third level, *the operational guidelines* that the accountant uses in establishing and applying accounting standards include the recognition criteria,

*EXHIBIT 6 CONCEPTUAL FRAMEWORK FOR FINANCIAL ACCOUNTING
AND REPORTING*

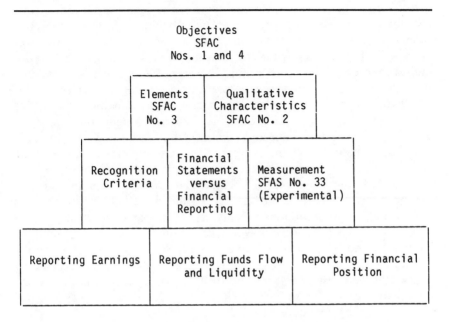

financial statements versus financial reporting, and measurement (Statement of
Financial Accounting Standard No. 33).

4. At the fourth level, the *display mechanisms* that accounting uses to convey
accounting information include reporting earnings, reporting funds flow and
liquidity, and reporting financial position.

The FASB's conceptual framework is by now an established and eagerly
watched project for the creation of an accounting constitution. Its major
benefit is that it will facilitate the resolution of conceptual disputes in the
standard-setting process. To be effective, this constitution must gain
general acceptance, represent collective behavior, and protect the public
interest in areas in which it is affected by financial reporting. Can this be
achieved? Several issues must be resolved before this question can be adequately answered. Some of these issues are:

1. The conceptual framework may not be sufficient to resolve certain
standard-setting problems. Some of these problems are related to the social-
choice aspect of accounting standard setting. One prevailing idea is that it is
impossible to develop a set of accounting standards that can be applied to
accounting alternatives in a way that will satisfy everybody. In response to
this pessimistic view, one may suggest that the problem may be overstated
and that a partial, piecemeal approach may succeed.

2. The conceptual framework must be workable and acceptable to all in-

terested parties. The workability of the conceptual framework may be hampered by the level of abstractness of some of the concepts and objectives and by the infeasibility of some of the qualitative characteristics and other recommendations. The acceptability of the conceptual framework may be hampered by the difficulty of resolving the conflicts of interest of all users and by the fear that the framework may be calling for radical changes in business reporting. One way of determining acceptability is to reaffirm the soundness of the reasoning underlying the elements of the framework. The more plausible the assumptions and the more compelling the analysis of the facts, the greater the chance of winning the support of diverse interests and retaining and enhancing the board's power.

3. The ultimate test of the conceptual framework is its implementation and survival. In substance, the conceptual framework should exist in more than form. In fact one accepted feeling is that following the publication of the conceptual framework, the board will probably feel obligated to pay lip service to it in future pronouncements. But these pronouncements will not be affected in any substantive way by what is contained in the content of the conceptual framework. One way of dismissing this view is to ensure that the conceptual framework be used to resolve the controversial accounting issues. But the question still remains: will the conceptual framework guide the FASB in correcting some of the accounting problems? The answer will have to wait for future developments.

NOTES

1. Financial Accounting Standards Board, "The Mission of the Financial Accounting Board," *Facts about FASB, 1983* (Stamford, Conn., 1983), 9.
2. Financial Accounting Standards Board, *The Conceptual Framework for Financial Accounting and Reporting: Elements of Financial Statements and Their Measurement* (Stamford, Conn., 1976), 4.
3. Ibid., 14.

V

THE SECURITIES AND
EXCHANGE COMMISSION

1. THE SECURITIES AND EXCHANGE COMMISSION: A TOUGH ACT AHEAD

Legal Acts

The period between 1929 and 1933 saw a dramatic decline in stock prices, creating social upheaval and concern about the viability of the capital market system in the United States. More and better disclosure about corporate affairs was needed to allow for a better evaluation of the soundness of corporate endeavors. Congress intervened and passed the Securities Act of 1933 to require registration of new securities offered for public sales and the Securities Exchange Act of 1934 to require continuous reporting by publicly owned companies and registration of securities, security exchanges, and certain brokers and dealers. Both acts gave the Securities and Exchange Commission (SEC) the authority to protect the public interest by calling for the disclosure of adequate information when securities are exchanged or sold. Other acts were passed later to broaden and strengthen the responsibility of the SEC, namely, (a) the Public Utility Holding Act of 1935, which requires registration of interstate holding companies covered by this law; (b) the Trust Indenture Act of 1939, which requires registration of trust indenture documents and supporting data; (c) the Investment Company Act of 1940, which requires registration of investment companies; (d) the Investment Advisors Act of 1940, which requires registration of investment advisers; (e) the Securities Investor Protection Act of 1970, which provides a fund through the Securities Investor Protection Corporation for the protection of investors; and (f) the Foreign Corrupt Practices of 1977, which governs questionable and illegal payments by U.S. corporations to foreign political officials and requires accurate and fair record-keeping and internal-control systems by all public companies.

Organization and Requirements

The SEC is organized into five divisions (Division of Corporate Finance, Division of Corporate Regulation, Division of Market Regulation, Division of Investment Management, and Division of Enforcement), three staff offices (Chief Accountant, General Counsel, Chief Economic Adviser), and two judicial offices (Office of Administrative Law Judges and Office of Opinions and Review). Of interest to accounting are (a) the Division of Corporate Finance, which is responsible for setting financial and accounting standards for firms under SEC jurisdiction and for reviewing registration statements; and (b) the chief accountant, who is responsible for all of the rules and regulations that govern the form and content of financial statements of firms under SEC jurisdiction. In effect, the firms under SEC jurisdiction must provide a continuous flow of specific information to the SEC by filing a finite list of forms. The most widely used forms are the following:

1. *Registration Statement:* Following the 1933 act, all firms making a public offering of their securities must file various forms (or registration statements) to provide information such as the nature of their business, the type of securities being registered, and audited financial statements. This information is the result of specific SEC regulations, either Regulations S-X or Regulations S-K. Regulations S-X specify the form and content of the financial statements and related schedules and notes required under all acts administered by the SEC. Regulations S-K specify certain nonfinancial information that must be included.

If a registration statement is found to be deficient, the SEC will ask for an amended registration statement that must be found acceptable before the company is allowed to proceed with the sale of securities. But not all is regulation at the SEC; in fact, the SEC has tried to simplify certain registration requirements. The agency's shelf registration rule, for example, lets large corporations issue stock without delay as proof of the commission's willingness to rethink original dogma and apply economic analysis to rule making. In a *shelf registration*, the corporate issuer registers a large number of shares with the SEC at one time, placing them "on the shelf" for sale at a future date and in an amount of the company's choosing. Rule 415, "Shelf Registration," affords more ease of access to capital markets. The rule permits the sale of securities at opportune times of the registrant's choosing within two years after filing a shelf-registration statement. Under the shelf procedure, the issuer does not have to supply a lead investment banking underwriter in the registration, creating at the same time substantial savings to the corporate issuers and greater competition among banking firms bidding to bring issues to the market. This simplified procedure for registering securities has significantly cut investment-banking underwriting profits on bringing shares to the market and is not popular with the securities industry. To make their case, the

Securities Industry Association has reprinted and circulated a Pennsylvania State University doctoral dissertation that found that stock prices were depressed an average of 8.77 percent by the announcement of shelf registration, a cost to the issuer that was four to twelve times greater than the savings from shelf registration. The debate will continue for a long time about whether shelf registration is or is not a boon for issuers.

Recent changes in the SEC requirements are aimed at reducing cost to registrars, protecting investors, and maintaining fair and orderly securities markets. The integrated disclosure program brought an end to an impenetrable jungle of duplication, inconsistency, and deadwood. The SEC also started EDGAR, an electronic information-analysis and retrieval system. This system will be beneficial to filers and users of the filed information. The EDGAR data base will be structured to permit easy access and to allow manipulation of the data base by a variety of industry software.

2. *10-K Report*: Following the 1934 act, all firms under SEC jurisdiction file an annual form, the 10-K Report, within 90 days of the end of the company's fiscal year. It includes much of the information in the company's annual report plus detailed information on the company's various corporate activities.

3. *8-K Report*: Following the 1934 act, all firms under SEC jurisdiction file a special report, the 8-K Report, to explain a material event (such as an acquisition, a lawsuit, or a change of auditors) within fifteen days after the material event has occurred.

4. *10-Q Report*: Following the 1934 act, all firms under SEC jurisdiction file a quarterly report, the 10-Q Report, within 45 days of the end of each quarter. Although less detailed than the 10-K, it includes audited financial statements and a narrative analysis by management of the results of the quarter covered by the report with appropriate explanation of the differences between the results of the consecutive quarters.

To facilitate the filing of these forms and provide guidance about the compliance with the various disclosure requirements, the SEC issues the following guidelines:

1. *Accounting series releases* (ASRs): The SEC issues these pronouncements to provide guidance on its financial-information requirements. Beginning in 1982 the SEC began issuing new pronouncements, called financial reporting releases (FRRs), intended to replace the ASRs.

2. *Staff accounting bulletins* (SABs): The SEC staff issues these bulletins to describe the interpretations and practices followed in administering the SEC's disclosure requirements. In fact, the SEC staff is known to apply its own understanding of the correct application of the GAAP, especially with respect to judgments about the correct accounting for specific facts and circumstances consistent with general GAAP guidance. The SABs are important documents to accountants filing reports to the SEC, given that at all times the staff may be operating with some ideas, points of view, policies, and practices that have been codified neither by the SEC nor the FASB.

3. *Accounting and auditing enforcement releases* (AAERs): Beginning in 1982 the SEC began issuing these pronouncements to deal with enforcement-related matters.

The issuance of these guidelines are not the last of the SEC's activities. Review for improper accounting practices is an important item on the SEC staff agenda. One of the goals of the Division of Corporate Finance is to review more than half of the 10-Ks. It is important to note that the division will not disclose its criteria for selecting 10-Ks for review. The review process is similar to any investigative reporting with the staff going through an exhaustive review of prior filing, industry data, and other sources of information as well as the current filing. Whatever the result of the review process by the Division of Corporate Finance, executives can appeal and request a conference with the chief accountant. An SEC "accounting court" composed of the chief accountant and members of his or her staff examine the controversial reporting issue; study all of the positions, those of the registrants and those of the Division of Corporate Finance; and render a decision.

In general, decisions taken by the chief accountant or SEC staff come with a bias for common sense when deciding questions about the proper application of the GAAP and Regulation S-X. This bias holds the concept of "fair presentation" as the highest and most appropriate standard. It gives a predominance to substance over mere form resulting from a superficial compliance with the GAAP requirements. The conflict is basically between the interpretations of the GAAP experienced in the registrant's position and the judgment by the chief accountant and his or her SEC accounting court about what "fair presentation" is. Accountants and executives dealing with the SEC should be aware of the enforcement activities of the SEC, as performed by the separate Division of Enforcement. Enforcement is conducted whenever the SEC believes there is a violation of a potential isolation of its laws and rules. It takes the form of (a) investigations, (b) suits for injunction, (c) administrative disciplinary proceedings, and (d) criminal references.

Standard Setting and the SEC

The Securities Acts of 1933 and 1934 gave the SEC the power to determine accounting standards. Basically, the SEC is top management and the private sector's standard-setting body is lower management. The process by which the disclosure system would be established, revised, and evaluated remained unclear until April 1938, when the SEC issued Accounting Series Release No. 4 (ASR No. 4), "Administrative Policy on Financial Statements." It reads as follows:

In cases where financial statements filed with this Commission pursuant to its rules and regulations under the Securities Act of 1933 or the Securities Exchange Act of

1934 are prepared in accordance with accounting principles for which there is no substantial authoritative support, such financial statements will be presumed to be misleading or inaccurate despite disclosures contained in the certificate of the accountant or in footnotes to the statements provided the matters involved are material. In cases where there is a difference of opinion between the Commission and the registrant as to the proper principles of accounting to be followed, disclosure will be accepted in lieu of correction of the financial statements themselves only if the points involved are such that there is substantial authoritative support for the practices followed by the registrant and the position of the Commission has not previously been expressed in rules, regulations, or other official releases of the Commission, including the published opinions of its chief accountant.

This 1938 ARS established the concept of *substantial authoritative support* as the basis for acceptable accounting principles to be used in preparing financial statements filed with the Securities and Exchange Commission.

Although the SEC has the power to regulate accounting practices and disclosure, it has in general relied on the accounting profession, using its power to set constraints and exert veto power. The SEC has generally concurred with most of the profession's pronouncements, APB opinions, and FASB statements. Nevertheless, it has retained the right to express its views. The SEC has sometimes disagreed with the accounting profession's pronouncements. Some of its accounting series releases on accounting, auditing, and financial matters have been in conflict with or have in fact amended or superseded standards set by the standard-setting bodies. Three examples are (1) ASR No. 96, in which the SEC rejected APB Opinion No. 2 and gave acceptance to several methods of handling the investment credit; (2) ASR No. 147, in which the SEC characterized lease disclosures required by APB No. 31 as inadequate and imposed additional disclosure requirements of its own; and (3) ASR No. 146, in which the SEC provided an interpretation of APB Opinion No. 16, which prompted a CPA firm to sue the SEC.

After the failure of the APB and the creation of the Financial Accounting Standards Board (FASB), the SEC issued a policy statement—Accounting Series Release No. 150—that specifically endorsed the FASB as the only standard-setting body whose standards would be accepted by the SEC as satisfying the requirements of the federal securities laws. The release states that "principles, standards and practices promulgated by the FASB will be considered by the Commission as having substantial authoritative support, and those contrary to such FASB promulgations will be considered to have no such support." It also states, however, that "the Commission will continue to identify areas where investor information needs exist and will determine the appropriate methods of disclosure to meet these needs." The SEC continues to permit the establishment of accounting standards by the private sector, and the commission's intervention as the federal government's major participant in the accounting standard-setting process is in the form of cooperation, advice, and sometimes pressure, rather than in the form of rigid controls. In other words, the SEC endorses the FASB with some reservations, in that it has not delegated any of its authority or given up any right to reject, modify, or supersede FASB pronouncements through its own rule-making procedures. The SEC has been compared to the sand in the oyster resulting in a pearl. Although accounting techniques are not exactly a pearl, the SEC has been, since its inception in 1934, a principal source of creative irritation in accounting, and the practicing public accounting profession has generally served as the host that builds on it. The SEC has always viewed its role with regard to setting accounting standards as one of oversight rather than regulation. This role is consistent with the view that the private sector can regulate itself more effectively than the government can do it. To quote one commissioner, "The accounting profession is forging a model of self-regulation which may well serve as an example for the other segments of the economy." In fact, the tendency has been for the commission to rely heavily on the Public Oversight Board's oversight of the peer-review program in fulfilling the SEC's responsibilities. This somewhat harmonious relationship between the SEC and the accounting profession and the standard-setting body has not been without its critics. There was a call for more regulation by the SEC, and as a result, the SEC began in 1984 to revert somewhat to its incarnation as a tough regulator. The regulatory mood is exemplified by (a) a legislative package to outlaw certain defensive tactics used in corporate takeover battles, (b) a crackdown on bankholding companies that overstate earnings and disguise their troubles, and (c) an investigation of the misuse of the "generally accepted accounting principles," "cooked books," "cute accounting" and "creative accounting," accounting irregularities, reckless application of the GAAP and GAAS, and improprieties arising from "shopping" for auditors' opinions.

The situation is characterized by the SEC still relying on the profession's self-regulation program but also using sharper enforcement criteria. Of particular importance to the SEC's enforcement effort is the financial fraud and insider trading issues. The financial-fraud enforcement program is designed to include a broad variety of misconduct including:

1. Liquidity problems, such as (a) decreased inflow of collections from sales to customers; (b) the lack of available credit from suppliers, banks, and others; and (c) the inability to meet maturing obligations when they fall due

2. Operating trends and factors affecting profits and losses such as (a) curtailment of operations, (b) decline of orders, (c) increased competition, and (d) cost overruns on major contracts

3. Material increase in the problem loans of financial institution

4. Deceptive and fraudulent accounting practices used by declining and failing companies that have (a) prematurely recognized income, (b) improperly treated operating leases as sales, (c) inflated inventory by improper application of the last in-first out (LIFO) inventory method, (d) included fictitious amounts in in-

ventories, (e) failed to recognize losses through write-offs and allowances, (f) improperly capitalized or deferred costs and expenses, (g) included unusual gains in operating income, (h) overvalued marketable securities, (i) created "sham" year-end transactions to boost reported earnings, and (j) changed their accounting practices to increase earnings without disclosing the changes.[1]

The enforcement program is not limited to the preparers of financial statements and to corporate accounting irregularities. It is also geared toward the accountants and the accounting firms guilty of "going along" with these corporate accounting irregularities and of "relaxed" auditing procedures. Four criteria are to be used by the SEC Division of Enforcement in determining action to be taken against accounting firms or individual CPAs:

1. The adequacy in applicable audit engagements of review practices or procedures and the extent to which those procedures were adhered to in the audit inquiry
2. The selection, training, supervision, and conduct of members or employees of the firm involved
3. The role played by the firm's top managers—the attentiveness to and the constant reminding of the need for top-level quality control and the continued updating of practice procedures and policies
4. A look at other problems or deficiences in which the firm or the individual CPA may have been involved

2. THE SEC, INSIDE TRADING, AND THE ACCOUNTANT

An insider trading bill, sponsored by Senator Alfonso d'Amato, who headed the Senate Banking Subcommittee at the time, would outlaw the "unfair use" of nonpublic information in securities and options trading. It would be illegal for any person to profit, or avoid a loss, by using such nonpublic information if it meant violating his or her "fiduciary or contractual obligations." In addition, it would be illegal for anybody else to take advantage of a tip if that person knew the tipster was violating his or her obligations in passing on the information. Such a bill would have expanded the definition of *insiders* beyond corporate officials, directors, and major shareholders to include "outsiders" such as financial printers, secretaries, and journalists. It also would have allowed the SEC not to rely so heavily on legal theories such as "misappropriation of information" and "breach of duty" in prosecuting insider cases. One would expect the SEC to favor such a bill. Instead, the director of the SEC enforcement program at the time suggested that (a) a rigid definition would reduce the SEC's flexibility in prosecuting new types of insider-trading schemes; (b) it was not one of the SEC's budget legislative-type priorities; and (c) it would be better to strengthen insider trading schemes. The advice was followed, and Congress approved tougher insider trading sanctions. The bill provides that the SEC can bring an action against anyone who aids and abets another person's violation by communicating material nonpublic information, without, however, providing a definition of *insider trading* or of *material nonpublic information.* Other provisions of the bill include:

1. Allowing the courts to levy civil fines three times greater than the profits or losses avoided through insider trading
2. Increasing the criminal fines for market manipulation, securities fraud, and other misconduct to $100,000 from a current maximum of $10,000
3. Explicitly stating that insider trading in stock options is illegal

Many academics and corporate executives would argue that there is nothing improper about most insider trading. They would contend, for example, that insider trading actually benefits all investors by speeding information about stock prices to the market. The SEC has not seen it that way and has been on a big drive against insider trading. For example, it sued a printer, Vincent Chiarella, who made a killing in the market by deriving the names of corporate takeovers from coded disclosure documents he was printing. The Supreme Court threw out the case. The SEC was more successful in a second case, when it sued a trader, James Newman, who got tips from investment bankers at Morgan Stanley. In this case, the Supreme Court declined to consider Newman's appeal. That success got the SEC on a witch hunt for "outsiders" who trade on inside information.

Among the "outsiders" considered by the SEC are journalists who trade stocks in anticipation of the market's reaction to their columns or articles. One of these journalists is the Wall Street reporter R. Foster Winams, who acknowledged leaking upcoming items from the influential "Heard on the Street" column, which features stock tips to investors. In this case, the government charged that (a) Winams violated his duty of loyalty as an employee by misappropriating confidential information from the journal; (b) he violated a fiduciary obligation to his readers by failing to disclose to them his role in the alleged trading scheme; and (c) consequently, by breaking these two duties in a scheme to make quick trading profits, he and his coconspirators committed securities fraud in violation of SEC Rule 1010-5. In all of this, the "duty-to-readers" theory used by the government is being criticized as inappropriate, because unlike investment advisors, journalists do not come under SEC jurisdiction. It seeks to base securities law violations on an alleged breach of duty to a reporter's readers rather than to his or her employer. Critics maintain that Winams' conduct is analogous to "scalping," which occurs when an investment adviser purchases shares of a security for his or her own account, recommends that security to customers, and then sells at a profit following these recommendations. In fact, the Investment Adviser Act, which regulates investment advisers, specifically excludes journalists from its restrictions.

The lesson from all of this is that all professionals who find themselves in the conduct of their professional activities in possession of any news having informational content are potential targets of the SEC. The most obvious examples of such professionals are lawyers and accountants. Lawyers and accountants may be constructive fiduciaries. In the past they have not been treated as "corporate insiders." However, the new legal theories used by the SEC may easily translate to lawyers and accountants owing the same duty to the corporation's shareholders as to corporate management. Hence lawyers and accountants found trading while in possession of material nonpublic information may be found in violation of the law.

3. MISLEADING FINANCIAL STATEMENTS AND THE SEC

"Cooked books," "cute fraud," or both are an evidence of the feature of corporate stewardship and a breakdown in management's accountability to shareholders. In fact, false or misleading financial statements are not a rare occurrence. They may result from practices such as the following: (a) willfully and extensively falsifying company records, (b) lying to auditors, (c) improperly applying a violation of accounting principles, and (d) making false disclosures concerning accounting principles. This type of activity seriously undermines the integrity of financial statements and may hinder the efficient working of the capital market. When false or misleading financial statements are found or suspected, the SEC may conclude that it is appropriate to seek extensive auxiliary relief, such as (a) a restatement of prior years' financial statements; (b) the appointment of new directors acceptable to the commission, thus diluting incumbent management's control; (c) heightened responsibility of the audit committee; and (d) even the retention by the audit committee of its own accounting firm, acceptable to the commission, as an advisor. The SEC is serious about false or misleading financial statements.

What are the causes of financial-statement fraud? In a 1984 speech, SEC Commissioner James C. Treadway, Jr., singled out three possible causes:

Aggressive corporate executives who manage by objectives, and who see the manipulation of financial statements as an acceptable, if not entirely proper, means to achieve that end.

A Board of Directors which is either isolated, indifferent, unquestioning, insensitive, or simply unwilling to ask tough questions.

Insufficient regard or respect for the auditing and accounting functions.

The SEC has to crack down on financial-statements fraud, whatever the cause, to restore the integrity of financial statements and the confidence of both the corporate community and the market in the reliability and integrity of financial statements and financial data. The future offers more puzzling questions:

1. Will the incidence of misleading financial statements continue and thereby taint the image of integrity asked of the accounting profession?

2. Will the increasing role of the SEC in cracking down on financial-statements fraud lead to a quasi-public regulation of accounting at the expense of actual private regulation?

3. Is there a link between the "quality" of the audit committee's work and the incidence of misleading financial statements?

4. Is there a link between the incidence of misleading financial statements and economic troubles experienced by the company? More precisely, is the incidence of misleading financial statements indicative or predictive of potential bankruptcies?

4. WHAT EXACTLY IS THE POSITION OF THE SEC ON NONAUDIT SERVICES AND AUDITOR INDEPENDENCE?

The SEC has always shown some concern about auditor independence in general. On December 13, 1977, it issued ASR No. 234, "Independence of Accountants," in which it reaffirmed that the "major value" of an outside audit of financial statements is that an "independent" viewpoint "not connected with management" is obtained. The concern with auditor independence took a more pronounced dimension with the growth of nonaudit services. First, on June 29, 1978, the SEC issued ASR No. 250, "Disclosure of Relationships with Independent Public Accountants," and on June 14, 1979, it issued an "interpretation" in ASR No. 264, "Scope of Services by Independent Accountants." Both releases heightened the importance of the issue of auditor independence when nonaudit services are also rendered. In ASR No. 250 the SEC required each registrant to disclose which nonaudit services their independent accountants performed, what percentage relationship the fee bore to the audit fee, and whether the board of directors, or its audit committee, reviewed and approved each of the nonaudit services. ASR No. 264 followed a 1979 report of the Public Oversight Board (POB) of the American Institute of Certified Public Accountants (AICP), which examined the scope-of-services issue and concluded that it was not necessary or desirable to impose any new rules limiting the scope of services. ASR No. 264 was, in fact, intended to help evaluate how performing nonaudit services might affect auditor independence. The SEC did not agree with the conclusions of the POB report. ASR No. 264 stated that it was necessary to "sensitize the profession and its clients to the potential effects on the independence of accountants of performance of nonaudit services for audit clients." It also affirmed that public confidence would be significantly lessened if auditors engaged in activities and services that the public perceives as foreign to the suspected role of the auditor.

The two positions taken by the SEC in ASR No. 250 and ASR No. 264 generated fiery arguments from the AICPA and public accounting firms. One of the noticeable arguments is that both releases are merely restrictions on the scope of services performed by CPAs and could be costly to both auditors and clients. What was the reaction of the SEC to this fiery response? In 1982 the SEC rescinded ASR No. 250 and decided not to reimpose ASR No. 264. It used the arguments that (a) ASR No. 250 was no longer necessary, since the SEC practice section of the AICPA division for CPA firms had amended its annual report form to require that member firms furnish information on the relationship of nonaudit fees to total fees for all SEC clients; and (b) ASR No. 250 and No. 264 created much confusion and resulted in unwarranted curtailment of nonaudit services.

Given this situation, what led the SEC to give up its regulatory power in cases like nonaudit services in which auditor independence is strongly alleged to happen? Is it not a major issue that deserves direct oversight by the SEC? Would not the required disclosure in proxy statements of nonaudit services be important information to the investors, the market, and those relying extensively on the auditor's report? Is direct regulation not necessary where directors, audit committees, and management have not in the past been vigilant enough and sensitive enough to the possible impact of nonaudit services on audit independence? Is public confidence in the integrity of financial reporting going to be maintained without direct SEC regulation of auditor independence?

NOTE

1. J. M. Fedders and L. G. Perry, "Policing Financial Disclosure Fraud: The SEC's Top Priority," *Journal of Accountancy*, July 1984, 59.

VI

AUDITING

1. THE AUDITOR'S STANDARD REPORT: PAST, PRESENT AND FUTURE

> Reading the so-called auditor's letter in an annual report gives you the impression that there is some omniscient force protecting your interests, and guaranteeing that protection with a nicely sculpted signature. But, of course, this is wrong.
>
> *Forbes*, December 22, 1980, 55

The audit report is the only formal means to communicate the results of the audit function to the users of financial statements. Over the years its format, content, and importance have changed in various attempts to increase or change its educational and informational value.

The origins began in England, where its contents were prescribed by the English Companies Act of 1900 and were introduced as such in the United States. Until 1948 auditors were required to state whether, in their opinion, the balance sheet presented a true and correct view of the financial condition of the company after a detailed examination of the books was made. No standard report existed. An example is the following unaddressed certificate in the 1907 Sears, Roebuck and Company financial statement: "We have attended at Chicago, Illinois, and audited the accounts of the company for the year ended June 30, 1907, and certify that the balance sheet, in our opinion, correctly sets forth the position of the company as shown by the books of accounts. Deloitte, Plender, Griffiths & Co., Auditors, 49 Wall Street, New York City, September 7, 1907."

Another good example is the following report from the first annual report of the United States Steel Corporation:

Certificate of Chartered Accountants

New York
March 12, 1903

To the Stockholders of the United States Steel Corporation:

We have examined the books of the U.S. Steel Corporation and its Subsidiary Companies for the year ending December 31, 1902, and certify that the Balance Sheet at that date and the Relative Income Account are correctly prepared therefrom.

We have satisfied ourselves that during the year only actual additions and extensions have been charged to Property Account; that ample provision has been made for Depreciation and Extinguishment, and that the item of "Deferred Charges" represents expenditures reasonably and properly carried forward to operations of subsequent years.

We are satisfied that the valuations of the inventories of stocks on hand as certified by the responsible officials have been carefully and accurately made at approximate cost; also that the cost of material and labor on contracts in progress has been carefully ascertained, and that the profit taken on these contracts is fair and reasonable.

Full provision has been made for bad and doubtful accounts receivable and for all ascertainable liabilities.

We have verified the cash and securities by actual inspection or by certificates from the Depositories, and are of opinion that the Stocks and bonds are fully worth the values at which they are stated in the Balance Sheet.

And we certify that in our opinion the Balance Sheet is properly drawn up so as to show the true financial position of the Corporation and its Subsidiary Companies, and that the Relative Income Account is a fair and correct statement of the net earnings for the fiscal year ending at that date.

Price Waterhouse & Co.

Following World War I, the *Ultramares* case in 1931, the stock market crash in 1929, the *McKesson and Robbins* case in 1938, the passage of the securities acts of 1933 and 1934, and the release of SAP No. 5 and No. 6 in February 1941 and March 1941, both titled "The Revised SEC Rule on 'Accountants' Certificates,' " the audit report was subjected to various changes in format and content. Finally, in October 1948 the American Institute issued SAP No. 24, "Revision in Short-form Accountant's Report or Certificate." It amended the scope paragraph to read: "We have examined the balance sheet of X Company as of ———, and the related statements of income and surplus for the year then ended. Our examination was made in accordance with generally accepted auditing standards, and accordingly included such tests of the accounting records and such other auditing procedures as we considered necessary in the circumstances." Other changes followed in 1963 with the substitution of the word *surplus* for the phrase *retained earnings* and in 1971 with the addition of *statement of changes in financial position*. As a result the current form of the auditor's standard report reads as follows:

We have examined the balance sheet of X Company as of (at) December 31, 19XX, and the related statements of income, retained earnings and changes in financial position for the year then ended. Our examination was made in accordance with generally accepted auditing standards and, accordingly, included such tests of the accounting records and such other auditing procedures as we considered necessary in the circumstances.

In our opinion, the financial statements referred to above present fairly the financial position of X Company as of (at) December 31, 19XX, and the results of its operations and the changes in its financial position for the year then ended in conformity with generally accepted accounting principles applied on a basis consistent with that of the preceeding year.

Although it has stood the test of time, the present form of audit report has been criticized for its failure to describe the auditor's function adequately. It gives the false impression that all is well financially for those firms receiving unqualified opinions and that the whole truth is being disclosed in the annual reports. What is in fact happening is that the financial statements are prepared by management and reflect only management's version of the truth. In addition, the audit report is not only appearing to the general public as a guarantee that is far from correct but is becoming more of a symbol than an important indicator. The Cohen Commission alerted the profession to the situation. It called for the profession to indicate explicitly that (a) the financial statements are representations of management, (b) that the accounting principles deemed appropriate were used, and (c) that the auditor's opinion is the result of judgments exercised by the auditor in his or her work. The commission thought that the present auditor's standard report is unsatisfactory and requires a thorough revision to clarify the present intended meaning and add important aspects of the audit function not presently covered explicitly. The commission also gave the following example of tomorrow's auditor's report:

Report of Independent Auditors

The accompanying consolidated balance sheet of XYZ Company as of December 31, 19X6, and the related statements of consolidated income and changes in consolidated financial positions for the year ended, including the notes, were prepared by XYZ Company's management, as explained in the report by management.

In our opinion, those financial statements in all material respects present the financial position of XYZ Company at December 31, 19X6, and the results of its operations and changes in financial position for the year then ended in conformity with generally accepted accounting principles appropriate in the circumstances.

We audited the financial statements and the accounting records and documents supporting them in accordance with generally accepted auditing standards. Our audit included a study and evaluation of the company's accounting system and the controls over it. We obtained sufficient evidence through a sample of the transactions and other events reflected in the financial statement amounts and an analytical review of the information presented in the statements. We believe our auditing procedures were adequate in the circumstances to support our opinion.

Based on our study and evaluation of the accounting system and the controls over it, we concur with the description of the system and controls in the report by management (or, based on our study and evaluation of the accounting system and controls believe the system and controls over it, we have the following uncorrected material weaknesses not described in the report by management: . . .) (or other disagreements with the description of the system and controls in the report by management) (or a description of uncorrected material weaknesses found if there is no report by management.) Nevertheless, in the performance of most control procedures, errors can result from personal factors. Also, control procedures can be circumvented by collusion or overridden. Furthermore, projection of any evaluation of internal accounting control to future periods is subject to the risk that changes in conditions may cause procedures to become inadequate and the degree of compliance with them to deteriorate.

We reviewed the process used by the company to prepare the quarterly information released during the year. Our reviews were conducted each quarter (or times as explained). (Any other information reviewed, such as replacement cost data, would be identified.) Our review consisted primarily of inquiries of management, analysis of financial information, and comparisons of that information to information and knowledge about the company obtained during our audits and were based on our reliance on the company's internal accounting control system. Any adjustments or additional disclosures we recommended have been reflected in the information.

We reviewed the Company's policy statement on employee conduct, described in the report by management, and reviewed and tested the related controls and internal audit procedures. While no controls or procedures can prevent or detect all individual misconduct, we believe the controls and internal audit procedures have been appropriately designed and applied.

We met with the audit committee (or the board of directors) or XYZ Company sufficiently often to inform it of the scope of our audit and to discuss any significant accounting or auditing problems encountered and any other services provided to the company (or indication of failure to meet or insufficient meetings or failure to discuss pertinent problems).

Test Check & Co.
Certified Public Accountants

Following the publication of the Cohen Report, the Auditing Standards Executive Committee (now called the Auditing Standards Board) of the AICPA formed a task force to examine possible revisions of the auditor's report. It agonized for three years before concluding that the report, the primary means of communication between the auditor and the users of his or her work, should be modified to clarify the character of the audit and the extent of the auditor's responsibility. The proposed changes were disclosed in September 1980 in a proposed SAS titled "The Auditor's Report." The proposed form of the independent auditor's standard report will be as follows:

The accompanying balance sheet of X Company as of (at) December 31, 19XX, and the related statement of income, retained earnings and changes in financial position for the year ended are management's representations. An audit is intended to provide reasonable, but no absolute, assurance as to whether financial statements taken as a whole are free of material misstatements. We have audited the financial statements referred to above in accordance with generally accepted auditing standards. Application of those standards requires judgment in determining the nature, timing and extent of testing and other procedures, and in evaluating the results of those procedures.

In our opinion, the financial statements referred to above present the financial position of X Company as of (at) December 31, 19XX, and the results of its operations and the changes in its financial position for the year then ended in conformity with generally accepted accounting principles.

The following seven changes in the wording of the report were made:

1. The first change was the proposed deletion of the word *fairly* from the opinion paragraph. The word *fairly* has always generated some controversy; in 1964 an AICPA committee, the Seidman Committee, asserted in its 1965 report that:

[I]n the standard report of the auditor, he generally says that financial statements "present fairly" in conformity with generally accepted accounting principles. What does the auditor mean by the quoted words? Is he saying: (1) that the statements are fair *and* in accordance with generally accepted accounting principles; or (2) that they are fair *because* they are in accordance with generally accepted accounting principles; or (3) that they are fair only *to the extent* that generally accepted accounting principles are fair; or (4) that whatever the generally accepted accounting may be, the *presentation* of them is fair?

The challenge to the profession did not go unchallenged. In 1975 the AICPA Auditing Standards Executive Committee issued Statement on Auditing Standards No. 5 on "The meaning of 'Present Fairly' in conformity with Generally Accepted Accounting Principles in the Independent Auditor's Report." In it, the idea of fairness was set as follows (Paragraph 4):

(a) The accounting principles selected and applied have general acceptance . . . ;

(b) The . . . principles are appropriate in the circumstances . . . ;

(c) The financial statements, including the related notes, are informative of matters that may affect their use, understanding, and interpretation . . . ;

(d) The information presented in the financial statements is classified and summarized in a reasonable manner, that is, neither too detailed nor too condensed . . . ;

(e) The financial statements reflect the underlying events and transactions . . .
     within a range of acceptable limits, that is, limits that are reasonable and prac-
     ticable to attain in financial statements.

In spite of these clarifications the debate on the usefulness of "present
fairly" continues today. Those in favor of its deletion argue that (a) it is
wrongly interpreted as an opinion on the fairness of financial statements
rather than an opinion about their conformity with the GAAP, and (b) it is
subjective and unnecessary, given that fairness is already embodied in the
GAAP. Those in favor of its inclusion argue that (a) it may indicate to the
nonsophisticated users of financial statements that the auditors are reneging
on their responsibilities, (b) it is an overriding principle of accounting recognized by both the profession and the users, and (c) it acts as a "modifier"
without which the audit process might appear more exact than it really is.

   2. The second change was the assertion that financial statements are
management's representations. Such change is believed to give a true
picture of the relationships between management and the auditors. Management prepares or finds somebody to prepare the financial statements to be
verified by the auditors. Those arguing against the deletion maintain that
(a) it may be more confusing to the users, (b) it may give the idea that the
statements are used by management to present less than a factual picture of
the financial condition of the company, and (c) it may give the impression
that the auditors are backing away from any responsibility to find "material
misstatements." The most relevant argument against the change is that it
would be redundant given the usual presence of a management report in the
annual report.

   3. The third change was the deletion of the reference to consistency. The
deletion is justifiable, because APB Opinion No. 20 requires disclosure of
changes in accounting principles. Therefore, reference to consistency is redundant in view of the requirements of APB Opinion No. 20. Those
arguing against the deletion maintain that most users may not be aware of
APB Opinion No. 20 and therefore need the reference to consistency.

   4. The fourth change was the addition of the word *independent* to
comply with the standard of independence and as a reminder to auditors,
management, and users.

   5. The fifth change was the replacement of the word *examined* with the
word *audited* to emphasize the exhaustive work accomplished in an audit.
Some think, however, that either word may be confusing to users and may
mean anything from a perusal to a probe.

   6. The sixth change is a statement in the scope paragraph that the
application of the generally accepted auditing standards (GAAS) requires
judgment in determining the nature, timing, and extent of testing and other
procedures and in evaluating the results of those procedures. Such change
was expected to give a better picture of the nature of the opinion and help

the users in their interpretation of the opinion. It admits that audits do not guarantee complete accuracy, much less any firm protection against fraud. Some think, however, that the change is redundant, since the judgmental nature of the opinion is reflected in the current report wording: "included such tests . . . as we considered necessary in the circumstances." Others believe that the change sounds as if the accountants are trying to retreat even further and take even less responsibility; they appear to be doing less than the users thought they were.

7. The seventh change is the statement that an audit is intended to provide reasonable, but not absolute, assurance about whether financial statements as a whole are free of material misstatements. It is clearly a confession that an audit is only an audit and not a guarantee.

All of these changes, however, proved to be politically and practically difficult to accept, and the proposed SAS was shelved. More on the subject awaits us in the future. The best given is that the format and content of the auditor's report is bound to change with an emphasis on providing more *assurances* than *opinions* on the financial health of audited firms.

2. THE AUDITOR'S STANDARD REPORT: CONTENT AND NATURE OF THE OPINION

The auditor process is not random. It is guided by the profession. Since 1972 the AICPA has issued statements on auditing standards (SAS) to serve as the most authoritative references available to auditors. These statements, however, provide less direction to auditors than may be assumed. They are used by practitioners as minimum rather than ideal standards of performance. They do not provide defined and detailed guidelines for determining the specific auditing procedures and the extent of evidence to be accumulated. They do, however, specify that a report must be issued any time a CPA firm is associated with financial statements. If the CPA is providing help in the preparation of the financial statements, a compilation or review report is required. If the CPA is conducting an audit, an audit report is required. It is this auditor's standard report that is the most important to the users of financial statements' information. To aid auditors in fulfilling their professional responsibilities, the accounting profession issued in 1947 ten *generally accepted auditing standards.* These ten standards, summarized in Exhibit 7, have not drastically changed since 1947. The last standard requires explicitly that the auditor express an opinion about the overall financial statements or a specific statement that an overall opinion is not possible, along with the reasons for not expressing an opinion. This opinion is communicated as the final phase of an audit in what is known as the auditor's report. The language of the auditor's report is standardized to cover specific points.

EXHIBIT 7 GENERALLY ACCEPTED AUDITING STANDARDS

GENERAL STANDARDS

1. The examination is to be performed by a person or persons having adequate technical training and proficiency as an auditor.
2. In all matters relating to the assignment, an independence in mental attitude is to be maintained by the auditor or auditors.
3. Due professional care is to be exercised in the performance of the examination and the preparation of the report.

STANDARDS OF FIELD WORK

1. The work is to be adequately planned, and assistants, if any, are to be supervised properly.
2. There is to be a proper study and evaluation of the existing internal control as a basis for reliance thereon and for the determination of the resultant extent of the tests to which auditing procedures are to be restricted.
3. Sufficient competent evidential matter is to be obtained through inspection, observation, inquiries, and confirmations to afford a reasonable basis for an opinion regarding the financial statements under examination.

STANDARDS OF REPORTING

1. The report shall state whether the financial statements are presented in accordance with generally accepted accounting principles.
2. The report shall state whether such principles have been consistently observed in the current period in relation to the preceding period.
3. Informative disclosures in the financial statements are to be regarded as reasonably adequate unless otherwise stated in the report.
4. The report shall either contain an expression of opinion regarding the financial statements, taken as a whole, or an assertion to the effect that an opinion cannot be expressed. When an overall opinion cannot be expressed, the reasons therefore should be stated. In all cases where an auditor's name is associated with financial statements, the report should contain a clearcut indication of the character of the auditor's examination, if any, and the degree of responsibility he or she is taking.

Unqualified Report

The most common type of audit report is one in which the auditor expresses an *unqualified opinion.* It is used when the financial statements have been presented in accordance with generally accepted accounting principles. It implies the belief that the financial statements have the following qualities:

1. The accounting principles selected and applied have general acceptance;
2. The accounting principles are appropriate in the circumstances;
3. The financial statements, including the related notes, are informative of matters that may affect their use, understanding, and interpretation;
4. The information presented in the financial statements is classified and summarized in a reasonable manner, that is, neither too detailed nor too condensed; and
5. The financial statements reflect the underlying events and transactions in a manner that presents financial position, results of operations, and changes in financial position stated within a range of acceptable limits, that is, limits that are reasonable and practicable to attain financial statements.

Wording of an unqualified opinion covers (a) the address of the auditee, (b) the *scope paragraph* in which the auditor explains what was done in the audit process, (c) the *opinion paragraph* in which the auditor expresses his or her opinion about the financial statements, (d) the name of the CPA firm conducting the audit, and (e) the audit report date. It generally appears as follows:

Monti and DeAngelo, CPAs
1255 Campbell Avenue
Chicago Heights, IL 60680

Tel._____

Address	To the Stockholders
	Total Zribi Corporation
Scope	We have examined the balance sheets of Total Zribi Corporation as of December 31, 198A and 198B, and the related statements of income, retained earnings, and changes in financial position for the years then ended. Our examinations were made in accordance with generally accepted auditing standards and accordingly included such tests of the accounting records and such other auditing procedures as we considered necessary in the circumstances.
Opinion	In our opinion the financial statements referred to above present fairly the financial position of Total Zribi Corporation at December 31, 198A and 198B, and the results of its operations and the changes in its financial position for the years then ended, in conformity with generally accepted accounting principles applied on a consistent bases.
CPA Firm	Monti and DeAngelo, CPAs

Audit Report Date
(date audit field   February 15, 1980
work is completed)

The reference to consistent application in the opinion paragraph is essential information to the users of the financial statements. It means that, in the auditor's opinion, there has been no change in the application of accounting principles during the current year that significantly affects the comparability of the financial statements with those of the preceding year or that may affect comparability in the future. Some unqualified reports come with modified wording when the auditor feels that it is important to provide additional information.

Audit Reports Other Than Qualified

Occasionally, the auditor will not be able to give an unqualified opinion on the financial statements and may find it necessary to render a *qualified opinion*, an *adverse opinion*, or a *disclaimer*. The auditor may conclude that a qualified opinion is not required when one of the following five conditions seems to prevail:

1. The scope of the auditor's examination is restricted by the client or by circumstances beyond either the client's or auditor's control.
2. The financial statements have not been prepared in accordance with the generally accepted accounting principles.
3. The accounting principles used in the financial statements have not been consistently applied.
4. There are material uncertainties affecting the financial statements that cannot be reasonably estimated at the date of the auditor's report.
5. The auditor is not independent.

A *disclaimer of opinion* is issued when the auditor is unable to arrive at a judgment on fairness for some pervasive reason such as financial precariousness, limitation of scope of the engagement, or a nonindependent relationship. The disclaimer of opinion arises because of the lack of knowledge necessary to form *any* opinion on the financial statements, and that can occur only under the three situations described above. All of the other types of opinions indicate that the auditor has sufficient knowledge to form an opinion.

An *adverse opinion* states that the auditor has concluded that the financial statements deviate materially from the GAAP in some specified manner or are otherwise so materially misstated or misleading that they do not present fairly the financial position or results of operations in conformity with the generally accepted accounting principles.

A *qualified opinion* states that the auditor believes that the overall financial statements are fairly stated *"except for"* or *"subject to"* the effect of a specified matter.

An auditor uses "except for" in cases when (a) there is a lack of sufficient competent evidence or there are restrictions on the scope of the examination that preclude expressing an unqualified opinion; (b) the financial statements contain a departure from the GAAP, the effect of which is material; or (c) the use of different accounting principles during one of the years is included in the statement. The auditor uses "subject to" in cases when significant uncertainties affecting the financial statements have not been resolved as of the date of the auditor's report.

Is the "Subject-to" Audit Qualification Needed?

The question about the use of "subject to" has generated a heated debate. A "subject to" clause in the auditor's report says, in effect, "Subject to the outcome of thus-and-so contingency which no one can predict right now, these financial statements fairly reflect the condition of the company." It gives the user a *red flag* in addition to full disclosure. Such a position was not viewed favorably by the Commission on Auditor's Responsibility (Cohen Commission), which claimed that it places the auditor in the untenable position of being both a reporter and an interpreter of financial information. It also suggested that sufficient disclosure is all that is needed for each user to make his or her own assessment of the degree of uncertainty. It mainly concluded that:

1. Users of financial statements need enough information to make their own evaluation of uncertainties, and they are not served by a reporting requirement that diverts the auditor's attention from evaluating the disclosure of uncertainties to highlighting the existence of some uncertainties.

2. The auditor should issue a qualified opinion with respect to uncertainty only when disclosure is not full and fair.

Not all people share the views of the Cohen Commission. A November 1982 meeting at the AICPA on "subject to" for users of financial statements—mostly analysts and bankers—showed a consensus in favor of the clause as a red flag and a tip to the user. Although the debate continues in the United States, the Canadian profession abolished its version of "subject to" in 1980. It also allowed Canadian auditors reporting on a Canadian company that also submits audited financial statements to the SEC in the United States to issue a *split opinion*, which includes a comment to explain the situation to U.S. readers.

What Does an Emphasis Paragraph Mean?

Sometimes when the problem is estimated to be solvable, the CPA firm does not issue a qualified opinion but instead puts a less severe warning that auditors call an "emphasis paragraph." Emphasis paragraphs are, however, applied differently from one CPA firm to another. Some auditors use emphasis paragraphs to signal that the company may not be in immediate trouble, but if things are not improved, they will be given a qualified report. That naturally causes skeptics to ask the fundamental question: Does an emphasis paragraph mean it is a cheap, clean opinion? Or is it a cheap, qualified opinion?

From the companies' point of view an emphasis paragraph is preferable to a qualified opinion. The word *qualification* is an emotional word to the CPA firm, the firm audited, and the market. To the CPA firm, qualification is a delicate decision that involves subjective judgments and threatens auditors' fees and reputations. To the firm audited, qualification means a cloud hanging over its operations and the performance of management and various negative consequences. To the market, qualification triggers an immediate stampede by the investors with stock prices dropping and confidence shattered. But qualified opinions are on the increase; at the same time the number of publicly held firms firing their auditors in 1982 jumped 48 percent, to 442 from 298 the year before. Given this situation, one may expect to see an increase in "emphasis paragraphs."

3. THE AUDITOR'S STANDARD REPORT: MEANING OF "PRESENT FAIRLY . . . IN CONFORMITY WITH GAAP"

The current form of the auditor's standard report reads as follows:

We have examined the balance sheet of X Company as of (at) December 31, 19XX, and the related statements of income, retained earnings and changes in financial position for the year then ended. Our examination was made in accordance with generally accepted auditing standards and, accordingly, included such tests of the accounting records and such auditing procedures as we considered necessary in the circumstances.

In our opinion, the financial statements referred to above present fairly the financial position for the year then ended in conformity with generally accepted accounting principles applied on a basis consistent with that of the preceding year.

For more than 40 years, the second part of the auditor's report has expressed the auditor's opinion that financial statements "present fairly . . . in conformity with generally accepted accounting principles." The meaning of "present fairly" and the relationship between that phrase and "in conformity with generally accepted accounting principles" are not, however, clear and have been the subject of various interpretations. Each of the meanings and interpretations gives a view of what the responsibility of the auditor *should be* in reporting on financial statements. The situation is confusing enough to create three interpretations of the auditor's responsibility in expressing an opinion.

Opinion on Fairness

The first interpretation is that the auditor is expressing an *opinion on fairness*. This view maintains that the auditor can express an opinion on fairness based on his own private standard completely apart from the GAAP. It calls for every auditor to formulate his or her own view of fairness in auditing financial statements. But this view may lead to a very chaotic and highly subjective situation. A framework is needed to attain a high level of quality and comparability. The GAAP provide such a framework.

Those who maintain that the auditor can express an *opinion on fairness* based on his or her own private standards have either misunderstood or misinterpreted the *Continental Vending* case (U.S. v. Simon, 425 F. 2d 706 [2d Cir. 1969], Cert. den. 397 U.S. 1006 [1970]). This case concerned a footnote that was alleged to be affirmatively misleading. More precisely, the court found that the financial statements omitted material facts, principally because they did not state (a) that a receivable from a company controlled by a major stockholder of Continental Vending was essentially a loan to the stockholder who used the other company as a conduit for the loan and was unable to repay it and (2) that the "marketable securities" that served as collateral for the receivable consisted of stocks and bonds of Continental Vending. The defendant auditors contended that they had followed the GAAS in their examination and concluded that the financial statements conformed with the GAAP. The trial judge instructed the jury, however, that the "critical test" was whether the financial statements fairly presented the financial condition and to consider proof of compliance with professional standards as "evidence which may be persuasive but not necessarily conclusive" that the financial statements "were not materially false or misleading." Given these instructions, the jury found the defendants guilty. The appeals court heard the case and refused to reverse the decision. In its decision the appeals court considered the issue of whether the auditors had acted in good faith in not disclosing information that they were aware of but was not required by the GAAP—essentially in the form of published authoritative standards—to be disclosed:

We do not think the jury was . . . required to accept the accountants' evaluation whether a given fact was material to overall fair presentation, at least not when the accountants' testimony was not based on specific rules or prohibitions to which they could point out, but only on the need for the auditor to make an honest judgment and their conclusion that nothing in the financial statements themselves negated the conclusion that an honest judgment had been made. Such evidence may be highly persuasive, but it is not conclusive, and so the trial judge correctly charged.[1]

The decision of the court simply held that conformity with the GAAP, if established, does not by itself preclude a jury from inferring criminal intent from other evidence of the auditor's conduct, especially if the GAAP are silent on the subject. The court was calling the auditors to exercise individual judgments in areas in which no GAAP exist to determine that the statements are not misleading. It provided the following guidelines:

Generally accepted accounting principles instruct an accountant what to do in the usual case where he has no reason to doubt that the affairs of the corporation are being honestly conducted. Once he has reason that this basic assumption is false, an entirely different situation confronts him. Then . . . he must "extend his procedures to determine whether or not such suspicions are justified." If as a result of such extension or, as here, without it, he finds his suspicions to be confirmed, full disclosure must be the rule.[2]

A similar interpretation was expressed in the AICPA booklet titled *The Auditor's Report:*

Accounting for business transactions requires approximations and estimates. Unlike certain fields of science where a specific result can be achieved by the combination of certain elements, the amounts of many items in the financial statements cannot be measured with exactness but are subject to the application of professional judgment on an informed basis. Therefore, when the auditor refers to fairness of presentation, no claim is being made as to precise exactness. Rather, the auditor is saying that unlike a reasonable range of materiality, the financial statements have been presented on a basis which is fair to all segments of the financial community.[3]

The above guideline does not ask auditors to appraise presentations based on their own private standards completely apart from the GAAP. In short, the *Continental Vending* decision has been misinterpreted by those interpreting the auditor's responsibility in expressing an opinion on fairness based on his or her private standards. In any case, if that would ever become a fact, the situation would be incredibly confusing, with auditors presenting and arguing their own brands of accounting theory to support their own opinions about fairness. The accounting world can do without such a situation.

Dual Opinion

The second interpretation is that the auditor is expressing dual opinions—one on fairness and one on conformity to the GAAP. This would lead the auditor to draw one of four possible conclusions:

1. The presentations conform with the GAAP and are fair.
2. The presentations conform with the GAAP and are not fair.
3. The presentations do not conform with the GAAP and are fair.
4. The presentations do not conform with the GAAP and are not fair.

The opinions about fairness rest on conformity with the auditor's private standard of fair presentation. The dual opinion is explicitly stated by the Canadian Institute of Public Accountants (CICA). In the *CICA Handbook* (Section 5500.08) the Canadian Institute requires auditors to fulfill the following responsibilities:

The auditors should express an opinion, or report that they are unable to express an opinion, as to whether:

(a) the financial statements present fairly the financial position of the enterprise, the results of its operations and, where applicable, the source and application of its funds, and

(b) the financial statements were prepared in accordance with generally accepted accounting principles applied on a basis consistent with that of the preceding period.

The Canadian position implies that the auditor is responsible for appraising financial statement presentations based on his or her own private standard completely apart from the GAAP in addition to appraising conformity with the GAAP. In fact, to make sure that the auditors got the point, a letter dated May 16, 1972, to the members of the CICA from G. Mulcahy, then director of research, stated that a departure from the GAAP required a qualified opinion but only as to conformity with the GAAP. "This does not mean that auditors must necessarily qualify their opinion as to whether the financial statements present fairly the financial position of the enterprise, the results of operations and, where applicable, the source and application of its funds. That decision is a separate matter of professional judgment on the part of auditors."

Although the dual opinion seems to be acceptable to the Canadian profession, it is anathema for the U.S. counterpart. Again, the opinion on fairness above is perceived to undermine the GAAP and confidence in financial statements and to lead to a chaotic situation. For example, accounting firms may start competing on the basis of whose ideas on accounting theory agreed most with clients' situations.

Opinion on Conformity with the GAAP

The third interpretation is that the auditor is only expressing an opinion on conformity with the GAAP. Therefore, the GAAP are regarded as the only standard of reference to be used by the auditor in judging the quality of the audited financial statements. This interpretation can be inferred from the AICPA official pronouncements. Thus in its Statement No. 4 (paragraph 189), the AICPA Accounting Principles Board discussed fair presentation in conformity with the GAAP:

The qualitative standard of *fair presentation in conformity with generally accepted* principles of financial position and results of operations is particularly important in evaluating financial presentations. This standard guides preparers of financial statements and is the subjective benchmark against which independent public accountants judge that propriety of the financial accounting information communicated. Financial statements "present fairly the conformity with generally accepted accounting principles" if a number of conditions are met: (1) generally accepted accounting principles applicable in the circumstances have been applied in accumulating and processing the financial accounting information, (2) changes from period to period in generally accepted accounting principles have been appropriately disclosed, (3) the information in the underlying records is properly reflected and described in the financial statements in conformity with generally accepted accounting principles, and (4) a proper balance has been achieved between the conflicting needs to disclose important aspects of financial position and results of operations in accordance with conventional concepts and to summarize the voluminous underlying data in a limited number of financial statement captions and supporting notes.

In the statement it appears that conformity to the GAAP and application of the GAAP are the center of the auditor's responsibility in expressing an opinion. The GAAP appear then as a rule book to be followed without the exercise of personal judgment by the individual auditor, a body of principles and techniques agreed upon by authoritative professional studies. As such they constitute an ideal collective standard to be used to appraise financial statements. The auditor's opinion is a personal approval of financial statements, because they meet the standard adopted by the profession. For this interpretation to be valid, however, the GAAP need to be strengthend by a narrowing of the range of choices in accounting principles and a better identification of the circumstances in which a specific accounting principle is to be used.

Fairly or Exact Statements

The profession has struggled with the meaning attached to the phrase "Present fairly . . . in conformity with GAAP." The acceptable meaning was that adherence to professional standards—both accounting and auditing—cannot ensure absolute accuracy, given the nature of the financial statements. It meant that although the GAAP governed the preparation of the financial statements, and the GAAS (generally accepted auditing standards) governed their audit, the auditor's report does not connote absolute accuracy. The GAAP and GAAS rest on estimations, evaluations, and judgments to both prepare and audit the financial statements, which precludes the use of words such as *true* or *correct* but calls for the use of a word such as *fairly*. This interpretation of "present fairly" as meaning that the GAAP require estimations, evaluations, and judgments in their application and cannot lead to "exact" financial statements was supressed first in the AICPA booklet *Forty Questions and Answers about Audit Reports*:

What is the significance of the expression "present fairly" in the CPA's report? . . . No one can be in a position to state that a company's financial statements "exactly present" financial position or results of operations. Accordingly, the CPA usually states that the financial statements "present fairly" in the sense that he believes they are substantially correct. For the same reason, his findings are expressed in the form of an opinion. However, it should be borne in mind that the judgment involved is an informed one, and is guided by generally accepted accounting principles.[4]

NOTES

1. U.S. v. Simon, 425 F. 2d 706 (2d Cir. 1969), Cert. den. 397 U.S. 1006 (1970).

2. Ibid.

3. American Institute of Certified Public Accountants, *The Auditor's Report* (New York, 1967), 12-13.

4. American Institute of Certified Public Accountants, *Forty Questions about Audit Reports* (New York, 1956), 11.

VII

CONCLUSIONS

Inadequacies, issues, and unresolved problems are facing the accounting world. To most observers, it looks as though most of the actors in the accounting world have lost some of their cherished virtues. To the general public, the situation appears murky. Not only does the public not grasp the parameters of the situation, but it does not grasp effectively the specific roles of the actors involved, namely, the American Institute of Certified Public Accountants, the CPA firms and individuals, the Financial Accounting Standards Board (FASB), and the Securities and Exchange Commission (SEC). This book has attempted to close the gap by providing a critical examination of the role and issues facing accounting and auditing and the main actors. From that examination stem general conclusions and practical recommendations.

1. THE GENERALLY ACCEPTED ACCOUNTING PRINCIPLES AND FINANCIAL STATEMENTS

The generally accepted accounting principles (GAAP) are the guide to the accounting profession in the choice of accounting techniques and the preparation of financial statements in a way considered to be good accounting practice. The convention, rules, and procedures acquire the special status of being included in the GAAP when they have *substantial authoritative support*. The list of those principles, however, is either hard to compile or constantly changing. In addition, besides the widely known GAAP for business enterprises, there are not only special GAAPs (GAAP for governmental organizations, GAAP for regulated business enterprises, GAAP for not-for-profit organizations, GAAP for investment companies, and GAAP for banks, and so on) but alternatives to the GAAP, basically in financial statements prepared in accordance with other comprehensive bases of accounting (OCBOA). The crucial question to the profession is to decide what should it be: GAAP, special GAAPs, or OCBOA? Even if the profession chooses the GAAP, the question becomes one of determining whether any real difference exists between large and small businesses and between the needs of their respective information users to justify differences in the accounting rules in the form of two GAAPs: a little GAAP for smaller or closely held businesses and a big GAAP for larger companies. Even after this choice is made, two problems remain: First, are the accounting techniques being used in practice backed up by sound accounting theories or doctrines? Second, does the actual flexibility in the choice of accounting techniques make it easy for management to resort to income-smoothing behavior, namely, the intentional dampening of fluctuations about some level of earnings that are currently considered to be normal for a firm?

After all of these issues are resolved, the financial statements may be expected to be not only reflective of the financial structure, performance, and conduct of a firm for a given period but a reliable guide for the resource-allocation decisions of the average investor. A lot of issues need to be resolved before the GAAP and the resulting financial statements regain good virtues.

2. THE AMERICAN INSTITUTE OF CERTIFIED PUBLIC ACCOUNTANTS

The American Institute of Certified Public Accountants (AICPA) is the professional coordinating organization of practicing *certified public accountants* in the United States. It used to be the standard-setting body through the Committee on Accounting Procedure (CAP) and the Accounting Principles Board (APB) and is gradually moving toward a more advisory role to the FASB. It does not feel very comfortable in this new position. The continuous issuance of *statements of positions* shows some longing for the AICPA's previous predominant role in standard setting. One may wonder whether a clash might occur in the future between the AICPA and the FASB over the standard-setting process. However, before the AICPA regains any of the old predominant stature in standard setting, it has to field all of the calls for either public or private regulation of its activities and its efforts. Naturally, the profession is in favor of voluntary self-regulation as evidenced, for example, by its peer-review program. The peer review is essentially a quality control by peers. The performance of this voluntary program is important to the AICPA. It is perceived to be the best alternative available to regulate the activities of CPA firms and ensure that the quality of the services offered is adequate for the ultimate purpose of protecting the public from exploitation and inadequate services by accountants.

Besides standard setting and regulation of its activities, the AICPA faces a lot of issues needing examination. Of these issues, professionalism versus commercialism in accounting and specialization in the profession are of crucial importance. Commercialism is creeping into the accounting scene, and the AICPA has a stake in restoring professionalism as a voluntary commitment to achieve excellence. Similarly, specialization is unavoidable in accounting. Accreditation of specialists in accounting is going to be a great conceptual and practical challenge for the profession.

All of those and other issues place the AICPA in the public limelight and expose it to a continuous critical debate. Although these issues are continually being examined by various committees of the AICPA, progress is relatively slow. The AICPA is not a homogeneous organization. It includes large and small CPA firms, individuals, CPAs in other-than-public practice, academicians, and others. A consensus on a given position is difficult to achieve. Leadership is lacking and may be the key.

3. CPA FIRMS AND INDIVIDUALS

CPA firms and individuals are the subject of much criticism. Various famous cases show that auditors are missing the mark. In addition, there is the wide spread suspicion that by switching auditors, businesses may get the opinion they want. These two strong accusations head a list of other concerns, including "low balling" by CPA firms, loss of independence, a litigating explosion against accountants, the IRS access to accrual papers, client chasing by CPAs, bias applying to partnerships, and large firms invading the middle-market turf. Not only are solutions necessary to these problems but a whole new image of accounting is needed to liberate the accountant from a long siege and restore its image of a learned and complex profession.

4. THE FINANCIAL ACCOUNTING STANDARDS BOARD

Accounting standards dominate the accountant's work. The FASB is the authoritative, independent body charged with establishing and improving financial accounting and reporting standards—that is, these standards are concerned with meaningful information about economic events and transactions in a useful manner in financial statements. The setting of these standards follows an elaborate and formal due-process procedure. The FASB is not without its problems. First, its relations with both the AICPA and the SEC are at best uneven. Second, it is often accused of spending too much time on the balance sheet at the expense of the income statement, of focusing on narrow pieces of issues instead of complete questions, and of basing its decisions on the wrong economic theories. Third, there is the perception that too many standards are being issued, leading to a standards-overload problem. Finally, some question the desirability and the feasibility of a conceptual framework as an accounting constitution aimed at solving all problems. These are some of the important challenges facing the FASB that are examined in this book. They call for urgent solutions to avert a governmental intervention in the standard-setting process. The survival of the FASB rests on the ability to deal quickly and efficiently with all of these problems. The conceptual framework is one of the answers but not necessarily the only answer. Much remains to be done.

5. THE SECURITIES AND EXCHANGE COMMISSION

The SEC is top management, and the FASB is lower management. Although the SEC has the power to regulate accounting practices and disclosure, it has in general relied on the accounting profession, using its power to set constraints and exert veto power. It has generally concurred with most of the profession's pronouncements, APB opinions, and FASB statements. Nevertheless, it has retained the right to express its views and to disagree with the accounting profession's pronouncements. This creates a climate of general confusion among the FASB, the AICPA, and the SEC. Each is expressing its subjective views on similar issues, ending up most of the time disagreeing on the form rather than the substance and confusing the preparers and users of financial statements. What should be expected from the SEC is a general protection of the public interest through an active use of its oversight role and not through any obstructionist strategies. General and intelligent guidance rather than scare tactics of possible takeover of the standard-setting process is needed to create a better climate in the accounting world.

6. AUDITING

Central to the audit process is the issuance of the audit report as the only formal means to communicate the results of the audit function to the users of financial statements. The audit report contains the opinion of the auditor. Although it has stood the test of time, the present form of the audit report has been criticized for its failure to describe the auditor's function adequately. It gives the false impression that all is well financially for those firms receiving unqualified opinions and that the whole truth is being disclosed in the annual reports. The report needs revision to clarify the present intended meaning and add important aspects of the audit function not presently covered explicitly. With these changes, a lot of misunderstanding about the role of the audit and the measuring of the opinion will be avoided. A lot remains to be done—one more challenge for the accounting profession.

SELECTED BIBLIOGRAPHY

Abraham, S. C. *The Public Accounting Professional: Problems and Prospects.* Lexington, Mass.: Lexington Books, 1970.

"Accountants to Be Required to Tell Management of Internal-Control Weakness." *SEC Accounting Report*, March 1977, 3-4.

Adkerson, R. C. "Can Reserve Recognition Accounting Work?" *Journal of Accountancy*, September 1979, 72-81.

Alderman, C. W.; D. M. Guy; and D. R. Meals. "Other Comprehensive Bases of Accounting: Alternative to GAAP?" *Journal of Accountancy*, August 1982, 52-62.

American Accounting Association. "A Tentative Statement of Accounting Principles Affecting Corporate Reports." *Accounting Review*, July 1938, 187-91.

American Institute of Certified Public Accountants. "Institute Responds . . . to the Study by the Staff of the Subcommittee on Reports, Accounting and Management, U.S. Senate Committee on Governmental Affairs, entitled *The Accounting Establishment.*" New York, 1977, 40.

———.Auditing Standards Executive Committee. "Independent Auditor's Responsibility for the Detection of Errors or Irregularities." *Statement on Auditing Standards.* New York, 1977.

———. Commission on Auditor's Responsibilities. "Effect of Litigation on Independent Auditors," by H. A. Jaenicke. *Research Study, No. 1.* New York, 1977, 116 pp.

———. Commission on Auditor's Responsibilities. *Report, Conclusions, and Recommendations.* New York, March 1978.

———. Equity Funding Special Committee. *Report of the Special Committee on Equity Funding: The Adequacy of Auditing Standards and Procedures Currently Applied in the Examination of Financial Statements.* New York, 1975, 46.

———. Public Oversight Board. *Annual Report, 1978-79.* New York, March 1979.

"Are Auditors Ever Free of Liability? Equity Funding Case Equates Negligence with Fraud." *SEC Accounting Report*, July 1975, 1-2.

Armstrong, M. S. "Corporate Accountability: A Challenge to Business." *Conference Board Record*, August 1971, 29-31.

"Auditors Liability Limited in Draft of Law Codification." (News report) *Journal of Accountancy*, December 1973, 20, 22.

Austin, K. R., and D. C. Langston. "Peer Review: Its Impact on Quality Control." *Journal of Accountancy*, July 1981, 78-82.

Austin, R. H. "CAP's Social, Civic, and Political Responsibilities." (Statements in quotes) *Journal of Accountancy*, December 1971, 64-66.

Bab, D. S. "Current Thoughts about the Legal Liability of the CPA." *New York Certified Public Accountant* 41 (June 1971): 438-43.

Backer, M. "Comments on 'The Value of the SEC's Accounting Disclosure Requirements.' " *Accounting Review*, July 1969, 533-38.

Barker, R. E. "Legal Liability," Independence, Professional Ethics." *Cases in Auditing with Supplemental Readings*, 1969, 3-64.

Barr, A. "Relations between the Development of Accounting Principles and the Activities of the SEC." In *Eric Louis Kohler: A Man of Principles*, edited by W. W. Cooper and V. Ijiri. Reston, Va.: Reston Publishing Co., 1979, 41-61.

Barrett, E. "Extent of Disclosure in Annual Reports of Large Companies in Seven Countries." *International Journal of Accounting, Education and Research*, Spring 1977, 1-25.

Barron, R. A. "SEC to Act on Report of Advisory Committee on Corporate Disclosure." (Recent SEC developments) *Securities Regulation Law Journal*, Summer 1978, 176-79.

Baruch, H. "The Foreign Corrupt Practices Act." *Harvard Business Review*, January-February 1979, 1-7.

Beaver, W. H. "Current Trends in Corporate Disclosure." *Journal of Accountancy*, January 1978, 44-52.

_____. "Reporting Responsibility of the SEC." *Financial Executive*, March 1977, 14-19.

Bedford, N. M. "Corporate Accountability." *Management Accounting (NAA)*, November 1973, 41-44.

Berry, B. A. "Three Company Approaches [to the Foreign Corrupt Practices Act]: NCNB Corporation." *Financial Executive*, July 1979, 28-31.

Benjamin, J. J.; K. G. Stanga; and R. H. Strawger. "Disclosure of Information Regarding Corporate Social Responsibility." *Managerial Planning* July-August 1978, 23-27.

Benston, G. J. "Accountants Integrity and Financial Reporting." *Financial Executive*, August 1975, 10-14.

_____. "Accounting Standards in the United States and the United Kingdom: Their Nature, Causes and Consequences." (Symposium on Accounting and the Federal Securities Laws) *Vanderbilt Law Review*, January 1975, 235-68.

_____. "An Appraisal of the Costs and Benefits of Government-Required Disclosure: SEC and FIC Requirements." *Law and Contemporary Problems*, Summer 1977, 30-62.

_____. "Evaluation of the Securities and Exchange Act of 1934." *Financial Executive*, May 1974, 28-36, 40-42.

_____. "The Market for Public Accounting Services: Demand, Supply, and Regulation." (Working paper) Rochester, N.Y.: University of Rochester, March 1979.

_____. "Public (U.S.) Compared to Private (U.K.) Regulation of Corporate Financial Disclosure." *Accounting Review*, July 1976, 483-98.

_____. "Value of the SEC's Accounting Disclosure Requirements." *Accounting Review*, July 1969, 515-32.

Beresford, D. R., "Emerging Problems: How the Profession Is Coping." *Journal of Accountancy*, February 1981, 57-60.

_____. "Foreign Corrupt Practices Act—Its Implication to Financial Management." *Financial Executive*, August 1979, 26-32.

Beresford, D. R., and R. D. Neary. "SEC Responds to Advisory Committee's Report." (Financial reporting briefs) *Financial Executive*, May 1979, 8.

Bernstein, P. W. "Composition Comes to Accounting." *Fortune*, July 17, 1979, 88-96.

Biegler, J. C. "Who Shall Set Accounting Standards." *Financial Executive*, September 1977, 34-39.

Block, D. J., and E. J. Odoner. "Enforcing the Accounting Standards Provisions of the Foreign Corrupt Practices Act." *Financial Executive*, July 1979, 19-27.

Blough, C. G. "Early Development of Accounting Standards and Principles." In *Eric Louis Kohler: A Man of Principles*, edited by W. W. Cooper and V. Ijiri, Reston, Va.: Reston Publishing Co. 1979.

Blumberg, P. I. "Public's 'Right to Know': Disclosure in the Major American Corporation." *Business Lawyer*, July 1973, 1025-61.

Bowen, L. C. "Social Responsiveness of the Accounting Profession." *CPA Journal*, June 1978, 29-35.

Branson, D. M. "Progress in the Art of Social Accounting and Other Arguments for Disclosure on Corporate Social Responsibility." *Vanderbilt Law Review*, April 1976, 539-683.

Bremser, W. G. "The AICPA Division for Firms: Problems and a Challenge." *Journal of Accountancy*, August 1984, 98-110.

_____. "Peer Review: Enhancing Quality Control." *Journal of Accountancy*, October 1983, 78-88.

Brief, R. P. "Accountant's Responsibility for Disclosing Bribery: An Historical Note." *Accounting Historians Journal*, Fall 1977, 97-100.

Briloff, A. J. *Effectiveness of Accounting Communication, with a Foreword by Justice William O. Douglas.* New York: Frederick A. Praeger, 1967, 338.

_____. "Old Myths and New Realities in Accountancy." *Accounting Review*, July 1968, 404-95.

Brown V. H. "The Economic Impact of Financial Accounting Standards." *Financial Executive*, September 1979, 32-39.

Buchholz, D. L., and J. F. Moraglio. "IRS Access to Auditors Work Paper: The Supreme Court Decision." *Journal of Accountancy*, September 1984, 91-100.

Buchholz, R. A. "Corporate Cost for Compliance with Government Regulation on Information." Paper presented at the Round Table Conference on Government Regulation of Accounting and Information, Accounting Research Center, University of Florida, March 1979.

Buckley, J. W. "Accounting Principles and the Social Ethics." *Financial Executive*, October 1971, 32-34, 36, 38, 40, 42, 44, 46.

Burton, J. C. "Auditor of Record." (Statements in quotes) *Journal of Accountancy*, April 1977, 89-90.

_____. "Changing SEC Financial Disclosure and Accounting Rules—1975," chaired by John C. Burton and Manuel F. Cohen. *New York Law Journal*, 1975, 572.

_____. "A Critical Look at Professionalism and Scope of Services." *Journal of Accountancy*, April 1980, 48-56.

_____. "Educator Views the Public Accounting Profession." *Journal of Accountancy*, September 1971, 47-53.

_____. "Emerging Trends in Financial Reporting." *Journal of Accountancy*, July 1981, 54-66.

_____. "Ethics in Corporate Financial Disclosure." *Financial Analysts Journal*, January-February 1972, 49-53.

_____. "The Profession's Institutional Structure in the 1980's." *Journal of Accountancy*, April 1978, 63-69.

_____. "SEC Enforcement and Professional Accountants: Philosophy, Objectives, and Approach." (Symposium on Accounting and the Federal Securities Laws) *Vanderbilt Law Review* 78 (January 1975): 19-29.

_____. "A Symposium on the Conceptual Framework." *Journal of Accountancy*, January 1978, 53-58.

Carey, G. V. "Corporate Disclosure: How Much Is Enough?" *Bankers Monthly*, June 15, 1977, 12-13.

_____. "Problems of the Profession in the United States." *Accountancy* (England), February 1968, 77-80.

Carmichael, D. R. "The Auditor's Role and Responsibilities." *Journal of Accountancy*, August 1977, 55-60.

_____. "Auditor's Statutory Liability to Third Parties: A Landmark Decision." *Texas CPA*, October 1968, 5-12.

_____. "BarChris Case: A Landmark Decision on the Auditor's Statutory Liability to Third Parties." *New York Certified Public Accountant*, November 1968, 780-87.

_____. *Corporate Financial Reporting: The Benefits and Problems of Disclosure.* (Proceedings of a symposium, edited by D. R. Carmichael and B. Makels) New York, 1976, 274 pp.

_____. "Risk and Uncertainty in Financial Reporting and the Auditor's Role." In *Auditing Symposium III* (Touche Ross/University of Kansas Symposium on Auditing Problems, 1976) Lawrence, Kans., 49-73.

_____. "What Does the Independent Auditor's Opinion Really Mean?" Accounting and auditing) *Journal of Accountancy*, November 1974, 83-87.

Catlett, G. R. "Relationship of Auditing Standards to Detection of Fraud." *Arthur Andersen Chronicle*, October 1975, 50-62. Reprinted from *CPA Journal*, April 1975.

Causey, D. Y. "Foreseeability as a Determinant of Audit Responsibility." *Accounting Review*, April 1973, 258-67.

Chandra, G., and M. N. Greenball. "Management Reluctance to Disclosure: An Empirical Study." *Abacus*, December 1977, 141-54.

Chazen, C., and Benjamin Benson. "Fitting GAAP to Smaller Businesses." *Journal of Accountancy*, February 1978, 46-51.

Chirm, R. "Deception of Auditors and False Records." *Journal of Accountancy*, July 1979, 1-72.

Churchman, C. W. "On the Facility, Felicity, and Morality of Measuring Social Change." *Accounting Review*, January 1971, 30-35.

Cohen, M. H. "Regulation through Disclosure." *Journal of Accountancy*, December 1981, 52-62.

Connor, J. E. "Reserve Recognition Accounting: Fact or Fiction?" *Journal of Accountancy*, September 1979, 92-99.

Cook, J. M., and T. P. Kelley. "Internal Accounting Control: A Matter of Law." *Journal of Accountancy*, January 1979, 58-64.

Cooper K.; S. M. Flory; S. D. Grossman; and J. C. Groth. "Reserve Recognition Accounting: A Proposed Disclosure Framework." *Journal of Accountancy*, September 1979, 82-91.

Cowen, S. S. "Nonaudit Services: How Much Is too Much?" *Journal of Accountancy*, December 1980, 51-56.

Cummings, J. P., and M. N. Chetkovich. "World Accounting Enters a New Era." *Journal of Accountancy*, April 1978, 52-62.

Davies, J. "Changing Legal Environment of Public Accounting: Lower Court Applications of the Hochfelder Decision." (Case notes) *American Business Journal*, Winter 1978, 394-401.

Delfliese, P. L. "The Search for a New Conceptual Framework of Accounting." *Journal of Accountancy*, July 1977, 59-67.

Devine, C. T. "Professional Responsibilities: An Empirical Suggestion," with discussion by L. L. Vance and H. J. Davidson. In *Empirical Research in Accounting: Selected Studies.* (Conference on Empirical Research in Accounting) Chicago: University of Chicago Press, May 1966, 160-82. *Financial Executive*, July 1979, 50-57.

DeVos, B. H., Jr. "The Top-down Approach (to the Foreign Corrupt Practices Act)."

"Do the SEC Disclosure Rules Have an Impact on your Small Business?" *SEC Accounting Report*, May 1978, 5-7.

Doyle, B. R. "Three Company Approaches (to the Foreign Corrupt Practices Act): General Electric Company." *Financial Executive*, July 1979, 32-41.

Dyckman, T. R.; H. Downes; and R. P. Magee. *Efficient Capital Markets and Accounting: a Critical Analysis.* Englewood Cliffs, N.J.: Prentice-Hall, 1975, 130 pp.

Earle, V. M. "Accountants on Trial in Theatre of the Absurd." *Fortune*, May 1972, 227-28, 232.

Elliott, R. K., and P. D. Jacobson. "Is Regulation the Answer?" *World* (Peat, Marwick, Mitchell Co.), Spring 1979.

Ellyson, R. C., and W. H. Van Rensselaer. "Sunset—Is the Profession Ready for It?" *Journal of Accountancy*, June 1980, 52-61.

Emery, J. T. "Efficient Capital Markets and the Information Content of Accounting Numbers." *Journal of Financial and Quantitatives Analysis*, March 1974, 139-53.

Estes, R. W. "Accountant's Social Responsibility." *Journal of Accountancy*, January 1970, 40-43.

Fedders, J. M., and L. G. Perry. "Policing Financial Disclosure Fraud: The SEC's Top Priority." *Journal of Accountancy*, July 1984, 58-64.

Financial Accounting Foundation. Structure Committee. *The Structure of Establishing Financial Accounting Standards.* Stamford, Conn., April 1977.

Flom, J. H., and P. A. Atkins. "Expanding Scope of SEC Disclosure Laws." *Harvard Business Review*, July-August 1974, 109-19.

Francia, A. J., and N. J. Elliott. "Significant Differences in Accountants' Professional Liability Insurance Coverage." *New York Certified Public Accountant,* October 1970, 810-15.

Fritzemeyer, J. R. "Seven Rules for Minimizing the Risks of Liability. " (Accounting and auditing problems) *Journal of Accountancy,* June 1969, 64-65.

Gaertner, J. F., and J. A. Ruhe. "Job-Related Stress in Public Accounting." *Journal of Accountancy,* June 1981, 68-74.

Gavin, T. A.; R. L. Hicks; and J. D. Decosimo. "CPAs' Liability to Third Parties." *Journal of Accountancy,* June 1984, 80-88.

Gibson, C. "Analysis of Continental Vending Machine (United States versus Simon)." *Ohio CPA,* Winter 1971, 8-16.

Gregory, W. R. "Unaudited, but OK?" *Journal of Accountancy,* February 1978, 61-65.

Hagerman, R. L. "Metcalf Report: Selling Some Assumptions." *Management Accounting (NAA),* January 1978, 13-16.

Hanggi, G. A., Jr. "Media Advertising as a Practice Development Tool." *Journal of Accountancy,* January 1980, 54-58.

Hampson, J. J. "Accountants' Liability: The Significance of Hochfelder." *Journal of Accountancy,* December 1976, 69-74.

Hanson, R. E., and C. R. Lees. "IRS Examination of Accountants' Workpapers." *Journal of Accountancy,* April 1977, 60-65.

Hanson, R. E., and W. J. Brown. "CPAs' Workpapers: The IRS Zeroes In." *Journal of Accountancy,* July 1981, 68-76.

Hearn, L. "On the Philosophy of Sartor Resartus." *Interpretations of Literature.* Vol. 1, edited by J. Erskine. New York: Dodd, Mead and Co., 1915, 208-32.

Helstein R. S. "Guidelines for Professional Liability Insurance Coverage." *CPA Journal,* October 1973, 849-55.

Henry, W. O. E., et al. "Responsibilities and Liabilities of Auditors and Accountants." *Business Lawyer,* March 1975, 169-205.

Hepp, G. W., and T. W. McRae. "Accounting Standards Overload: Relief Is Needed." *Journal of Accountancy,* May 1982, 52-62.

Herwitz, D. R. "Right to Know." In *Objectives of Financial Statements, vol. 2, Selected Papers,* by the American Institute of Certified Public Accountants, Accounting Objectives Study Group. New York, 1974, 55-56.

Hickok, R. S. "Looking to the Future: A Key to Success." *Journal of Accountancy,* March 1984, 77-82.

Hill, T. W., Jr. "Public Accountant's Legal Liability to Clients and Others." *New York Certified Public Accountant,* January 1958, 21-31.

Hinsey, J. "The Foreign Corrupt Practice Act: The Legislation as Enacted." *Financial Executive,* July 1979, 12-18.

Horngren, C. "The Marketing of Accounting Standards." *Journal of Accountancy,* October 1973, 61-66.

Ihlanfeldt, W. J. "Three Company Approaches [to the Foreign Corrupt Practices Act]: Shell Oil Company." *Financial Executive,* July 1979, 42-49.

Ijiri Y. "Oil and Gas Accounting: Turbulence in Financial Reporting." *Financial Executive,* August 1979, 18-27.

————. *Theory of Accounting Measurement.* Sarasota, Fla.: American Accounting Association, 1975.

Isbell, D. B. "Overview of Accountants' Duties and Liabilities under the Federal Securities Laws and a Closer Look at Whistle-Blowing." *Ohio State Law Journal*, 1974, 261-79.

_____. "Rules for Being Sued." (Practitioners forum) *Journal of Accountancy*, April 1972, 84.

Jacobson, P. D., and R. K. Elliott. "GASS: Reconsidering the 'Ten Commandments.' " *Journal of Accountancy*, May 1984, 77-88.

Kaplan, R. S. "Should Accounting Standards Be Set in the Public or Private Sector?" (Working paper, Carnegie-Mellon University, Pittsburgh, April 1979). In *Regulation and the Accounting Profession* (proceedings). Los Angeles: University of California, 1980.

Kay, R. S. "How to Detect Illegal Activity." *Touche Ross Tempo*, 1976, 7-10.

Keane, J. G. "The Marketing Perspective: The CPA's New Image." *Journal of Accountancy*, January 1980, 60-66.

Killpack, J. R. "Disclosure—to Whom—and How Much." *Ohio CPA*, Summer 1977, 59-64.

Kirk, D. J.; J. J. Leisenring; and P. Pacter. "The FASB's Second Decade." *Journal of Accountancy*, November 1983, 89-96; December 1983, 94-102.

Kripke, H. *The SEC and Corporate Disclosure: Regulation in Search of a Purpose.* New York: Law and Business, Inc., a subsidiary of Harcourt Brace and Jovanovich, 1979.

_____. "Where Are We on Securities Disclosure after the Advisory Committee Report?" *Securities Regulation Law Journal*, Summer 1978, 99-132; *Journal of Accounting, Auditing and Finance*, Fall 1978, 4-32.

Krogstad, J. L.; M. E. Stark; K. L. Fox; and H. O. Lytle, Jr. "The Faculty Residency: A Concept Worth Considering." *Journal of Accountancy*, November 1981, 74-86.

Lantry, T. L. "Judges as Accountants." (Comments) *American Business Law Journal*, Spring 1975, 108-18.

Larson, C. B. "Directors for CPA Firms: A Provocative Proposal." *Journal of Accountancy*, May 1983, 86-94.

Larson, R. E., and T. P. Kelley. "Differential Measurement in Accounting Standards: The Concept Makes Sense." *Journal of Accountancy*, November 1984, 78-90.

Lee, B. Z.; R. E. Larson; and P. B. Chenok. "Issues Confronting the Accounting Profession." *Journal of Accountancy*, November 1983, 78-85.

Lev, B. "The Impact of Accounting Regulation on the Stock Market: The Case of Oil and Gas Companies." *Accounting Review*, July 1979, 485-503.

Levine, A. I., and E. S. Marks. "Accountants' Liability Insurance: Perils and Pitfalls." *Journal of Accountancy*, October 1976, 59-64.

Loscalzo, M. A. "What Is Peer Review All About?" *Journal of Accountancy*, October 1979, 78-82.

Madison, J. "The Federalist Papers." (Nos. 10 and 51) New York: New American Library, 1961, 77-84, 320-25.

Mautz, R. K. "Self-Regulation-Criticisms and a Response." *Journal of Accountancy*, April 1984, 56-66.

_____. "Self-Regulation-Perils and Problems." *Journal of Accountancy*, May 1983, 76-84.

Mautz, R. K., and R. D. Neary. "Corporate Audit Committee—Quo Vadis?" *Journal of Accountancy*, October 1979, 83-88.

Madnick, R. "Transaction Flow Auditing." *Financial Executive*, July 1979, 58-64.

Miller, H. E., and S. Davidson. "Accreditation: Two Views." *Journal of Accountancy*, March 1978, 56-65.

Minow, N. N. "Accountants' Liability and the Litigation Explosion." *Journal of Accountancy*, September 1984, 70-72, 76-86.

Moran, M., and G. J. Previts. "The SEC and the Profession, 1934-84: The Realities of Self-Regulation." *Journal of Accountancy*, July 1984, 68-80.

Mundhelm, R. H. "Selected Trends in Disclosure Requirements for Public Corporations." *Securities Regulation Law Journal*, Spring 1975, 3-32.

Murphy, T. A. "Setting Accounting Standards:A Suggestion from a Businessman." *Financial Executive*, August 1979, 52-57.

"National Student Marketing, Law Firm, and Auditors Sued." (News report) *Journal of Accountancy*, March 1972, 10, 12-13.

Nelson, A. T. "Accounting Education's Coming Crisis." *Journal of Accounting*, April 1983, 70-80.

Olson, W. e. "The Accounting Profession in the 1900s." *Journal of Accountancy*, July 1979, 54-60.

_____. "How Should a Profession Be Disciplined?" *Journal of Accountancy*, May 1978, 56-66.

_____. "Self-Regulation:What's Ahead?" *Journal of Accountancy*, March 1980, 46-49.

_____. "Specialization: Search for a Solution." *Journal of Accountancy*, September 1982, 70-79.

Pacter, P. A. "The Conceptual Framework: Make No Mystique about It." *Journal of Accountancy*, July 1983, 76-88.

Palmer, R. E. "Audit Committees:Are They Effective? An Auditor's View." *Journal of Accountancy*, September 1977, 76-79.

Pearson, D. B. "Will Accreditation Improve the Quality of Education?" *Journal of Accountancy*, April 1979, 53-58.

Pollock, K. "What's Been Happening to Auditing Since Equity Funding." *GAO Review*, Spring 1977, 62-64.

Prakash, P., and B. L. Lewis. "Consequences Issue: The Accounting Paradigm for the Eighties." (Working paper) Pittsburgh: University of Pittsburgh, April 1979.

Prentice-Hall. *Accountants on the Firing Line: What Accountants, Corporate Managers, and Lawyers Must Know about Accountants' New and Expanded Duties.* Englewood Cliffs, N.J., 1975, 16 pp.

Previts, G. J., and E. N. Coffman. "Practice and Education: Bridging the Gap." *Journal of Accountancy*, December 1980, 39-45.

"Proposed Regulation of the Profession." *Week in Review* (Deloitte Haskins and Sells), June 16, 1978, 1-3.

Rappaport, A. "The Strategic Audit." *Journal of Accountancy*, June 1980, 71-77.

Relser, R. E. "Financial Analysts Federation's Response to the Securities and Exchange Commission's Committee on Corporate Disclosure." *Financial Analysts Journal*, March-April 1977, 12-14, 174-75.

Rolfe, R. S., and R. J. Davis. "Scienter and Rule 10b-5." (Notes) *Columbia Law Review*, June 1969, 1057-83. Reprinted in *Securities Law Review*, 1970, 173-204.

Saxe, E. "Accountants' Responsibility for Unaudited Financial Statements." *New York Certified Public Accountant*, June 1971, 419-23; *Massachusetts CPA Review*, July-August 1971, 21-24; *Michigan CPA* November-December 1971, 5-7.

Schnepper, J. A. "Accountants' Liability under Rule 10b-5 and Section 10(b) of the Securities Exchange Act of 1934: The Hole in Hochfelder." *Accounting Review*, July 1977, 653-57.

"Scienter and SEC Injunction Suits." *Harvard Law Review*, March 1977, 1018-28.

"SEC Acts on Recommendations of Disclosure Advisory Group." (News report) *Journal of Accountancy*, April 1978, 12, 14.

"SEC and Accountants' Liability under Statute Law." In *Auditing Theory and Practice*, by R. H. Hermanson et al. (Homewood, Ill.: 1976), 85-117.

"SEC Disclosure Committee Issues Final Report." *SEC Accounting Report*, January 1978, 6-7.

"SEC Issues Plans to Implement Advisory Committee Recommendations." *SEC Accounting Report*, May 1978, 7-8.

"SEC Survey Shows Investor Reliance on Annual Reports." (News report) *Journal of Accountancy*, October 1977, 14, 16.

"Securities Acts—Federal Securities Exchange Act—Stock Purchases by Insiders Possessing Material Inside Information, and Misleading Corporate Press Release Unrelated to Securities Transactions by Corporation, Violate SEC Rule 10b-5-SEC V. Texas Gulf Sulphur Co." (Recent cases) *Harvard Law Review*, February 1969, 938-51.

Securities and Exchange Commission. Advisory Committee on Corporate Disclosure. *Report of the Advisory Committee on Corporate Disclosure*, November 1977.

Siegel, G. "Specialization and Segmentation in the Accounting Profession." *Journal of Accountancy*, November 1977, 74-80.

Simonetti, G. "Corporate Accountability System under Fire." *Price Waterhouse Review*, 1977, 2-9.

Skousen, K. F. "Accounting Education: The New Professionalism." *Journal of Accountancy*, July 1977, 54-58.

Slavin, N. S. "The Elimination of Scienter in Determining the Auditor's Statutory Liability." *Accounting Review*, April 1977, 360-68.

_____. "Origin of the Present Structure of the Public Accounting Profession:A Historical Analysis, Parts 1 and 2," *National Public Accountant*, August 1977, 15-18; September 1977, 38-42.

Sloan, D. R. "The Education of the Professional Accountant." *Journal of Accountancy*, March 1983, 56-60.

Smith, B. E. "Reaching the Public: The CPA's New Image." *Journal of Accountancy*, January 1980, 47-52.

Solomons, D. "The Politicization of Accounting." *Journal of Accountancy*, November 1978, 65-73.

Sommer, A. A. "Financial Reporting and the Stock Market: The Other Side." *Financial Executive*, May 1974, 36-40.

_____. "The Limits of Disclosure." *Financial Executive*, October 1975, 46-50, 52-54.

_____. "Neglected Dimension of Financial Reporting." (Statements in quotes) *Journal of Accountancy*, April 1974, 71-74.

Sommer, A. A., Jr. "The Lion and the Lamb: Can the Profession Live with 'Cooperative Regulation'?" *Journal of Accountancy*, April 1978, 70-76.

Spicer, B. H. "Investors, Corporate Social Performance, and Information Disclosure: An Empirical Study." *Accounting Review*, January 1978.

Sprouse, R. I. "The Importance of Earnings in the Conceptual Framework." *Journal of Accountancy*, January 1978.

Sterling, R. R. *Institutional Issues in Public Accounting*. Lawrence, Kans.: Scholars Book Co. 1974, 9.

Sunder, S. "Towards a Theory of Accounting Choice: Private and Social Decisions." (Working paper) Chicago: University of Chicago Press, January 1979.

"Texas Gulf Sulphur: Expanding Concepts of Corporate Disclosure under SEC Rule 10b-5." (Notes) *St. John's Law Review*, January 1969, 425-55; April 1969, 655-85.

Thorne, R. D. "AICPA's Special Advisory Committee on Management Reports." *Financial Executive*, July 1979, 65-67.

Touche Ross & Co. *Response to the Report of Tentative Conclusions of the Commission on Auditors' Responsibilities*. New York: Touche Ross & Co. July 22, 1977, i-vi.

Touche Ross/University of Kansas Symposium on Auditing Problems, *Auditing Looks Ahead*. Lawrence, Kans., 1972.

Trienens, H. J. "Legal Aspects of Fair Value Accounting." *Financial Executives* January 1973, 30-32, 34, 38.

Turner, J. N. "International Harmonization: A Professional Goal." *Journal of Accountancy*, January 1983, 58-66.

"Two Auditors Found Guilty in Student Marketing Case." (News report) *Journal of Accountancy*, January 1975, 8, 10.

United States Senate. Committee on Government Operations. Subcommittee on Reports, Accounting and Management. *Accounting and Auditing Practices and Procedures (Hearing)*, 1977.

_____. *Accounting Establishment: A Staff Study*, 1976.

Vance. L. L. "Changing Responsibilities of the Public Accountant." (Stanford, Calif.: Stanford University, 1970, 16. (*Stanford Lectures in Accounting*, presented by the Graduate School of Business, Stanford University, under Sponsorship of the Price Waterhouse Foundation, June 5, 1970.)

Warren, C. S. "Audit Risk." *Journal of Accountancy*, August 1979, 66-74.

Watts, R. L., and J. L. Zimmerman. "Auditors and the Determination of Accounting Standards." (Working paper) Rochester, N.Y.: University of Rochester, March 1979.

_____. "The Demand and Supply of Accounting Theories: The Market for Excuses." *Accounting Review*, April 1979, 273-305.

_____. "Toward a Positive Theory of the Determination of Accounting Standards." *Accounting Review*, January 1978, 112-34.

"When Accountants Hire Private Detectives." (Management) *Business Week*, June 30, 1975, 104.

White, G. I. "More on Current Trends in Corporate Disclosure: Comment and Reply." (Professional notes) *Journal of Accountancy*, August 1978, 42, 44-46, 48.

Wiesen, J. "Securities Acts and Independent Auditors: What Did Congress Intend?" In *Commission on Auditors' Responsibilities Research Study, No. 2* New York: American Institute of Certified Public Accountants, 1978, 52.

Williams, H. M. "Audit Committees: The Public Sector's View." *Journal of Accountancy* September 1977, 71-74.

"World's Most Audited Auditor." (Businessmen in the news) *Fortune*, August 1975, 38.

"You Can't Legislate Accounting Principles." *Forbes*, October 2, 1978, 90, 93, 95.

Zeff, S. A. "The Rise of 'Economic Consequences,' " *Journal of Accountancy*, December 1978, 56-83.

INDEX

AAERs, 152

Accountants. *See* Accounting profession; Certified Public Accountants

Accounting: accrual basis of, 43-44; cash-flow accounting, 43-44; creative, 49; defined, 3; financial, 17, 145-48; framework of, 3; future scope of, 39-47; human-resource, 41-42; reporting to employees, 44-45; socio-economic, 39-41; useful fields for, 3; value-added reporting, 45-47. *See also* Financial Accounting Standards Board

Accounting and auditing enforcement releases (AAERs), 152

Accounting and review services, knowledge, skills and abilities required of CPAs for, 58

Accounting and Review Services Committee (ARSC), 19

Accounting costs, reducing, 114

Accounting equation, 7, 25

Accounting Establishment, The, 11

Accounting firms. *See* "Big Eight" accounting firms; CPA Firms

Accounting needs, self-analysis of, 114

Accounting-period postulate, 24

Accounting postulates, 22, 23-24; accounting-period, 24; continuity, 23-24; entity, 23; going-concern, 23-24; unit-of-measure, 24

Accounting practices: in Colonial America, 7-8; history of, 6-9; impact of federal income tax on, 8-9. *See also* Generally Accepted Accounting Principles

Accounting principles, 22, 27-33; choice of, to smooth the net income series, 47; comparability, 32-33; conservatism, 31-32; consistency, 29-30; cost, 27; full-disclosure, 30-31; matching, 28-29; materiality, 32; need for standards for, 52; objectivity, 29; revenue, 27-28; substantive authoritative support concept as basis for, 153, 179; uniformity, 32-33. *See also* Generally Accepted Accounting Principles

Accounting Principles Board (APB), 10; accounting research studies issued by, 10; contribution to GAAP, 10-11; criticism of, 10-11; establishment of, 10, 52; financial statement user groups defined by, 17-18, 175-76; opinions issued by, 10; reasons for replacement of, 132; replaced as standard-setting body by Accounting Standards Board, 52, 132, 153; replacing Committee on Accounting Procedure, 10, 52; statements issued by, 10, 17-18, 175-76

Accounting procedures, justifying changes in, 30

Accounting profession: accreditation of specialists proposed for, 78-81; attitudes to, 107-9; common liability to clients, 122-23; common liability to third parties, 123-24; conflict between management-advisory services and audit function, 101; criminal liability under federal and state laws, 126; criticism of self-regulation in, 55-56; future issues for, 82-86; government regulation of, 53-54, 69-70; importance of independence to, 100-103; importance of sunset review to, 67-69; liability under Federal Securities laws, 124-26; liability under Foreign Corrupt Practices Act, 126; origin of, 10; peer regulation of, 54, 154; peer-review in, 54-55, 70-75, 154, 180; private regulation of, 53, 54, 70; privity-of-contract doctrine applied to, 123; professionalism vs. commercialism in, 75-77, 118, 181; public regulation of, 53-54, 69-70; regulation of, 53-56, 69-75, 154, 180; role of public oversight board in regulation of, 55; search for mandatory guidance for, 6; sex-bias applied to partnerships in, 109-11; sources of legal liability for, 122-26; specialization in, 77-82, 181; standard-setting for, 51-53 (*see also* Accounting standards; Financial Accounting Standards Board; Generally Accepted Accounting Principles); voluntary self-regulation preferred by, 54-56; women in, 109-11. *See also* Auditors; Certified Public Accountants; CPA firms

Accounting research bulletins (ARBs), 10, 52

Accounting research studies (ARSs), 10

Accounting series releases (ASRs), 5-6, 151, 152-53

Accounting standards: costs of compliance with, 15-16, 20-21, 142; first established in 1930s, 131-32; lead set by AICPA, 51-53; proliferation of bodies involved in, 140; shorter reports called for, 145. *See also* Accounting standards overload; Financial Accounting Standards Board; Generally Accepted Accounting Principles

Accounting Standards Executive Committee (AcSEC): issue papers prepared by, 53; responding to proposals from FASB and SEC, 52; statements of position issued by, 51, 52-53

Accounting standards overload, 14, 139-45, 181-82; AICPA recommendations and FASB responses, 143-44; effects of, 15-16, 20-21, 141-42: nature and cause of, 139-40; solutions of, 142-44

Accounting Terminology Bulletins (ATB), 10

Accounting theory: accounting postulates in, 22, 23-24; accounting principles in, 22, 27-33; structure of, 21-23; theoretical concepts of accounting in, 22, 25-27

Accounting Trends and Techniques, 6

Accrual basis of accounting, 43; compared with cash-flow, 43-44

Acquisition cost, 35

AcSEC. *See* Accounting Standards Executive Committee

ADAPSO. *See* Association of Data Processing Organizations

Additional paid-in capital, 35

Adequate disclosure, 30

Advertising by CPAs, AICPA policy statement on, 120

AICPA. *See* American Institute of Certified Public Accountants

AICPA Technical Practice Aids, 6

American Accounting Association, cosponsoring FASB, 132

American Institute of Certified Public Accountants (AICPA), 180-81; Accounting and Review Services Committee created by, 19; Accounting Standards Executive Committee of, 51-53; Accounting Principles Board established by, 10 (*see also* Accounting Principles Board); accounting research bulletins issued by, 10; accounting terminology bulletins issued by, 10; audit committees recommended by, 95-96; Commission on

Auditor's Responsibilities, 95, 101, 106, 163-65, 171, Committee on Accounting Procedure established by, 10 (*see also* Committee on Accounting Procedure); Committee on Scope and Structure, 78; Division for CPA firms established to promote peer-review, 54-55, 56, 71; examinations set by, 51, 108; issues considered by Future Issues Committee, 82-86; knowledge, skills and abilities list developed by, 56-63; and modification of GAAP for small businesses, 18-20; National Automated Accounting Research System of, 53; non-CPA associate membership proposed by, 81-82; peer-review proposed by, 54-55 (*see also* Peer review); position on non-audit services, 102-3, 158-59; position on scope of services provided, 102-3, 158-59; publications by, 6, 10, 14, 89-90; Public Oversight Board, 101, 102, 158; relationship with FASB, 4, 52, 136-37; report of Special Committee on Solicitation, 119-20; self-regulation favored by, 54-56, 180; Special Committee on Accounting Standards Overload, 14, 142-43 (*see also* Accounting standards overload); standard-setting role of, 11-13, 51-53, 180 (*see also* Accounting standards); Statements on Auditing Standards issued by, 14, 89-90; Wheat Committee, 132; work activities list developed by, 63-67. *See also* Accounting profession; Certified Public Accountants
American Institute of Certified Public Accountants Code of Professional Ethics: preventing specialization, 80-81; Rule 101 emphasizing independence, 100; Rule 203 defining relationship with FASB, 4, 52, 136; Rule 204 defining relationship with FASB, 4-6; Rule 502 on solicitation, 119, 120
Antitrust laws, applied to ban on solicitation of clients by CPAs, 119
APB. *See* Accounting Principles Board
ARBs, 10, 52

ARSC, 19
Arthur Andersen & Co., 111-12, 121. *See also* "Big Eight" accounting firms
Arthur Young & Co. *See* "Big Eight" accounting firms
ASR. *See* Accounting series releases
Assets: characteristics of, 33-34; current, 34; defined for entity theory, 26; defined for fund theory, 26; fixed, 34; intangible, 34; investments as, 34; valuation of, 35, 37
Association of Data Processing Organizations (ADAPSO), 102
ATB, 10
Audit, determining need for, 113
Audit committees, 92-99; bias of members of, 98; challenges facing, 97-99; Cohen Report recommending, 95; duties set down by Protection of Shareholders Act, 96-97; Metcalf Committee recommending, 96; New York Stock Exchange statements on, 95; qualified CPAs to serve on, 98; recommended by AICPA, 95-96; role of, 92-93; SEC outline of responsibilities of, 94-95; skills and qualifications required for members of, 97-98, support for, 93-94; variations in performance of, 99
Audit Committees 1984 (Deloitte, Haskins and Sells), 99
Auditing, 182; knowledge, skills and abilities required of CPA's for, 57-58
Auditing costs, reducing, 114
Auditing Standards Board, 164
Auditing Standards Executive Committee (AuSEC): on meaning of "present fairly", 165-66; proposing changes in auditor's report, 164-66; statements of position issued by, 51
Auditor independence: defined, 101-2; enhancing, 103; importance of, 100-103; "low balling" affecting, 106-7; sec position on, 158-59; threatened by performance of nonaudit services, 100-103, 158-59
Auditors: changing, 98-99, 104, 106; changing to obtain a different opinion,

111-12; Cohen Report on responsibilities of, 95, 101, 106, 163-65, 171; Internal Revenue Service access to work papers of, 90-92; rights and responsibilities under Securities Act of 1933, 124-26; role in evaluating internal control, 89-90; sources of legal liability for, 122-26. *See also* Audit committees; Auditor independence; Auditor's standard report
Auditor's opinion section in financial statement, 38-39
Auditor's Report, The, 174
Auditors standard report, 182; adverse opinion in, 170; current form, 162-63; current form criticized, 163; disclaimer of opinion in, 170; early forms of, 161-62; emphasis paragraph in, 171-72; generally accepted auditing standards for, 167-68; interpretations of auditor's responsibility, 172-77; interpreted as dual opinion, 174-75; interpreted as opinion on conformity with GAAP, 175-76; interpreted as opinion on fairness, 173-74; proposed changes in, 164-67; qualified opinions in, 170-71, 172; split opinion in, 171; "subject-to" qualification in, 170, 171; unqualified, 168-70
Audit work activities of Certified Public Accountants, 64-65
AuSEC. *See* Auditing Standards Executive Committee

Balance sheet, 33-35
Basic accounting method, 143
"Big Eight" accounting firms: in competition with local firms, 103-5; control of standard-setting process by, 11-13; moving from primary market to middle market, 103-4; small business divisions developed by, 104; women partners in, 110. *See also* CPA firms
Book value per share, 25
Business law, knowledge, skills and abilities required of CPAs for, 58-59

Canadian Institute of Public Accountants (CICA), 175
CAP. *See* Committee on Accounting Procedure
Capitalized value, 35
Capital stock, 35
Cash-flow accounting, 43-44; compared with accrual accounting, 43-44
Certified Public Accountants (CPAs), 181; accounting and revenue services, knowledge, skills and abilities required of, 58; auditing knowledge, skills and abilities required of, 57-58; audit work activities of, 64-65; business law knowledge, skills and abilities required of, 58-59; in corporate hierarchy, 108-9; cost/management accounting knowledge, skills and abilities required of, 61; effect of accounting standards overload on, 141; engagement management and administration activities of, 63-64; federal taxation knowledge, skills and abilities required of, 61-63; financial accounting knowledge, skills and abilities required of, 59-60; financial statement knowledge, skills and abilities required of, 57; improving image of, 107-9; knowledge, skills and abilities required by, 56-63; licensing examinations for, 51, 108; management advisory services work activities of, 66; office and firm administration work activities of, 67; privilege of confidentiality rejected by Supreme Court, 91; professional literature knowledge, skills and abilities required of, 56-57; professional services work activities of, 66-67; relationship with clients, 126-28; selection guide, 112-16; solicitation of clients by. *See* Solicitation of clients; tax work activities of, 65-66; types of services provided by, 112-13; work activities list for, 63-67; working paper knowledge, skills and abilities required of,

57. *See also* Accounting profession; Auditors; CPA firms

Certified Public Consultant (CPC), 79

Certified Public Examiner (CPE), 79

Certified Public Generalist (CPG), 79

Certified Public Tax Adviser (CPTA), 79

CICA, 175

CICA Handbook, 175

Circumstantial variables, 33

Cohen Report, 95, 101, 106, 163-65, 171

Commercialism in accounting, 75-77, 118, 181

Commission on Auditors' Responsibilities, 95, 101, 106, 163-65, 171

Committee on Accounting Procedures (CAP): accounting research bulletins issued by, 10, 52; ad hoc approach to problems, 52; contribution to GAAP, 10, 52, 132; criticism of, 10-11; establishment of, 10, 50; replaced by Accounting Principles Board, 10, 52

Common-stock equivalents, 36

Comparability principle, 32-33

Conservatism, reasons for, 31

Conservatism principle, 31-32

Consistency principle, 29-30

Continuity postulate, 23-24

Contractual liability, applied to accountants, 122

Coopers & Lybrand, 112, 121. *See also* "Big Eight" accounting firms

Corporate concept of income, 25

Corporate financial forecasts, public reporting of, 42

Corporate Report, The, 44

Cost, 27

Cost/managerial accounting theory and practice: knowledge, skills and abilities required of CPAs for, 61

Cost-of-goods sold, methods for valuing, 36

Cost principle, 27

CPA firms, 181; competition between, 103-5, 106-7; ideal for, outlined, 116-17; "low-balling" by, 106-7; providing consulting services for law firms, 105-6; selection of, 112-16; sex-bias applied to partnerships in, 109-11; "up-or-out" policy, 110-11; women partners in, 110. *See also* "Big Eight" accounting firms

CPAs. *See* Certified Public Accountants

CPC. *See* Certified Public Consultant

CPE. *See* Certified Public Examiner

CPG. *See* Certified Public Generalist

CPTA. *See* Certified Public Tax Adviser

Creative accounting, 49; defeasance as, 49-50

Current assets, 34

Current entry value, 35

Current exit value, 35

Current liabilities, 34

Defeasance, 49-50

Deloitte Haskins and Sells, 111, 112. *See also* "Big Eight" accounting firms

Dividend per share, 25

Double-entry bookkeeping, first described in 1494, 6-7

Earnings per share, 25; for income statement, 36-37

Economic Recovery Act of 1982, 14

EDGAR, 151

Employee reporting, 44-45

Engagement letter, contents of, 114

Engagement management and administration, work activities of CPAs involved in, 63-64

Entity equation, 25-26

Entity postulate, 23

Entity theory, 25-26

Equity, defined for entity theory, 26

Ernst & Whinney, 121. *See also* "Big Eight" accounting firms

Exchange price, 27

Expenses: defined for proprietary theory, 25; for income statement, 35-36

Extinguishment of Debt, FASB Statement No. 76, 49

FAF. *See* Financial Accounting Foundation

Fair disclosure, 30
Fair presentation concept, 152; debate on, 165-66, 172-77
FASB. *See* Financial Accounting Standards Board
Federal Securities laws, accountants' liability under, 124-26
Federal taxation, knowledge, skills and abilities required of CPAs for, 61-63
FIFO, 36
Financial accounting, basic features of, 17
Financial accounting and reporting, conceptual framework for, 145-48
Financial Accounting Foundation (FAF), 53, 132
Financial Accounting Standards Board (FASB): accounting series releases issued by, 6; conceptual framework project of, 138, 145-48, 182; cosponsoring organizations for, 132; creation of, 131-32; definition of public company by, 16; definition of small company by, 16; due-process procedure of, 134-35; endorsed by Rules 203 and 204 of AICPA Code of Professional Ethics, 4-6, 52, 136; establishment of, 11; interpretations made by, 4, 135; membership of, 132-33; mission of, 133-34; and modification of GAAP for small businesses, 19-20; political aspects of standard-setting process, 10-13; position of defeasance, 49; position on small businesses, 17-18; performance of, 137-38; relationship with accounting profession, 4-6; relationship with SEC and AICPA, 136-37, 181; relationship with SEC clarified, 5-6; replacing Accounting Principles Board as standard-setting body, 42, 132, 153; response to AICPA recommendations for relieving accounting standards overload, 143-44; standard-setting by, 53, 135-36, 181-82 (*see also* Accounting standards overload); statements issued by, 17, 19, 39, 49; statements of financial accounting stan-

dards issued by, 4, 135; structure of, 132-33; technical bulletins issued by, 135-36
Financial accounting theory and practice: knowledge, skills and abilities required of CPAs for, 59-60
Financial Analysts Federation, cosponsoring FASB, 132
Financial Executive Institute, cosponsoring FASB, 132
Financial Reporting and Changing Prices, FASB Statement No. 33, 39
Financial Reporting for Segments of a Business Enterprise, FASB Statement No. 14, 17
Financial statements, 33-39, 180; auditor's opinion section, 38-39; balance sheet, 33-35; differences among users of, 16-18; income statement, 33-37; knowledge, skills and abilities required of CPAs for, 57; misleading, 157-58; notes to, 38-39; reconciliation of retained earnings section, 38; statement of changes in financial position, 37-38; supplementary information on the effects of changing prices, 39; user groups identified, 17; value-added statement, 45-47
First in-first out method for cost of goods sold, 36
Fixed assets, 34
Foreign Corrupt Practices Act of 1977, 89, 126, 149
Foreseen party, legal liability to, 124
Forty Questions and Answers about Audit Reports, 176
Fox & Company, 121
Full disclosure, 30
Full-disclosure principle, 30-31
Fully diluted earnings per share, 36-37
Funds, defined for statement of changes in financial position, 37-38
Fund theory, 26-27

GAAP. *See* Generally accepted accounting principles
GAAS. *See* Generally accepted auditing

standards

Generally accepted accounting principles (GAAP): alternatives to, 14-15, 142-43, 179-80; authoritative support for, 4; contribution of Accounting Principles Board to, 10-11; contribution of Committee on Accounting Procedure to, 10-11; development of, 9-13; flexibility of, 48; importance of conformity with, for audits, 175, 176; management-contribution phase of development of, 9-10; meaning of, 3-6; professional-contribution phase of development of, 10-11; political phase of development of, 11-13; small business problems with, 15-16; specialized for different circumstances, 14, 179-80; standard-setting bodies involved in, 4-6 (*see also* American Institute of Certified Public Accountants, Financial Accounting Standards Board). *See also* Other Comprehensive Bases of Accounting

Generally accepted accounting principles for small businesses: debated, 15-18; objections to, 20; official positions on, 20, 180; suggested, 14, 180. *See also* Accounting standards overload

Generally accepted auditing standards (GAAS), 166, 167-68, 176

Going-concern postulate, 23-24

Government regulation, 53-54, 69-70

HR. 13175, 70-71

Human resource accounting, 41-42; defined, 42; measures for, 42

Improving the Accountability of Publicly Owned Corporations and Their Auditors, 96, 101

Income, defined for entity theory, 26

Income-smoothing, 47-48; characteristics of firms attempting, 48; motivations for, 47; options for methods, 48

Income statement, 33-37; categories in, 36; value-added statement derived from, 45-46

Insider trading, 155-57; definition of, 156; legislation to control, 155-56; SEC drive against, 156

Institute of Management Consultants, certified management consultants accredited by, 81

Intangible assets, 34

Internal accounting control, responsibility for, 89-90

Internal Revenue Service: authority to summons documents given by Section 7602 of Code, 90; court decisions on access to auditor's work papers, 90-91; questions raised by policy on seeking auditor's work papers, 91-92

Investment Advisors Act of 1940, 149, 156

Investment Company Act of 1940, 149

Investments, as assets, 34

Journal of Accounting, The, 51

Knowledge, skills and abilities, for CPAs, 56-63

Large company, defined, 16

Last in-first out method for cost of goods sold, 36

Law firms, CPA firms providing consulting for, 105-6

Liabilities, 34-35; characteristics of, 34; current, 34; defined for fund theory, 26; long-term, 35; valuation of, 35, 37

LIFO. *See* Last in-first out

"Little GAAP." *See* Generally accepted accounting principles for small businesses

Local CPA firms, in competition with "Big Eight" accounting firms, 103-4. *See also* CPA firms

Long-term liabilities, 35

"Low balling," 106-7

Management advisory services: contents of proposal for, 116; possible conflicts with audit function, 101; selecting a firm for, 115; types of, 115; work activities of CPAs involved in, 66

Managerial accounting; knowledge, skills and abilities required of CPAs for, 61

Matching, for accrual basis of accounting, 43

Matching principle, 28-29

Materiality: change criterion approach to, 32; size approach to, 32

Materiality principle, 32

Material non-public information, defined, 156. *See also* Insider trading

Metcalf Report, 96, 101

Middle market, for auditors, 104

Misleading financial statements, 157-58

Modern Corporation and Private Property, The (Berle and Means), 9-10

Moss Bill, 70-71

NAARS, 53

National Association of Accountants, cosponsoring FASB, 132

National Automated Accounting Research System (NAARS), 53

Negligence liability, applied to accountants, 122-23

Net realizable value, 35

New York Stock Exchange (NYSE), statements on audit committees, 95

Nonaudit services: AICPA position on, 102-3, 158-89; benefits of, for clients, 102-3; legal liability arising from, 123; performance of, threatening independence of auditors, 100-103, 158-59; SEC position on, 158-59

Notes to financial statements, 38-39

NYSE. *See* New York Stock Exchange

Objectivity principle, 29

OCBOA. *See* Other Comprehensive Bases of Accounting

Office and firm administration work activities of CPAs, 67

Opinion paragraph, in auditor's report, 169-70

Other Comprehensive Bases of Accounting (OCBOA), 143, 179-80; criteria for, 14; problems presented by, 14-15. *See also* Generally Accepted Accounting Principles

Owner's equity, 26, 35

Partnerships: bias applied to advancement, 109-11; federal law applied to, 110-11

PCPS. *See* Private Companies Practice Section

Peat, Marwick, Mitchell & Co., 111, 112, 121-22. *See also* "Big Eight" accounting firms

Peer regulation, 54

Peer-review, 54-55, 70-75, 154, 180; criticism of, 74-75; procedures of, 71-74

POB. *See* Public Oversight Board

Price Waterhouse & Co. *See* "Big Eight" accounting firms

Primary beneficiary, liability to, 123

Primary earnings per share, 36

Primary market, for auditors, 104

Private Companies Practice Section (PCPS), established for peer-review, 54-55, 71, 75

Private company, defined, 16

Private regulation, 53, 54, 70

Privity-of-contract doctrine, 123

Professionalism vs. commercialism in accounting, 75-77, 118, 181

Professional literature for CPAs, 56-57

Professional services activities of CPAs, 66-67

Property, plant and equipment, as assets, 34

Proprietary theory, 25

Protection of Shareholders Act of 1980, duties of audit committees set down by, 96-97;

Public company, FASB definition of, 16

Public Oversight Board (POB), 55, 101, 158

Public regulation, 53-54

Public Relations Guide for CPAs, 108

Public Utility Holding Act of 1935, 149

Recommendations and Comments on Financial Reporting to Shareholders and Related Matters (NYSE), 95

Registration requirements of SEC, 150-51

Regulation of accounting profession: government, 53-54, 69-70; peer, 54, 154 (*see also* Peer-review); private, 53, 54, 70; public, 53-55, 69-70; self, 54-56, 154, 180

Reliability, and objectivity principle, 29

Replacement cost, 35

Report of the Commission on Auditors' Responsibilities, 95

Report of the Special Advisory Committee on Internal Accounting Control, 89

Retained earnings, 35

Revenue, 27; defined for proprietary theory, 25; recognizing for income statement, 35; timing of, 28

Revenue principle, 27-28

SAB. *See* Staff accounting bulletins

SAS. *See* Statements on Auditing Standards

Scienter requirement, 124

Scope of Services by the CPA Firms, 102-3

Scope paragraph in auditor's report, 169

SEC. *See* Securities and Exchange Commission

SEC Practice Section (SECPS), established for peer-review, 54-55, 71, 75

SECPS. *See* SEC Practice Section

SECPS Manual, 1983, 74

Securities Act of 1933, 10, 149, 152-53

Securities and Exchange Commission (SEC), 182; accounting and auditing enforcement releases from, 152; accounting series releases issued by, 5-6, 151-53; audit committee responsibilities outlined by, 94-95; common-sense bias of, 152; control of "Big Eight" and AICPA over accounting standards approved by, 11-13; criteria for enforcement action, 155; enforcement

activities of, 152, 154-55; and financial statements fraud, 154-55, 157-58; and insider trading, 155-57; legislation giving power to, 149; organization of, 150; position on defeasance, 49; position on nonaudit services and auditor independence, 158-59; registration and reporting requirements of, 150-52; relationship with FASB, 136-37; review activities of, 152; rulings emphasising auditor independence, 101, 158-59; staff accounting bulletins issued by, 151; standard-setting power of, 152-55; supporting audit committees, 93-94

Securities and Exchange Commission Accounting Series Releases: No. 4, "Administrative Policy on Financial Statements," 152-53 No. 150, clarifying relationship with FASB, 5-6, 153

Securities Exchange Act of 1934, 10, 149, 152-53

Securities Investor Protection Act of 1970, 149

Security Industry Association, cosponsoring Fasb, 132

Self-regulation, 54-56, 154, 180. *See also* Peer-review

SFAC, 135

SFAS, 4, 135

Shelf-registration, 150-51

Size approach to materiality, 32

Small businesses: differences from large businesses, 16; FASB definition of, 16; modification of GAAP for, proposed, 17-20 (*see also* Generally accepted accounting principles for small businesses); problems with accounting rules, 15-16, 20-21 (*see also* Accounting standards overload)

Socio-economic accounting, 39-41; avenues for, 41; defined, 40; paradigms in social sciences applied to, 40-41

Solicitation of clients, 118-20; AICPA policy statement on advertising, 120;

ban on, illegal under anti-trust laws, 119; definition of, 118; opposition to ban on, 119; report of AICPA special committee, 119-20; support for ban on, 118-19

SOP. *See* Statements of position

Staff accounting bulletins (SABs), 151

State accountancy boards, sunset review of, 67-69

Statement of changes in financial position, 37-38

Statement of financial position. *See* Balance sheet

Statements of Financial Accounting Concepts (SFAC), 135

Statements of Financial Accounting Standards (SFAS), 4, 135

Statements of position issued by Accounting Standards Executive Committee and Auditing Standards Executive Committee, 51, 52-53, 180

Statements on Auditing Standards (SAS), 167

Stewardship function, 43

Sunset review of state accountancy boards; 67-69, criticism of, 69

Sunset Review of Accounting Principles, 20

Supreme Court, decisions relevant to accounting profession, 90-91, 110-11, 119

Suspension of Reporting of Earnings per Share and Segment Information by Nonpublic Enterprises, FASB Statement No. 21, 19

Tax accounting, separating from GAAP accounting, 14

Tax accrual papers, access of Internal Revenue Service to, 90-92

Tax preparation. *See* Federal taxation

Tax work activities of CPAs, 65-66

Technical bulletins issued by FASB, 135-36

Theoretical concepts of accounting, 22, 25-27; entity theory, 25-26; fund theory, 26-27; proprietary theory, 25

Touche Ross & Co., 120; *See also* "Big Eight" accounting firms

Trust Indenture Act of 1939, 149

Uniformity principle, 32-33

Unit-of-measure postulate, 24

Valuation of assets and liabilities, 35

Value-added reporting, 45-47

Value-added statement, 45-47; advantages of, 46; disadvantages of, 47

Weighted-average method for cost of goods sold, 36

What Is Peer Review?, 54

Wheat Committee, 132

Women in accounting, 109-11

Work activities performed by CPAs, 63-67

Working papers: Internal Revenue Service access to, 90-92; knowledge, skills and abilities required of CPAs for, 57

About the Author

AHMED H. BELKAOUI is Professor of Accounting at the Chicago campus of the University of Illinois. He is the author of *Industrial Bonds and the Rating Process, Socio-Economic Accounting, International Accounting* (Quorum Books, 1983, 1984, 1985), *Accounting Theory, Conceptual Foundations of Management Accounting, Cost Accounting, Theorie Comptable,* and numerous articles.